Emily Dickinson
Perception and the Poet's Quest

Emily Dickinson (Robert Frost Library, Amherst College)

Emily Dickinson

Perception and the Poet's Quest

Greg Johnson

THE UNIVERSITY OF ALABAMA PRESS

Copyright © 1985 by
The University of Alabama Press
University, Alabama 35486
All rights reserved
Manufactured in the United States of America

Publication of this book was made possible, in part,
by financial assistance from the Andrew W. Mellon Foundation
and the American Council of Learned Societies.

Library of Congress Cataloging in Publication Data
Johnson, Greg
Emily Dickinson: perception and the poet's quest.
Bibliography: p.
Includes index.
1. Dickinson, Emily, 1830–1886—Criticism and interpretation.
2. Perception in literature. I. Title.
PS1541.Z5J56 1985   811'.4   84-16849
ISBN 0-8173-0247-6

To the memory of Ernest White
(1951–1982)

Pass to thy Rendezvous of Light,
Pangless except for us—
Who slowly ford the Mystery
Which thou hast leaped across!
P 1564

*Paradise is no Journey because it is
within—but for that very cause though—
it is the most Arduous of Journeys—*
PF 99

Contents

Acknowledgments

I am particularly indebted to William B. Dillingham of Emory University, who offered his good-humored support and enthusiasm to this project from its inception to its present form, and whose magisterial achievement as a Melville scholar provided an inspirational model of criticism as literary art.

I am also grateful to Laurence Perrine, whose graduate seminar on Dickinson and subsequent professional guidance helped lay the groundwork for this book; to Peter W. Dowell and Lore Metzger, who read the manuscript at an early stage and made valuable suggestions; and to W. Paul Elledge and Willard Spiegelman, who enriched my understanding of the Romantic tradition from which Dickinson's work emerges. For their dedication to teaching and to the exacting art of writing about literature, I am grateful to Jerome Beaty, Judith Eubank, and Ronald Schuchard.

The texts of Emily Dickinson's poems are reprinted by permission of the publishers and the Trustees of Amherst College from *The Poems of Emily Dickinson,* edited by Thomas H. Johnson, Cambridge, Mass.: The Belknap Press of Harvard University Press, Copyright 1951, © 1955, 1979, 1983 by the President and Fellows of Harvard College; from *Emily Dickinson Face to Face* by Martha D. Bianchi, Copyright 1932 by Martha Dickinson Bianchi, Copyright © renewed 1960 by Alfred Leete Hampson, reprinted by permission of Houghton Mifflin Company; from *Life and Letters of Emily Dickinson* by Martha D. Bianchi, Copyright 1924 by Martha Dickinson Bianchi, Copyright renewed 1952 by Alfred Leete Hampson, reprinted by permission of Houghton Mifflin Company; and from *The Complete Poems of Emily Dickinson,* edited by Thomas H. Johnson, Copyright 1914, 1929, 1935, 1942 by Martha Dickinson Bianchi, Copyright © 1957, 1963 by Mary L. Hampson, by permission of Little, Brown and Company.

The texts of Emily Dickinson's letters are reprinted by permission of the publishers from *The Letters of Emily Dickinson*, edited by Thomas H. Johnson, Cambridge, Mass.: The Belknap Press of Harvard University Press, Copyright © 1958 by the President and Fellows of Harvard College, © 1914, 1924, 1932 by Martha Dickinson Bianchi.

Portions of this book previously appeared in the following journals:

" 'A Pearl of Great Price': The Identity of Emily Dickinson,"
ESQ: A Journal of the American Renaissance 26 (4th Quarter, 1980).
   "Broken Mathematics: Emily Dickinson's Concept of Ratio,"
Concerning Poetry 13 (Spring, 1980).
   "Emily Dickinson: Perception and the Poet's Quest," *Renascence* 35 (Autumn, 1982).

To the editors, acknowledgment and thanks are due.

Emily Dickinson
Perception and the Poet's Quest

Introduction

Emily Dickinson was a divided being: two impulses contended in her, one which sought to solve the riddles of existence through poetry, endowing her experience with both human and spiritual meaning, and another which refused with a peculiar, grim scrupulosity to accept received notions about man, God, or the natural world. Her empirical method, in fact, was so fiercely at odds with her deeply religious longings that her arguments with "received notions" can seem relatively minor when compared to her intricate, brooding arguments with herself. The most purely rebellious of the American Romantics, Dickinson found it necessary to remake the universe through the medium of her own seeing, her own perceived evidence—to undertake, in short, a major poetic quest. Her poems, partaking of an established Romantic mode, both narrate the progress of this quest and express the quester's self-conscious reactions—her moments of ecstasy, doubt, and fear. They are the record of a lifelong, agonizing journey, one whose lyric narration required a heroine (Dickinson's ubiquitous "I") of nearly mythic stature, a heroine whose energy, honesty, and inner strength could withstand the rigors of the quest experience. Clearly, Dickinson saw herself as such a heroine—both in the literal and literary sense—and her poems provide a breathtaking view of a mind at war with the world and itself, a mind whose "solitary prowess"[1] sought nothing less than to achieve, within her mortal consciousness, the peace of immortality.

Despite her deeply felt sense of deprivation and spiritual longing, Dickinson's skepticism toward orthodox religion and literary convention—indeed, toward all received ideas—became steadfast; and although she described her poetic mission as "The spreading wide my narrow Hands / To gather Paradise" (P 657), she remained the most pragmatic of visionaries. These central tensions in Dickinson's personality drove her to develop her artistic skills to the degree that she became the greatest American poet of her century, and give to her work its compelling sense of intellectual and emotional strife. The following chapters will argue Dickinson's central place in the thrust of American Romanticism toward a unity between mind—the poet's "fallen" consciousness, adrift in the sea of experience—and a spiritual identity from which the mind perceives itself as mysteriously estranged. As Bernard Rosenthal remarks, "The successful romantic quests, such as those found in *Nature*, *Walden*, or 'Song of Myself,' all posit the fallen figure seeking to *restore* a diminished or lost spirituality."[2] The poems of Emily Dickinson also belong to this list of "successful romantic quests," if we measure success by unflagging effort and intellectual honesty rather than by the presence of optimistic "resolution." Nevertheless, Dickinson's identity as a private poet, and the ensuing critical problem of the poet's biography and its relation to her art, forces us to examine the poems on their own terms even while noting their relationship to the work of her great contemporaries; we must now view the problem itself as a key to a deeper understanding of Dickinson. The line between Dickinson the autonomous poet-quester and Dickinson the isolated, suffering human being very often cannot be drawn, so readily do the two aspects of the poet merge in the drama of her quest's narration. It is the degree to which Dickinson *lived* her art—more exclusively even than Emerson, Whitman, or Thoreau—that impresses us, that makes us see the close, mutually enriching relationship between her biography and her poems.

Dickinson's poetic canon comprises a drama whose theme is the adventure of consciousness, whose goal is a *visionary* (Dickinson's terms are clear) apprehension of spiritual reality, and whose implied heroine—appearing as the lyric "I"—is the poet herself. She was clearly engaged in a kind of myth-making, as even her contemporary reputation in Amherst makes evident, with herself at its dynamic center; and in this sense, despite her celebrated eccentricities, she is the most intense and the most typical of the American Romantics. The famous intensity, resulting in a mythologizing of self through which she made her life the literal and symbolic center of her poetry, permitted a special clarity of insight. Dozens of poems testify to the value of extreme personal conditions: " 'Tis Thirsting—vitalizes Wine—" (P 313), "Power is only Pain—" (P 252), "To comprehend a nectar / Requires sorest need" (P 67). No poet was ever more enamored of the things of this world than Dickinson, yet none ever went to greater lengths to avoid possessing them. In *Walden*, Thoreau remarks that "If we would enjoy the most intimate society . . . we must not only be silent, but commonly so far apart bodily that we cannot hear each other's voice,"[3] and Emerson, discussing "Our American literature and spiritual history," speaks of ideal leaders (whom he calls "admirable radicals," "unsocial worshippers") in terms strikingly descriptive of Dickinson: "They are lonely; the spirit of their writing and conversation is lonely; they repel influences; they shun general society; they incline to shut themselves in their chamber in the house, to live in the country rather than in the town, and to find their tasks and amusements in solitude."[4] Thus Dickinson, physically alone, now seems to us at the center of the nineteenth-century antinomian impulse, understanding more clearly and proving more definitively than anyone that virtual incarceration was the necessary condition of the largest, most encompassing freedom. "Capitivity is Consciousness— / So's Liberty" (P 384); she insisted that "We grow accustomed to the Dark" (P 419)—"dark" being her frequent metaphor for spiritual blindness— through the acuteness and accuracy of our best perceptions. Isolated in her radicalism, she could permit herself the witty observation that " 'Faith' is a fine invention / When Gentlemen can *see*" (P 185) and elsewhere simply exclaim, "Consult your Eye!" (P 420).

The first part of this study, "The Errand of the Eye: Poetic Strategies," considers the marked emphasis Dickinson places upon her human perception as the agent of poetic quest and stresses the extent to which she partook of a climate of thought and sensibility whose elements included the Puritan tradition of her region, the Transcendentalism of Emerson and Thoreau, and distinct modes of perception common to American Romanticism. In discussing Emerson, Todd M. Lieber remarks that "A very fine line exists between the apocalypse of the imagination into the independence of idealism and the renunciation of self to a divine world soul; this was the line to which Emerson tried to adhere, this the balance that organicism helped him to express. But the instability of the compromise pushed him now toward one extreme and now toward the other."[5] Dickinson shares this typically Romantic oscillation, and in her poems human perception seems to move simultaneously in two directions: toward a comprehensive vision of existential life in its contexts of the natural universe, the forces of time and eternity, and the unexplained agonies of consciousness; and toward a shrewd, empirical perceiving (one far more stringent than Emerson's) of reality through her own eyes. The emphasis Dickinson places upon empiricism combined with her deracinated awareness often seems, in fact, to make her kinship with modern writers more striking than her relationship to the Transcendentalists. Her poetry, as a number of recent critics have stressed, is peculiarly modern in its prescient foreshadowing of contemporary philosophical stances and literary sensibility. Since her central vision, again typically Romantic, is of life and nature as an organic, ongoing *process* continuing within "The Admirations—and Contempts—of time" (P 906), it is surely appropriate and perhaps necessary to view Dickinson's own achievement, unique as it is, within a conception of the American Romantic impulse as it reaches even to the present day. Such an approach should result in a clarity of perspective that will stress her own enormous contribution and the continuing power of her influence.

Despite her intellectual ties to other major writers, her own contemporaries and ours, the unusual physical isolation of her life must remain in constant view as we read the poems. In a central theoretical statement she wrote that "Perception of an object costs / Precise the Object's loss" (P 1071), and her way of life may be viewed as a stubborn dramatization of this insight. Although potent social and psychological forces undoubtedly encouraged her withdrawal, her unusual strategies for coping with existence, particularly in the realm of human relationships, represent the conscious choice of an artist, and have an intimate connection with her way of perceiving reality and with the conclusions she drew from her perceptions. Presumably she had decided, by her early thirties, that she was willing to pay the price of renunciation (recommended but only intermittently practiced by Emerson, Thoreau, and Whitman) for the privilege of a heightened perception; her isolation seems to have solved both psychological and poetic quandaries, and it certainly sharpened her discernment in the quest for essential truths. Because Dickinson insists that visual perception is the fulcrum of all experience that matters and the only reliable guide toward a more comprehensive and synthetic vision, I will briefly discuss biographical factors relevant to her intense concern with perception, including her self-consciousness as a poet whose female selfhood refused to be stifled and the possibly crucial event (particularly in this context) of Dickinson's eye disease of the early 1860s. I have also emphasized the way in which the poet's identification of physical seeing as a means toward glimpsing immortality leads inevitably to her poems dealing with "extra-visual" perception—spiritual intuition or apprehension—as a means toward the longed-for comprehensive vision.

Although she did not so label it, perception is her true "flood subject," since her great themes of nature, death, and immortality are equally vitalized by the central tension in her poetry between the perceived and the unknown, between what can be empirically verified and what is only hauntingly suggested by the visible. My second part, "Broken Mathematics: Ratio, Transience, Essence," explores Dickinson's stubborn empiricism as confronted by the intractable mysteries of existence and indicates how this confrontation caused Dickinson to view her poetry as a process of gauging and valuation, an attempt to gain spiritual knowledge through a close scrutiny and measurement of earthly conditions. In this process, it will be seen that Dickinson's perception is again of paramount importance, since she is concerned to make keen, precise observations of the natural world in order to explore the spiritual implications of its phenomena, investing them with symbolic—and often contradictory—values.

Finally, in "Death: The Great Romance," Dickinson's major theme is explored in terms of perception, since death marks the passage from human seeing into an unknown which contains either extinction or a full revelation. This section analyzes Dickinson's concern with death as phenomenon and death as theme, as the shaping force of her quest romance, and it stresses her self-consciousness as a quest poet who is fully aware of the conditions—especially the poetic irresolution—of her internalized journey. In the death poetry, as in all her work, Dickinson's eyes are the tense, single point of connection between herself and the universe, her perception the single opportunity for discovering a meaningful correspondence. Her poems are the record of this correspondence, and in her finest work she transforms her perception into an art which is both the process and the achievement of a transcendent vision.

I should add, at this point, a few remarks about procedure. I have focused upon the subject of perception in Dickinson's work not in order to isolate a single theme or cluster of imagery, but rather to provide a reliable lens through which the entire range of her work might be viewed. As Adrienne Rich has noted, "Wherever you take hold of [Dickinson], she proliferates,"[6] and maintaining an accurate perspective upon a mind so restless, energetic, and seemingly self-contradictory as Dickinson's may seem a foredoomed endeavor. In general, however, I have found that the central subject of perception has enabled me to frame appropriate critical questions bearing on all aspects of the poet's work and has further proved helpful in the attempt to probe beyond apparent contradictions in the hope of discovering hidden relationships and patterns. Discussing the relationship in the poetry between visionary revelation and what Dickinson called her "unfurnished eyes" (P 685), Sharon Cameron remarks: "as if to jar vision from the modesty of its limitations, her poems spin out new attempts at defining the relationship, each time catching it at a different angle."[7] Thus the typical Dickinson poem, angling outward from unfurnished eyes toward visionary fulfillment, tries to form a bridge, a unitary moment of insight, and though moments pass and insight often falters (or even, at times, proves delusive), Dickinson's incremental progress can be observed as the quest continues and she begins to master "that precarious Gait / Some call Experience" (P 875). The chapters which follow will therefore argue the centrality of this relationship between perception and Dickinson's religious quest—or, more accurately, her epistemological quest narrated with religious intensity, and often employing Christian imagery. My chief aim has been to provide a comprehensive reading of the poems, and to do so according to the design inherent in her canon itself, rather than to one externally imposed.

The most obvious design I have followed in reading Dickinson's work pertains to chronology. In each of the three major parts, I have begun my study of her poetic quest with the earliest poetry and followed its argument into the mature work. Two assumptions underlie this approach. First, it is my belief that there is a more discernible pattern of development in Dickinson's work than has heretofore been acknowledged. Even in 1981 David Porter asserts that Dickinson's work exhibits no artistic development: "Its form, its language ploys, its unarranged mosaic of glimpses did not alter, did not evolve."[8] Other recent critics, however, have suggested the validity of a developmental approach—notably Thomas M. Davis, Joanne Feit Diehl, and Roland Hagenbüchle—and my conception of Dickinson's quest as a traceable progression through time owes much to their valuable leads. Although the poet's major themes do indeed remain constant throughout her life, I have found that her emotional and psychological attitudes toward these themes increase in complexity as the quester's identity continues to develop greater authority and confidence. Second, the conception of poetic quest itself (and Dickinson is acutely conscious of the nature of her endeavor and even, perhaps, of its literary precedents) implies a linear narrative, for which certain crucial poems represent definable stages of the quester's progress. Although many of her poems typically describe lyric "moments" of insight, these moments may be safely placed at various points along a critically conceived map of the poet's movement toward knowledge and a final, idealized illumination. Such a "map," in fact—guiding the quester from blindness toward vision, from despair toward confidence, from a "barefoot rank" toward a monarchial status—is continually implied in the imagery of the poems themselves.

Another principle of organization developed from my sense of the major obstacles to Dickinson's quest and the increasing skill and subtlety she employs in attempting to overcome them. I deal first, therefore, with the basic techniques—mainly poetic, but personal as well—which the poet evolves as a means of profitably initiating and then conducting her quest. Under the rubric of "poetic strategies" I have discussed the poet's youthful sense of disorientation and her subsequent development of a solid identic base; her modes of perception themselves and the literary influences which helped to shape them; and her sense of a world beyond human perception, a "Glimmering Frontier" (P 696) which is the object of her deepest longings. In the second part I deal with her poetic development, her increasing store of knowledge, as well as the highly original techniques—her "broken mathematics"—she employs as a means toward this continuing progress. And in the final part on death I treat Dickinson's ultimate obstacle, the "White Exploit" (P 922) which stands as an impenetrable mist between the quester and her holy grail, but which paradoxically inspires much of her best art.

Recent Dickinson scholarship has shown an amplitude and originality worthy of its subject, and any new study of the poet must not only acknowledge indebtedness but also clarify its extension or qualification of existing critical contexts. Contemporary scholars, for the most part, have admirably followed the suggestion made by Charles R. Anderson in his own pioneer study of the poetry: "To give her poetry the serious attention it deserves is the real task that remains. To study it intensively, to stare a hole in the page until these apparently cryptic notations yield their full meanings—this is the great challenge to modern readers."[9] Careful reading of Dickinson has produced several excellent studies within the past decade, each assuming a distinct critical viewpoint and often reaching sharply divergent conclusions about the aims, processes, and achievement of Dickinson's work. This divergence has been a healthy one, however, and viewing the scholarship as a whole, one is less struck by continuing disagreement than by the demands this far-ranging, enigmatic poet places upon the critical intelligence. Several studies are worthy of special note. Sharon Cameron's *Lyric Time: Dickinson and the Limits of Genre* (1979) provides a closely reasoned examination of the relationship of lyric form to Dickinson's epistemological quest and focuses upon the poet's defiance of temporal order. Joanne Feit Diehl's *Dickinson and the Romantic Imagination* (1981) delineates literary relationships between Dickinson—a writer too often considered within a vacuum—and her major precursors in the Romantic tradition. Robert Weisbuch's brief, brilliant study, *Emily Dickinson's Poetry* (1975), is simultaneously the most ambitious and most tautly concentrated work yet to appear on the poet; through close and sympathetic reading, Weisbuch defines Dickinson's major techniques and analyzes in detail the typological cast of her thought. His book is essential reading for any serious student of Dickinson's work.

Another major study is David Porter's *Dickinson: The Modern Idiom* (1981), one which represents a considerable departure from his previous, "formalist" approach in *The Art of Emily Dickinson's Early Poetry* (1966).

Porter now characterizes Dickinson as a thoroughgoing modernist who employs her dazzling linguistic gifts in the service of "utter miscellaneousness." He asserts that Dickinson is "the only major American poet without a project" and that "The Dickinson strain of modernism . . . inaugurates in American literature two main characteristics: the menacing ascendance of consciousness and the disappearance of an artistic goal."[10] The present study will emphasize the menacing quality of consciousness in Dickinson's work by examining its intensification of the poet's perception and her need to establish perceptual correspondences, but will also argue the centrality of Dickinson's "artistic goal": the narration of a mind's heroic battle with existential fear and its constant striving toward spiritual knowledge. As Hawthorne once remarked of Melville, "He can neither believe nor be comfortable in his unbelief; and he is too honest and courageous not to try to do one or the other":[11] Dickinson's art, like much of Melville's, typifies this fruitful opposition between intellectual honesty and emotional longing. What may appear to be "utter miscellaneousness" is actually the vast range of a mind that will not relent in its quest for knowledge and is compelled to record every stage of the quest and each random pressure, whether menacing or fortuitous, upon the poet's intensely focused awareness. The scope and eloquence of Porter's work are impressive, and though I have disagreed with his central thesis, I have also benefited from his original insights into Dickinson's technique and habits of composition, and from his meticulous examination of the texts. Porter has, in fact, taken Anderson's plea for close reading a step farther:

> Finding Dickinson requires an intricate going-back-through. A reader must penetrate the print that she did not authorize, with its straight lines and capitals, its even margins and spacing, the stanzaic regularity, the *visual definiteness;* go through the contorted syntax and beyond the unanchored tropes; back despite the absent tissue of her work and through her reclusion and her silence to the immediacy of the scraps and pencil.[12]

Now that a facsimile edition of Dickinson's manuscripts is available, beautifully edited by Ralph W. Franklin,[13] one may in fact study many of the poems just as Dickinson left them, in all their "immediacy" and idiosyncratic formal authority.

Other recent critics who have been particularly influential upon my study of Dickinson's perception include Inder Nath Kher, Roland Hagenbüchle, and Jean McClure Mudge. Todd M. Lieber's *Endless Experiments: Essays on the Heroic Experience in American Romanticism* (1973), though not dealing directly with Dickinson, has defined important attributes of American Romanticism which bear directly upon my own view of her work. A number of critics who emphasize a feminist perspective upon the poetry—Albert Gelpi, Adrienne Rich, Sandra M. Gilbert and Susan Gubar—have encouraged my own emphasis upon the poet's identity as a woman and its effect upon her perception of a world (spiritual, familial, and literary) ruled by male authority-figures. Every student of this and all other aspects of Dickinson's life is indebted, of course, to Richard B. Sewall's monumental biography, *The Life of Emily Dickinson* (1974), which amplifies in often startling detail the cultural, interpersonal, and psychological contexts in which Dickinson wrote her poems.

Because it is with the poems that we are ultimately concerned, I have attempted to provide explications of major texts when relevant to an understanding of the poet's quest, and especially when I feel that the poems have been misinterpreted by previous critics. It has been a special satisfaction to place poems like "Before I got my eye put out" and "One Blessing had I than the rest" within a context which simultaneously illuminates Dickinson's quest and showcases the individual poem as an impressive, previously undervalued achievement. In one of her many poems about poetry, Dickinson spoke wistfully about having the art "to stun myself / With Bolts of Melody!" (P 505). In my close examination of her work, I have found Dickinson's verbal melodies far more subtle and accomplished than I had previously considered them, and have proved—to myself, at least—that Dickinson had every reason to be stunned by the range, the complexity, and the austere beauty of her achievement.

Part One

The Errand of the Eye: Poetic Strategies

Perception of an object costs
Precise the Object's loss—
P 1071

I am pleasantly located
in the deep sea. . . .
L 209

1   The First League Out From Land

"The Child's faith is new," Dickinson writes in a characteristic deprecation of innocence, "Wide—like the Sunrise / On fresh Eyes—" (P 637). Throughout her poetry the pious childlike believer, who "Never had a Doubt" and "Believes all sham / But Paradise" and, perhaps worst of all, who "Credits the World," is the object of the poet's most withering scorn. She seems from the beginning to follow Emerson's lead: "To take on trust certain facts is a dead faith, inoperative. *A trust in yourself* is the height, not of pride, but of piety, an unwillingness to learn of any but God himself."[1] Yet Dickinson's attitude even toward God is one of suspicion, mistrust, and resentment; she parts with Emerson in her existential awareness of absolute solitude, an estrangement so stark and terrifying that she must invert a central, inherited Romantic concept: in her poems "experience" becomes a positive good, "innocence" the most perilous form of delusion. Unlike any of her contemporaries, Dickinson acknowledges an absolute, potentially debilitating fear of such delusions as the impetus of her quest for knowledge.

This state of fearfulness is objectified in her early poetry as a threatening sea, buffeting mercilessly the bewildered, flailing quester. This elemental chaos threatens her perception, her identity, her life itself. In Dickinson's early work we sense an urgent need for orientation, one which the poet gradually defines as perceptual leverage: perception orients the perceiver in a necessary isolation from chaos, endowing her with identity and specially acute vision even as it grants her an ambiguous "polar privacy" and even though the experiencing self of the poet, as distinct from the detached artist, continues to cope with emotional flux and peril. The poet's quest begins by adopting Emerson's "trust in yourself" almost by default, for her identity as a quest poet emerges after a horrified recoiling from a world that cannot be "credited" and that is possibly malevolent.

In her enforced perceptual isolation, Dickinson looks back with mingled contempt and longing toward an abandoned world, often imaged as "the shore," which yet embodies the tantalizing promise of reunion, an establishment of spiritual order. The possible reality of this order, usually described in Christian terms, haunts Dickinson's work from beginning to end. Yet she maintains her chosen estrangement in what often seems—to recall Emerson's phrase—an "impious" trust in her own gifts.[2] Though affected by Emersonian self-reliance and by his emphasis upon a personal confrontation with spirit, and though sharing with Thoreau the need to live "deliberately" and with the most stringent economy, she stands alone in her single-mindedness, her intensity, her shunning of compromise. Plunging into the sea of experience, armed with poetic genius and a desperate determination to see clearly and comprehensively, she seeks to discover the "pearl" of spiritual knowledge and to possess it on no one's terms but her own. From the outset her work shows a notable self-consciousness regarding her youthful, relatively inchoate identity as opposed to her distant, rarefied goal; like Whitman she understands herself as an "outsetting bard," one whose highly individuated quest is already distinctly conceptualized, both in its conditions and in its particular demands upon the quester's poetic gifts.

One of Dickinson's earliest poems may be read as a statement of poetic mission, and as a remarkably accurate sketch of this conception; the poem's imagery defines perception as her central means of poetic achievement, and in its intriguing combination of themes creates a tension maintained throughout her work:

> Whether my bark went down at sea—
> Whether she met with gales—
> Whether to isles enchanted
> She bent her docile sails—
>
> By what mystic mooring
> She is held today—
> This is the errand of the eye
> Out upon the Bay.
> (P 52)

The two stanzas of this poem hold an apparent contradiction which is at the heart of its meaning and which indicates at the outset of Dickinson's career a primary correspondence in her concept of poetic perception. The first stanza depicts a quest in which the persona identifies her poetic self with a "bark"; her concern is for the fate of this bark, and the four lines posit alternatives which decrease in their tragic potentialities. The first possibility is that ever-present one in Dickinson's poetry, that of death, perceptual extinction, here importantly related to the poetic quest. In the second line Dickinson suggests the possibility of stormy crossings—personal or imaginative crises—which will inevitably affect the poetic endeavor: "gales" are not assigned a qualitative value, however, since Dickinson's feelings about storms are almost always ambivalent; they symbolize destruction but also the intellectual or emotional turmoil which can result in great art. The third possibility of smooth sailing, a home among "isles enchanted," hints at imaginative complacency (recalling the delusive beckonings of the Sirens that threatened the quest of Odysseus), a deterred quest that leaves the bark far short of its potential achievement.[3] But rather than completing the dialectic of the first stanza, the second immediately suspends all choices and seems to suspend doubt itself (the tense shifts from past to present, "today" locating a specific moment in the quest) in the assertion of a presumably timeless "mystic mooring" which holds the bark, as if in readiness to be discovered by the poet's intuitive eye. Stanza one depicts the quest as a process resulting in a variety of possible outcomes; stanza two begins by positing an ever-present stasis in which the immortal self is held suspended and seeming to await discovery.[4] The poem finally asserts that it is "the errand of the eye" to discover the nature of this mooring.

The combination of process and stasis in the poem illustrates the dynamic relationship between two separate quests: the active, poetic quest imaged by the bark and its possible fates, and the perceptual quest imaged by the bodiless "eye." The poet realizes that her imaginative quest into the unknown is an uncertain setting out, perhaps already a failed one: only perception can aid her, and it is the eye's errand—this poem's "eye" of generalized intuitive seeing finally being subsumed into the poet's physical eye—which will represent the crucial action toward poetic fulfillment. The comfortable union in the poem of two Dickinson typologies—that of poetic quest and that of the larger ultimate quest for immortality and final meaning of which the poetic quest is itself a type—comes about through the dual relevancies of perception as the agent of poetic mission and as the intuitive seeker in the "mystic" realm of immortality and ultimate meanings.

This poem is a useful beginning for a study of Dickinson's perceptual quest for several reasons. First, it implies a full consciousness of poetic risk, of the conflict between mind and experience at the heart of Dickinson's poetry. It also places Dickinson's art within the larger Romantic context of the internalized quest,[5] and in fact seems formally to begin that quest, giving us a convenient entry into her enormous canon by hinting at the seriousness of her theme through a central typology: the individual afloat upon a complexly dangerous sea, with the threat of extinction never far distant. The enormous range, tension, and complexity of the poetry are foreshadowed, effectively deterring any critical quest to limit (and distort) its meaning through the creation of a false pattern or through excessive selection.[6] In this and in many other early poems dealing with Dickinson afloat in the sea of experience, we are also made aware of her kinship to other American Romantics who, though their methods and emphases may differ sharply from hers, nonetheless envisioned themselves also as embarked upon a lonely antinomian venture. Emerson's use of the sea metaphor, for instance, is pervasive; throughout Melville's work the sea remains the ambiguous and inescapable home of the human "orphan." Even such a normally optimistic poet as Whitman often noted his sense of disorientation and aimlessness. In "As I Ebb'd With the Ocean of Life" he addresses the Paumanok shore:

> I too Paumanok,
> I too have bubbled up, floated the measureless float,
>   and been wash'd on your shores,
> I too am but a trail of drift and debris,
> I too leave little wrecks upon you. . . . [7]

Returning to Dickinson's "Whether my bark went down at sea," we see that the poem, perhaps most importantly, places the landscape of poetic quest within the larger metaphorical landscape of a universe where flux and death are the formidable antagonists to the creative mind. To grasp the nature of this quest we must follow Dickinson's eye as it goes upon its crucial errand, noticing in particular the dynamic, complex interrelationships between her perception and her poetics, between her omnivorous eye and the progress of her artistic "bark."

This image of the bark recurs in several of Dickinson's poems, all of them written early in her career. Some of these develop one or more of the dramatic possibilities implied by the central poem just examined, and in each case the dramatization isolates a specific moment in the quest. Two poems of this group—and chronologically they are two of the earliest—are songs of innocence recreated by the experienced poet;[8] their speakers remain serene in their assurance that the bark will be saved through the intervention of an established spiritual world. The earliest of these dramatizes the moment when "night" is approaching—night being a symbol throughout Dickinson's poetry for times of doubt, despair, even madness—but rather than a night of perceptual extinction, it represents here the passage toward a new "dawn," a new existence that does not sacrifice identity:

> Adrift! A little boat adrift!
> And night is coming down!
> Will *no* one guide a little boat
> Unto the nearest town?
>
> So Sailors say—on yesterday—
> Just as the dusk was brown
> One little boat gave up it's strife
> And gurgled down and down.
>
> So angels say—on yesterday—
> Just as the dawn was red
> One little boat—o'erspent with gales—
> Retrimmed it's masts—redecked it's sails—
> And shot—exultant on!
> (P 30)

Even this song of innocence acknowledges death, but it rejects human perceptions of death in favor of an orthodox faith, articulated with characteristic zest in the last stanza: the poem is an attractive example of Dickinson's frequent dramatizations of wish-fulfillment, poems which answer to her desire rather than to her intelligence. Despite the conventional imagery of salvation—the coming dawn, the angels—and the rather sentimental attitude taken here to the "little boat," the poem rises above the commonplace in its fervent expression of this desire.[9] And, in the startling verb of the last line, it foreshadows the self-conscious power of the mature poet, a power later described in such poems as "On my volcano grows the Grass" (P 1677) and "My Life had stood—a Loaded Gun—" (P 754).

In a second poem the angels once again save the boat from threatening gales:

> A poor—torn heart—a tattered heart—
> That sat it down to rest—
> Nor noticed that the Ebbing Day
> Flowed silver to the West—
> Nor noticed Night did soft descend—
> Nor Constellation burn—
> Intent upon the vision
> Of latitudes unknown.

> The angels—happening that way
> This dusty heart espied—
> Tenderly took it up from toil
> And carried it to God—
> There—sandals for the Barefoot—
> There—gathered from the gales—
> Do the blue havens by the hand
> Lead the wandering Sails.
> (P 78)

There are significant differences here, however; the poem seems to take place somewhat later in the quest, since night has already descended and the poet is "torn" and "tattered" rather than merely apprehensive.[10] Moreover, the seriousness of the quest has intensified: the speaker is so "Intent upon the vision / Of latitudes unknown" that she has remained unaware that night has fallen. Despite the quester's increased energy and commitment, however, the value of human perception in trying to pierce through doubt—so the poem implies—is practically negligible. Once again the help of angels is required, for thus "Do the blue havens by the hand / Lead the wandering Sails."

Another pair of poems, employing the same cluster of images, continues to move the quest forward, and not surprisingly the movement is from the relative complacency of the two songs of innocence discussed above toward an increasing awareness of danger. Both of these poems deal, in fact, not with salvation but with being lost, and the focus shifts from the happy stasis of another world to the dark and dangerous flux of this world; they may be viewed, therefore, as the turning point in this group of poems as a whole. In "A poor—torn heart—a tattered heart" the speaker's bark was so intent upon finding the unknown world that it was unaware that night had fallen and was effectually blinded to the complexity of its own world; the first poem of this next pair shows a similar lack of awareness, but here a gratuitous salvation does not follow, and the symbolic night gives way to an explicit sense of peril:

> 'Twas such a little—little boat
> That toddled down the bay!
> 'Twas such a gallant—gallant sea
> That beckoned it away!
>
> 'Twas such a greedy, greedy wave
> That licked it from the Coast—
>   [*no stanza break*]

Nor ever guessed the stately sails
My little craft was *lost!*
(P 107)

The poem's argument is clear, and seems marred by the extremely childish tone; yet the tone, the *voice,* is exactly appropriate to the level of awareness the poem represents. The speaker describes a time of innocence when
she could not "guess" that she was lost; but now, looking back, she can recreate this precise moment in her quest for uncompromised vision and place
all the symbolic elements in true perspective, even as she recreates the pathet-
ically innocent voice in order to dramatize the moment, to lend it emotional
immediacy. The repetition of three key adjectives—*little, gallant,* and *greedy*—
helps achieve this perspective. The "little" individual is pitted hopelessly against
rapacious ("greedy") nature, and the most interesting word choice, "gallant,"
describes the sinister cordiality of death which fascinates the speaker even at
this early stage (this idea of death's gallantry will recur in some of the best
poems of Dickinson's maturity). Viewing the poem as a whole, therefore,
understanding that its speaker is writing in a state of experience about the
dangers of innocence, we see that the poem is an explicit warning against a
lack of awareness, against complacency. The poem does not warn against
being "lost"—for this is an ineluctable fact of existence—but against the failure to mature, to grow out of a childish sense of safety, of unquestioning faith
in a benevolent universe. In a similar context—his essay titled "Experience"—
Emerson warns that "An innavigable sea washes with silent waves between
us and the things we aim at," and Dickinson, though never conceding that
the sea is "innavigable," shares Emerson's awareness of the daily confusions
of experience, its barriers to knowledge.[11]

The second poem, apparently written a year later, deals with being lost
in a more complex way; though it also describes a state of innocence, and
therefore focuses upon the desirability of salvation, the conventional religious
imagery has given way to a more personalized vision of eternity. The poem
also looks forward to the best of Dickinson's mature work in its dramatization of the crucial moment of death—frequently envisioned as the moment
of fulfillment, of completed quest. Though death is not realized here, its nearness creates emotional upheaval and sharpened insight:

Just lost, when I was saved!
Just felt the world go by!
Just girt me for the onset with Eternity,
           [*no stanza break*]

When breath blew back,
And on the other side
I heard recede the disapppointed tide!

Therefore, as One returned, I feel,
Odd secrets of the line to tell!
Some Sailor, skirting foreign shores—
Some pale Reporter, from the awful doors
Before the Seal!

Next time, to stay!
Next time, the things to see
By Ear unheard,
Unscrutinized by Eye—

Next time, to tarry,
While the Ages steal—
Slow tramp the Centuries,
And the Cycles wheel!
(P 160)

As in her later, more famous poem, "Safe in their alabaster chambers," the final stanza presents the characteristic Dickinson vision of individual existence out of time, freed from "Centuries" and from the "Cycles" of natural process. But here, importantly, the speaker's yearning for a oneness with eternity involves a specific goal:

Next time, the things to see
By Ear unheard,
Unscrutinized by Eye—

Even at this early stage, therefore, the "errand of the eye" necessitates a confrontation with death, one which will presumably allow the speaker a transcendent visionary experience.[12] In this sense, one may say that the entire shape of Dickinson's career is already set: inevitably, following through with her peculiarly intense Romanticism, the goal of her quest can be reached only through the "White Exploit," death itself. The answers lie just beyond the "awful doors." But, as has been noted, the speaker who reasons in this way remains in a state of innocence, and her rather breathless sense of absolutes—being lost or saved, blindness and vision, life and death—does not take into account the complexity of the natural world, the disorientation she seems so eager to leave behind. Her stance is emotional, exuberant, reckless, still focused on what is "unscrutinized by Eye"; and it is extremely naive. The process of the speaker's maturing, her passage into a state of experience, involves a shift of this focus to what *can* be scrutinized, her human perception gaining slowly in her trust until it is literally all she trusts. This pattern of her maturing process—her increasing dependency on her perceptions—becomes the pattern of her quest as a whole.

But the exuberance of her questing spirit should not be underestimated, for it provides the energizing force behind her later, more thoughtful poems as well as these early, intensely emotional lyrics which image a stark confrontation between the little bark and a frightening universe. Even at age nineteen, Dickinson had shown this exuberance, using the same imagery that would dominate her earliest surviving poems. She writes to Abiah Root: "The shore is safer, Abiah, but I love to buffet the sea—I can count the bitter wrecks here in the pleasant waters, and hear the murmuring winds, but oh, I love the danger!" (L 39). It was not all darkness and terror, after all:

Exultation is the going
Of an inland soul to sea,
Past the houses—past the headlands—
Into deep Eternity—

Bred as we, among the mountains,
Can the sailor understand
The divine intoxication
Of the first league out from land?
(P 76)

Here Dickinson becomes the adventurous, Adamic poet described by Roy Harvey Pearce: "the extreme American Protestant self which, when it comes fully alive in its greatest poems, is in effect able to set its institutional and religious commitments aside and be radically and unflinchingly itself, radically and unflinchingly free."[13] She is the most typical American romantic because she is the most intense, the most purely rebellious; unlike Emerson and Whitman, she is not limited by an adherence to any philosophical ideology or political vision and is thus free to be *herself*. Pearce remarks further: "She is the Puritan diarist who no longer has to believe that her acutely sensed private experiences are vulnerable and explicable only as types of something larger than they—something given from above, from outside herself."[14] Her

"polar privacy," and her exclusive fastening upon a single, egocentric drama—
that of the "inland soul" venturing out upon the sea of "deep Eternity"—thus
allows her, paradoxically, a nearly unlimited range of vision.[15]

All of the poems discussed above, written early in her career[16] and dealing metaphorically with the quest that would become her life's work, show
her moving in a single direction: toward an awareness of the value of experience. A poem written a few years later, also employing the sea image, speaks
explicitly of experience in terms of her quest and its progress:

> I stepped from Plank to Plank
> A slow and cautious way
> The Stars about my Head I felt
> About my Feet the Sea.
>
> I knew not but the next
> Would be my final inch—
> This gave me that precarious Gait
> Some call Experience.[17]
> (P 875)

Yet it is experience of a specially refined, purposeful kind, almost entirely
inward. She becomes intent upon a vision of her own world, seen with her
own two eyes, but she cannot seek the actual shore: she must renounce it.
Because "Water, is taught by thirst. / Land—by the Oceans passed" (P 135),
the internalized quest itself, progressing through oceans of experience, is the
means toward any meaningful achievement by her poetic bark. Like Emerson, she understood that "He in whom love of truth predominates will keep
himself aloof from all moorings, and afloat."[18] In her own most concise explanation of her way of thought, her way of seeing, she notes that "Perception
of an object costs / Precise the Object's loss" (P 1071), and as she matures she
can frequently be observed in the act of relating her perceptual quest to its
ultimate "Object" (her distance from that object is a given). Her new, more
considered stance thus allows for and occasionally demands irony and skepticism, even toward her own most fervent religious impulses. As Robert Weisbuch remarks, "The intelligence that could cry 'foul' against its most cherished
visions is Dickinson's chief, glorious anomaly—glorious because its skepticism makes the visions which survive it real."[19]

Pretending intellectual subservience, she asked bluntly in her first letter
to T. W. Higginson: "What is true?" (L 260). But by 1862 she knew that her
own answers were the only ones she could accept. The moment the brunt of

such a question falls on her marks the beginning of her mature quest: her focus is no longer upon fulfillment but upon the quest itself, intensified through frustration. The early, naive, wholly egocentric stance—crucial at the outset because it ensures purity of vision and freedom from distorting influences—must give way to an awareness of exteriority and of the division between mind and nature, for this awareness alone can bring about self-orientation, identity, and visionary perspective. She once wrote that "God was penurious with me, which makes me shrewd with Him" (L 207); this kind of shrewd self-reliance insisted upon absolute accuracy of vision, upon distance and the power of her own leverage. "Sighting land,"[20] to continue the sea metaphor, could otherwise prove "fictitious," and she preferred a dark truth to a comforting illusion:

> I many times thought Peace had come
> When Peace was far away—
> As Wrecked Men—deem they sight the Land—
> At Centre of the Sea—
>
> And struggle slacker—but to prove
> As hopelessly as I—
> How many the fictitious Shores—
> Of any Harbor be—
> (P 739)

Or, as she stated more bluntly in a later poem: "Peace is a fiction of our Faith" (P 912).

If in the early poems she pictures the novice quester as adrift, involved in a senseless process of disorientation and despair, she comes to insist that the poet must learn to trust her own perception to guide her. As the poems exhibit an increasing awareness of the quester's poetic identity, it becomes necessary to bring her entire personality into alignment with her paramount need to perceive accurately: poetically this involved placing herself at the center of her own mythology, seeing herself as a heroine setting out upon a quest of epic dimensions, "intent upon the Vision / Of latitudes unknown." Yet she remained a heroine with a "fallen" consciousness, one whose effort to see would involve severe adjustments in her personal life, highly individuated responses to inherited religious and literary assumptions, and above all, a shaping of her creative power into specifically useful poetic techniques. Emerson states the dilemma:

It is very unhappy, but too late to be helped, the discovery we have
made that we exist. That discovery is called the Fall of Man. Ever after-
wards we suspect our instruments. We have learned that we do not see
directly, but mediately, and that we have no means of correcting these
colored and distorting lenses which we are, or of computing the amount
of their errors. Perhaps these subject-lenses have a creative power; perhaps there are no objects. Once we lived in what we saw; now, the
rapaciousness of this new power, which threatens to absorb all things,
engages us.[21]

Dickinson's self-consciousness, her discovery that she existed, was a shock
from which she never fully recovered—and the gain was both hers and ours.
Despite a constant suspicion of her own instruments, however, Dickinson's
engagement with her "power" continued to deepen.

"I dwell in Possibility," Dickinson wrote (P 657), indicating that the atmosphere of her poetic endeavor was the same as that of her life as a whole; and while this poem, like many others, stresses her sense of blissful privilege in her identity as poet, she was constantly (and often angrily) aware of the enormous sacrifices her gift demanded. The confluence of social pressures and her own uncompromising temperament created an exclusivity so great that we cannot always readily separate Dickinson the woman from Dickinson the poet:[1] her mature work, in fact, often insists upon a merging of the two into "A Woman—white" (P 271) whose identity is self-sufficing in its fervent devotion to poetic vocation. This woman was, of course, the self-created mythic heroine Dickinson needed as the Romantic protagonist of her quest, as well as the literal woman, Emily Dickinson, who actually did begin wearing white in the early 1860's and who showed every sign of deliberately turning social and psychological disadvantages into a daily triumph of consciousness, a freedom both exalting and terrifying. To attain this freedom, it was necessary at the outset of her career to develop various private strategies—emotional and psychic, as well as poetic—in her effort to fulfill her "errand" of perception and to assume the heroic, queenly status befitting a quester whose goal was to "gather Paradise." Her chief antagonist in this orienting process was nature, an Emersonian nature nevertheless re-envisioned as a "haunted house" (P 1400); as a dweller in possibility, Dickinson had to verify natural facts and interpret natural signs, reversing what Emerson called "the despotism of the senses"[2] into the tyranny of an omnivorous perception.

Dickinson's chief struggle in all aspects of her life was to maintain the dangerous "unmoored" condition so crucial to the genuine truth-seeker, and simultaneously to achieve a necessary degree of psychic and emotional safety. Her need to perceive clearly and accurately, as we have already stressed, necessitated distance from the "object" (i.e., everything "other" than Dickinson) of her perception. Dickinson's potent, highly personal mythmaking, which biographical distortion earlier in this century did so much to obscure, was actually the proclamation of freedom allowed by this distance. We can only guess at Dickinson's slow, excruciating progress toward her freedom: if Thomas H. Johnson's dating is correct, we have almost no poems from the poet's early and middle twenties—a time of life in which poetic creativity is typically at flood tide—and it would seem likely that these years were occupied not only in practicing her craft and discarding unsatisfactory work, but also in developing those psychic and emotional attitudes which were to set the shape of her remaining life.

Recent criticism and biography have dispelled the long-prevailing, sentimental notions which imaged Dickinson as a fragile, scarcely human creature whose oddity resulted from a love disappointment and a spinsterish excess of sensibility; we may now assume that, following upon her early sense of estrangement and inchoate poetic selfhood, she also underwent a severe emotional and psychological crisis, probably in the winter of 1861–62, which may have resulted in a psychotic break.[3] The nature of this crisis remains a mystery, but in critical estimation the lovelorn poetess seeking to vent her frustrations through her verses has now been replaced by the skeptical, tough-minded thinker whose poetry shows a magnificent individualism and unwavering courage. Dickinson's famous "lover," even if he brought on the major crisis, was only one element in the larger design—already part of Dickinson's awareness, I believe, long before 1862—which formed Dickinson's psychic, and finally her poetic, method of dealing with reality. Her disorientation first manifests itself, we must remember, with her inability to accept conventional moorings and with her fear (paradoxical enough, considering her religious nature) that she was too worldly, and therefore "lost." Certainly her adolescent letters show little inclination to renounce the world; considering the oppressively religious atmosphere of her region, and especially considering the assumption that young girls were naturally docile, pious, and more attuned to spiritual matters than their grosser male counterparts, these letters show a rebelliousness, however uneasy, that is nonetheless stubborn and fully formed. In 1848 (aged 17) she writes to her pious friend, Abiah Root:

> The older I grow, the more do I love spring and spring flowers.
> . . . While at home there were several pleasure parties of which I was a
> member, and in our rambles we found many and beautiful children of
> spring. . . . Abiah, you may be surprised to hear me speak as I do, know-

ing that I express no interest in the all-important subject [accepting Christ]. . . . It is not now too late, so my friends tell me, so my offended conscience whispers, but it is hard for me to give up the world.

(L 23)

In a letter to Jane Humphrey, written two years later, she becomes more explicit:

The path of duty looks very ugly indeed—and the place where *I* want to go more amiable—a great deal—it is so much easier to do wrong than right—so much pleasanter to be evil than good, I dont wonder that good angels weep—and bad ones sing songs.

(L 30)[4]

A few months later she writes that she has begun to heed "beautiful tempters, yet I do not think I am wrong," and speaks of "one gold thread . . . a long, big shining fibre" which causes her great joy and indicates that, at last, "life has had an aim." (L 35)

In these early letters Dickinson indulges frequently in Emersonian lyricism, as well as in halfhearted self-mockery by picturing herself as a child of the devil, someone irretrievably lost. In time, the losses became actual: her important friendships with Abiah Root and with Susan Gilbert, later to become her sister-in-law, were shaken by Dickinson's lack of piety. In an 1854 letter to Susan, a letter rightly emphasized by Dickinson's two most recent biographers, her tone assumes a self-dramatizing wistfulness; yet self-dramatization was to become a way of life, and the letter represents a religious, sexual, and artistic declaration of independence. Here are the key passages:

Sue—you can go or stay—There is but one alternative—We differ often lately, and this must be the last. . . .

Sue—I have lived by this. It is the lingering emblem of the Heaven I once dreamed, and though if this is taken, I shall remain alone, and though in that last day, the Jesus Christ you love, remark he does not know me—there is a darker spirit will not disown it's child.

. . . Perhaps this is the point at which our paths diverge—then pass on singing Sue, and up the distant hill I journey on.

(L 173)

In a sense, Dickinson's "independence" here is a forced one: though the nature of this particular argument with Sue is unclear, much of Dickinson's bitterness clearly is in response to the coming marriage between Susan and the poet's brother, Austin. John Cody, in his Freudian analysis of Dickinson's inner life, remarks that after the marriage "she would go about her affairs indifferent to the fact that her life, now rendered meaningless, was ebbing away as through an open wound." He emphasizes her helplessness: "Emily has no choice but to accept the loss and continue on her way alone."[5] Conversely, Richard B. Sewall implies that the letter marks a new decisiveness: "The letter starts bluntly, goes straight to the point, and ends with finality. . . . [It] is an extraordinary one for Emily, the nearest approach to surliness and dismissal of any that survive."[6] Dickinson's necessary exclusion from the married intimacy of Susan and Austin seems to have made her, at last, acutely conscious of herself as dismissing the conventional existence Sue represented: marriage, Christian piety, a life in which Sue can "pass on singing" while Dickinson must journey "up the distant hill." The last phrase, foreshadowing her pervasive figure for poetic quest, hardly bears out Cody's contention that Dickinson's life was now "rendered meaningless." The letter conveys the bleak isolation of Dickinson's choice, but must be read in the context of the exuberant letter to Jane Humphrey: there was still that "gold thread" to be followed, and in her freedom there would be radical joy in addition to radical bereavement.

The "gold thread" of poetry, imaged by Dickinson as "a long, big shining fibre," seems unconsciously linked in her early letters with sexual power. Other early letters express a desperate anxiety regarding male sexual domination,[7] and part of Dickinson's fear that she is heeding "beautiful tempters" surely arises from a recognition that her interior potency implied an ambiguous sexual role. Though Dickinson often referred to herself in both poems and letters with a masculine pronoun—even calling herself "Brother Emily," or "Uncle Emily"—we need not assume that Dickinson was homosexual (although this case has been cogently argued).[8] Rather, as recent feminist criticism of Dickinson has demonstrated, the extremely stultifying role of the nineteenth-century woman naturally caused, in a woman of genius, an often bewildered confrontation with her own power (since women were thought to be powerless) and a tendency to consider herself as masculine—or even as a "madwoman"—rather than to consider power as a normal part of her feminine selfhood.[9] Sandra M. Gilbert and Susan Gubar have accurately described Dickinson's unique method of dealing with this dilemma:

> Where almost all late eighteenth- and nineteenth-century women writers . . . secreted bitter self-portraits of madwomen in the attics of their novels, Emily Dickinson herself became a madwoman—became

... both ironically a madwoman (a deliberate impersonation of a madwoman) and truly a madwoman (a helpless agoraphobic, trapped in a room in her father's house).[10]

This complex emotional circumstance, as we shall see, led into equally complex artistic strategies. Her deliberate adoption of a variety of "poses," her cunning uses of poetic personae, her frequent (and still frequently unnoticed) uses of dramatic irony, and especially, underlying all these, the tense, carefully maintained poise of her perceiving consciousness at the furthest bearable remove from outer phenomena—all these evolved from her identity as a woman poet in a particular cultural circumstance, and from the adjustments that circumstance forced upon her. We shall also see that her emphasis upon perception, upon *seeing*, which perhaps arose in the anxiety and defenselessness of her isolated, ambiguous selfhood, paradoxically became the means toward poetic and personal fulfillment.

Although we cannot know how great a degree of choice was involved in Dickinson's decision to renounce a conventional existence, we can evaluate this intensification of her perception and its crucial effect upon her work. In comprehending this effect, it is important to accept the terms of her renunciation of outer personalities and phenomena, to attempt to view the world from her own unique perspective. Far from the Whitmanesque conception of the poet as a highly vocal prophet, "the true son of God," a chief aspect of her poetic role was its deracinated privacy. When she included her poems in letters to friends, or even when she requested advice from her "preceptor" Higginson, she presented only various and oblique glimpses of herself and her profound engagement:[11] thus the extent of her posing, especially in letters to Higginson, is not a measure of the "coyness" of which she has often been accused, but rather of the complex delicacy of her position. She had increasingly to seek a sense of personal safety as a key condition of her enhanced perception (in her later years she would credit Higginson with "saving her life"—an uncharacteristically straightforward remark that one is inclined to take at face value), and this goal had continually to be aligned with her engagement in poetry, the liberty of poetic perception which was the special, hard-won quality of her existence. Dickinson did indeed live within a "polar privacy," and this extreme state, she instinctively knew, represented the necessary climate of her poetic creation.

Every aspect of Dickinson's existence, therefore, may be related to this strategy of conditioning whose goal was the most advantageous possible perspective for creative perception. Since her life and poetry are so continually a *process* of this perceiving (an ongoing cycle of what she often called "revelations"), and since her emotional impulse is so often that of aspiration toward oneness, Dickinson has rightly been discussed within the context of American Romanticism, particularly in its Transcendentalist phase. Yet her extreme individuality and lack of an acknowledged status within her literary world make such discussion a delicate task, even when it seems crucial to a full understanding of her art. Because of the quality of privacy in her poetic mission, and perhaps because the intensity of her quest excluded other concerns, it is not surprising that she left no formal theory of poetics (which, like Keats's letters or Emerson's journal entries, might provide the poet's own view of her intentions or her sense of literary affiliation); but Dickinson implies her own theory precisely in the act of declining to formulate one at all. She complained to Higginson that her thoughts, when "dressed" in the gowns of her poetics, "look alike, and numb" (L 261), and no doubt she would have felt this sense of frustration even more keenly had she attempted to theorize about poetry or the processes of her perception. If her poetic structures seemed too rigid and confining to the dynamism of her continual thought, a further codifying would surely have been unthinkable to her—only retreating an additional step backward from her main business of "Circumference," from her creative perception. Thus her method itself provides all the theory we need. She persuades by her very privateness, by the *exemplary* rather than the hortatory nature of her mode of life and communication; and she is fully aware of herself as one whose venture into the unknown can provide inspiration to others. "The Province of the Saved / Should be the Art—To save—" (P 539); she counted herself among the "Martyr Poets": "when their mortal name be numb— / Their mortal fate—encourage Some—" (P 544). Despite her privateness, she is nonetheless a leader; adjuring the reader to trust "the Infinite," she makes an important distinction: "trust him, Comrade— / You for you, and I, for you and me" (P 350).

David Porter is surely correct when he writes that "What we recognize [in Dickinson] is a language as well as a life withdrawn from contingent experience. The idiom of this reclusion is private and without adherence to the authority of either the actual world or literary tradition but eccentric in a fierce freedom." But this does not mean that we have "An art without progress," a "poet without a project."[12] Despite her isolation and fierce freedom, her progress was toward knowledge and her project was to narrate this lifelong journey in all its complexity. The following poem stresses her solitary fixation upon the infinite, but in its last line defines her own conception of her project:

The Only News I know
Is Bulletins all Day
From Immortality.

The Only Shows I see—
Tomorrow and Today—
Perchance Eternity—

The Only One I meet
Is God—The Only Street—
Existence—This traversed

If Other News there be—
Or Admirabler Show—
I'll tell it You—
(P 827)

In a poem that seems a reminder to herself about her mediating function, she notes: "Tell all the Truth but tell it slant— / Success in Circuit lies" (P 1129). She labored to be an Orphic truth-teller, making the truth visible to others. Because "Effort—is the sole condition" (P 750), she had to work alone; because she herself had a "fallen" consciousness, she could tell the truth only bit by bit, making her way along a circuitous and frequently agonized course.

As we have noted, Dickinson follows the prescription offered by Emerson in "Intellect":

> God offers to every mind its choice between truth and repose. Take which you please,—you can never have both. . . . He in whom love of truth predominates will keep himself aloof from all moorings, and afloat. He will abstain from dogmatism, and recognize all the opposite negations between which, as walls, his being is swung. He submits to the inconvenience of suspense and imperfect opinion, but he is a candidate for truth, as the other is not, and respects the highest law of his being.[13]

For Dickinson, too, "Truth—is stirless—" (P 780), the "Twin identity" of God (P 836); her constant impulse is to establish lasting connection with this absolute reality. As Sharon Cameron remarks, "a central feature of Dickinson's poetry is its resolute departure from temporal order and its reference to another absent or invisible order that is invoked as 'Immortality' or alluded to . . . as 'Centre.' "[14] Yet this "invisible order" is blocked by nature and by Dickinson's own benighted perception as a natural creature. She hardly shared Emerson's confidence that "The visible creation is the terminus or the circumference of the invisible world"; his transformation of nature's Platonic reflection of spirit into an ideal, ever-present interpenetration failed to clarify either reality for her.[15] Yet it was Emerson, whose high spiritual goals prompted him toward his own brand of radicalism, who most influenced Dickinson. Their difficult relationship helps to clarify, in fact, Dickinson's theory of perception, both regarding the natural world—our immediate subject here—and the conditions of her quest as a whole.

One way to approach this relationship is through Emerson's essay, "The Skeptic." Emerson places the skeptic midway along a spectrum that has the "abstractionist" at one extreme and the "materialist" at the other. For Emerson, the skeptic's credo is a self-defeating empiricism: "I see plainly, [the skeptic] says, that I cannot see."[16] Emerson's attitude toward the skeptic is grudgingly admiring but finally dismissive: we may free ourselves of skepticism, he insists, because "the expansive nature of truth comes to our succor, elastic, not to be surrounded. Man helps himself by larger generalizations. The lesson of life is practically to generalize; to believe what the years and the centuries say, against the hours; to resist the usurpation of particulars; to penetrate to their catholic sense."[17] In his final paragraph, he advises:

> Let a man learn to look for the permanent in the mutable and fleeting; let him learn to bear the disappearance of things he was wont to reverence without losing his reverence; let him learn that he is here, not to work but to be worked upon; and that, though abyss open under abyss, and opinion displace opinion, all are at last contained in the Eternal Cause. . . .[18]

Here we can observe that while Dickinson shares Emerson's aspirations, she cannot share his methods. Though she too searches for the permanent in nature, mutability is her persistent theme; though she also retains her reverence for the numinous (or, more darkly, the "haunted") dimension of nature, she is not satisfied to be passively "worked upon." Rather, she must work, and her means toward completing that work is to conjoin empirical perception and religious awe. Because Dickinson, like her Puritan forbears, no longer lives within a defined, logically ordered universe, she has an intense drive for precisely that certitude from which—in her Adamic, "fallen" state[19]—she has been disinherited; and it is not merely her uncertainty as a fallen creature (which the Puritans shared) that torments her, but a vaster, more chaotic, more generalized uncertainty regarding not only her relation to the spiritual order but also, horrifically, that order's possible nonexistence.[20] Her estranged vantage point makes her into Clark Griffith's "post-Romantic child," a poet who bitterly senses "Nature's wanton disregard for human welfare";[21] yet her stubborn questing spirit and religious temperament (those vestigial yet active Puritan virtues) force her, as well, to acknowledge and attempt to recreate in language those same phenomena—sublime, mysterious, piercingly beautiful—that represent a block to spiritual vision.[22] Where nature is concerned she is both acolyte and heretic, finding herself in an opaque environment, a moral wilderness that is nonetheless touched—and occasionally redeemed—by wonder.

The complex relation between Dickinson's perception and nature sets the basic conditions of her continuing quest for spiritual truth. Her nature poems, large in number and ranging from ardent Emersonian lyrics to austere, depressed notations reminiscent of Thomas Hardy, fall into two general categories: those which attempt to limn the natural universe as a whole, indicating its frightening vastness in relation to a single perceiving mind; and those which deal with minute particulars, discrete and isolable phenomena which can be perceived clearly and evaluated accurately. In both kinds of poems her central concern is the speaker's own relationship to a particular aspect of nature and the enhanced orientation, identity, and knowledge her understanding of the relationship might produce.

Dickinson's most exclusively Emersonian poetry is found mainly in the early work;[23] viewing nature as beneficent, such poems are analogous to the earliest "bark" lyrics in their blind faith that beyond torturous and chaotic conditions there resides an ultimate good, what Emerson confidently named the "Eternal cause."[24] Also in the early lyrics, however, are suggestions of nature's stubborn opacity, though most often Dickinson's tone is curious or awestruck rather than bitter:

Who built this little Alban House
And shut the windows down so close
My spirit cannot see?
(P 128)

This initial curiosity leads toward a central dilemma in Dickinson's work, well-described by Joanne Feit Diehl:

[Dickinson] asserts that nature is not the sacred text, ready to reveal all if we read it right. She contends not only that we can never attain to full knowledge of nature, that our view is dominated by our eye. . . . If nature is no longer at the center and cannot hold the answers she seeks, what of vision, the significance of sight? What becomes of the crucial

Emersonian "eye" if the "text" cannot be read anyway? Although vision remains a major concern, she antithetically praises what she cannot see, either because the moment is past, distant, or denied.[25]

Because of Dickinson's sense of natural withholding—what Inder Nath Kher calls "the landscape of absence"[26]—her poems, even the early ones, seldom begin with a preordained notion of transcendence which the poem must argue. Rather her poems are tentative, delicately exploratory, the argument of a particular poem to be inferred from the experience it depicts. Understanding of the relationship often produces terror, and the argument to be inferred is usually a dark one; but at least the relationship is defined, the chaotic "sea" of disorienting fear momentarily calmed. Whereas in the early poem "Whether my bark went down at sea" the natural universe is a largely symbolic seascape, it becomes in most of her work a literal antagonist, placing her in distinct contrast not only to Emerson but to most of the major Romantic writers—particularly Wordsworth—who conceived of nature as nurse, healer, and savior. Unlike Wordsworth, Dickinson does not deny her knowledge of isolation and danger, and the tension in her poems does not arise from the buried Wordsworthian anxiety that such denial is hopeless and immature; she does share, however, in the fear that relationship is wholly subjective and therefore delusional, so that in her poems the awareness of the speaker's apartness, the stark reality of division, produces a thrust toward objectivity, perspective, even producing the occasion for irony. Emerson again provides the sharpest imaginable contrast: "Whether nature enjoy a substantial existence without, or is only in the apocalypse of the mind, it is alike useful and alike venerable to me. Be it what it may, it is ideal to me so long as I cannot try the accuracy of my senses."[27] Here Emerson deliberately blurs subject and object in his desperate pursuit of an ideal optimism; for Dickinson the distinction was paramount, however, and when she could not "try the accuracy of [her] senses," she fell into despair. What was for Emerson "the splendid labyrinth of my perceptions"[28] was for Dickinson more often a terrifying maze of contradictory signs.

Dickinson, haunted by subjectivity, took as a major theme what Harold Bloom has called the "dark undersong" that creates the most significant tension in Wordsworth's "Tintern Abbey" and ultimately in Romantic nature poetry as a whole.[29] Bloom in fact locates Wordsworth as a signal turning point not only in the antagonisms between poet and nature but in the subject matter of poetry itself: "Before Wordsworth, poetry had a subject. After Wordsworth, its prevalent subject was the poet's own subjectivity. Before

Wordsworth, any poet, professional or amateur, would in some sense *choose a subject* in order to write a poem. After Wordsworth, this is no longer true, and so a new poetry was born."[30] And as R. P. Blackmur notes, "All her life [Dickinson] was looking for a subject, and the looking *was* her subject. . . ."[31] These insights help in gaining an appropriate perspective on Dickinson, both in relation to her Romantic ethos and in viewing her quest as the central ongoing concern (or "subject") of her poetry. They also aid us in defining her nature poems in terms of her perceptual stance: we see her both attempting to distrust her subjectivity yet also realizing that this is the essential condition of her perception and therefore of her artistic endeavor.[32]

Dickinson knew that the bodiless "eye" of her early poem represented a function that required a personal, psychic, emotional "mooring" even as it attempted to seek out a "mystic" one. In this aspect of perception especially she parts company with Emerson. Vivian Hopkins, in her study of Emerson's aesthetics, notes that for him considerations of "perception are inseparable from 'the immaterial aspect of vision' and that 'perception' or 'impression' of an object on the mind indicates that it is well on its way to becoming an 'image' of the imagination, since the mind's 'perception' of the object implies the interpretation which will inform the work of art."[33] Dickinson's perception of external reality involves a far less facile procedure, since she shares the Romantic anxiety over the absolute separation of mind and nature, and since her perception rarely implies a transcendence of the world of time. As Robert Weisbuch comments, "Her poems do not dramatize the projection of mind onto matter but the organization of a mind-world continuum in a pattern of chosen language."[34] It is helpful to bear in mind this concept of a "mind-world continuum" in examining the two major aspects of Dickinson's perception of nature.

For even her poems which deal, often lovingly, with discrete "particulars" of the natural world are nonetheless informed by a sharp, anti-Emersonian consciousness of subjectivity and of a continuity which conflicts with any attempt to "fix" her perceptions. Her famous poem of the snake may serve as a paradigm for these various tensions, since above all it emphasizes the link between particularity and the larger "ghost" of nature which can never be fixed or comprehended through perception. The poem begins with two stanzas which capture the movement of the snake while indicating the snake's effect on anyone encountering him:

A narrow Fellow in the Grass
Occasionally rides—
          [*no stanza break*]

> You may have met Him—did you not
> His notice sudden is—
>
> The Grass divides as with a Comb—
> A spotted shaft is seen—
> And then it closes at your feet
> And opens further on—
> (P 986)

The first stanza contains a warning which the second brilliantly justifies: the snake is characterized through his ability to elude perception, the description focusing on the snake's disturbance of the grass by which his presence is inferred. The use of the passive voice in the single line of the snake's brief appearance emphasizes that the creature has the upper hand and that *seeing* him is the chance occurrence of an instant. Later in the poem, the snake's deceptiveness is dramatized:

> . . . when a Boy, and Barefoot—
> I more than once at Noon
> Have passed, I thought, a Whip lash
> Unbraiding in the Sun
> When stooping to secure it
> It wrinkled, and was gone—

"Barefoot" and "Noon" in Dickinson's poems are often equated with naiveté and fulfillment, and the child's natural gesture toward "security" is understandable but short-lived. At this point in the poem two qualities of the snake have been stressed: its evanescence and its delusiveness. By the end of the poem the primary emotion of the speaker is fear (tinged with the sexual dread of the "worm" which appears in the dream poem "In winter in my room") and a sensation ("Zero at the Bone") which suggests both the deathly cold of "Safe in their alabaster chambers" and a brutally physical realization of the emptiness of her perception:

> Several of Nature's People
> I know, and they know me—
> I feel for them a transport
> Of cordiality—
>
> But never met this Fellow
> Attended, or alone
> Without a tighter breathing
> And Zero at the Bone —
> (P 986)

Dickinson stresses the tension and implicit division between herself and "Nature's People": the oxymoronic quality of her "transport / Of cordiality" indicates an innate emotional response qualified by a caution learned through experience; "transport" suggests an emotional aspiration toward oneness, but "cordiality" indicates a more measured response, an awareness of distance.[35] And as so often in Dickinson, colloquial diction effectively heightens emotional terror: this apparently harmless "Fellow" brings to the speaker's mind her sense of estrangement within nature, and in his mythic implications becomes a reminder of mortality as well.

 "A narrow Fellow in the Grass" is perhaps an extreme example of Dickinson's sense of the implicit terror in her sharp observation of nature, but few of the poems in this group are without the suggestion that perception increases consciousness of estrangement, and all serve ultimately as intimations of death. Admiring the "soundless travels" of a caterpillar she finds on her hand, envious of its "velvet world," she concludes by observing: "Intent upon its own career / What use has it for me—" (P 1448). Elsewhere she notes, in a similar tone, "How happy is the little Stone" whose integrity and fulfillment seem far greater than her own since the stone is "Fulfilling absolute Decree / In casual simplicity—" (P 1510). Even "A Route of Evanescence," in describing the hummingbird's vibrancy of color and movement, stresses the elusiveness of beauty, and in Dickinson's brilliant conceit of "The mail from Tunis, probably / An easy Morning's Ride—" (P 1463), the bird becomes a harbinger of death.[36] Also elusive is the firefly, "A speck of Rapture—first perceived / By feeling it is gone" (P 1468). "I'll tell you how the Sun rose" (P 318) ends with the speaker's deliberately faltering attempt to describe the sun's setting—which seemed "A Dominie in Gray"—and again views a natural process in a context symbolic of death.

 One of Dickinson's most haunting (and most undervalued) lyrics creates a natural scene of absolute bleakness, the perceiver's calm, disaffected voice serving to intensify the poem's inherent terror. Dickinson never wrote a more starkly "existential" poem than this:

Four Trees—upon a solitary Acre—
Without Design
Or Order, or Apparent Action—
Maintain—

The Sun—upon a Morning meets them—
The Wind—
No nearer Neighbor—have they—
But God—

The Acre gives them—Place—
They—Him—Attention of Passer by—
Of Shadow, or of Squirrel, haply—
Or Boy—

What Deed is Their's unto the General Nature—
What Plan
They severally—retard—or further—
Unknown—
(P 742)

The poem's "Four Trees," suggesting the points of a compass or, as a startling inversion of Whitman's "square deific," a shapeliness that is solid, blocklike, and permanent, nonetheless "Maintain"—desperately, meaninglessly—in a universe of solitariness and disorder. Relationship between the trees and other phenomena—even the "Attention of Passer by," the speaker's single oblique reference to herself—is mere contingency, lacking in substantive or even relative value. A shadow, a squirrel, a boy, a mature perceiver—all are leveled horribly in the undesigned, orderless "General Nature" that is the poem's universe. "God" is so hopelessly distant that he is only a word, signifying nothing, while the poem in its despair turns upon a handful of more ominous words: *solitary, haply,* and especially *Unknown.* Even the poem's stanzas, with their truncated second and fourth lines (excepting line 10, where the speaker's appearance disorders even the versification), create the impression of weariness, of estrangement, of a minimal and colorless world.[37] The poem itself may be said barely to exist: it speaks in a soft monotone at the very edge of silence, able only to sketch the lack of order in nature, to suggest the speaker's lack of knowledge, and to haunt the reader with its own ghostly yet profound uneasiness.

This uneasiness, often unclarified but always inescapable, underlies nearly all Dickinson's nature poetry. David Porter has suggested that Dickinson's impulse is to achieve a "scrupulous indecorum" in refusing to adopt the "uncritical habit" of her contemporaries in perceiving nature: "[S]he sought not to clarify existence but rather to restore its density and mystery. . . ."[38] But the emphasis here seems misleading: to clarify existence was in fact one of her chief aims, and her refusal to adopt the "uncritical habit" of an Emerson simply indicates her stubborn honesty in pursuing such clarification—again, in Robert Weisbuch's words, her "skepticism makes the visions which survive it real." Rather than seeking to "restore" the density and mystery of nature, she is acknowledging it, occasionally finding beauty in it; but Dickinson would surely trade the "mystery," however sublime, for certain knowledge. In one poem, charting her frustrating struggle toward this knowledge, she notes that "nature is a stranger" whose "ghost" can never be "simplified": "those who know her, know her less / The nearer her they get" (P 1400). She optimistically begins another poem, " 'Nature' is what we see—" but then proceeds to qualify this statement until she concludes that

> Nature is what we know—
> Yet have no art to say—
> So impotent Our Wisdom is
> To her Simplicity.
> (P 668)

In these latter two poems she defines the problem both in terms of perception and of art; in a letter to Higginson, she combines the ideas in one of her rare theoretical statements: "Nature is a Haunted House—but Art—a House that tries to be haunted" (L 459a).

For Dickinson, complacent "blindness" is a surrender to the opacity of nature. An important poetic aim, therefore, is her attempt to control its "density and mystery" through the dramatization of her perceptions; these dramatizations emphasize estrangement, fear, evanescence, and the inadequacy of human seeing in a mysterious natural world, even as they insist, with Emerson, upon the beauty and sublimity of the mystery. Dickinson's other perceptual approach to nature (and always implicit in her adjustment of focus is the quest for identity, for the poetic attainment of an accurate perspective) is the attempt to envision the natural world in its wholeness; perception shifts from minute particulars to the universal. Poems of this group tend to emphasize the self-sufficiency of the universe, occasionally hinting at a covert malignity in nature which anticipates Hardy; "Hap" would serve as an appropriate title, in fact, for several of Dickinson's poems, especially those in which she senses a veiled, indifferent God behind the inscrutable face of nature:

> The Perished Patterns murmur—
> But His Perturbless Plan
> Proceed—inserting Here—a Sun—
> There—leaving out a Man—
> (P 724)

In other poems this healthy anger toward indifference dissolves into paranoia:

> I could not find a Privacy
> From Nature's sentinels—
>
> In Cave if I presumed to hide
> The Walls—begun to tell—
> Creation seemed a mighty Crack—
> To make me visible—
> (P 891)

In this poem the speaker attempts to escape some outer, hostile perception—an extreme example of poetic perception externalized through placing the speaker (with maximum discomfort) into the natural landscape. It is in such poems that Robert Weisbuch's concept of Dickinson's "scenelessness" becomes valuable, since here the "scene" retains only its analogical value in illustrating the speaker's state of mind. In Dickinson, he writes, "scenes are not mimetic but illustrative, chosen, temporary, analogous . . . and this scenelessness is the fully unique quality which identifies Dickinson's lyric technique."[39] It is also the quality which makes her of all the American Romantics the most exclusively concentrated upon her internalized quest, using natural scenes only as they are relevant in creating the "mind-world continuum." Moreover, in nearly all the nature poems the speaker's perception of outer phenomena is relativistic—through her perceptions she attempts to assess her identity, her own "size." Again, this is part of the larger effort through which Dickinson attempts to establish her unthreatened yet stubbornly uncompromised perspective.

In poems where this perspective seems temporarily attained, however, the natural progress of Dickinson's thought is again toward consciousness of death. A well-known early poem may serve as the paradigm for Dickinson's awareness of natural process in contrast to her own mortality:

> Of Bronze—and Blaze—
> The North—Tonight—
> So adequate—it forms—
> So preconcerted with itself
> So distant—to alarms—
> An Unconcern so sovreign
> To Universe, or me—
> Infects my simple spirit
> [*no stanza break*]

With Taints of Majesty—
Till I take vaster attitudes
And strut upon my stem—
Disdaining Men, and Oxygen,
For Arrogance of them—

My Splendors, are Menagerie—
But their Competeless Show
Will entertain the Centuries
When I, am long ago,
An Island in dishonored Grass—
Whom none but Daisies, know.
(P 290)

This poem contains many implications characteristic of Dickinson's perception of phenomenal vastness in nature. Several intriguing word choices add
to the poem's complexity: "adequate" is in surprising juxtaposition to the
"Bronze—and Blaze" and contains a hint of irony in the speaker's awareness
of her own exclusion; the verb "forms" suggests the continual flux and process of the natural phenomenon set against her static perception. The "Unconcern so sovreign" of the northern sky is more than adequately dealt with
by Dickinson, however: rather than allowing the impressive sight to make
her feel insignificant or threatened, she pretends to partake imaginatively of
its rather smug self-sufficiency:

Till I take vaster attitudes
And strut upon my stem—
Disdaining Men, and Oxygen,
For Arrogance of them—

This represents a startling shift in the poem's manner, but the lines are surely
ironic: Dickinson's formidable wit is often used defensively in protesting the
"perturbless plan" of nature; she is at her best when she perceives with narrowed eyes. The wit continues in stanza two as she compares her own "Splendors" with those of the sky, but in the closing lines the poem takes on an
unexpected gravity to which the preceding ironies only lend substance and
weight.[40] When she becomes "An Island in dishonored Grass— / Whom none
but Daisies, know," she makes it clear that in death she will only be further
estranged, and truly ignored because forgotten, unknown; Dickinson pulls
the rug out from under her own wit. And it should be noted that for "Daisies"

she listed "Beetles" as a variant—a more macabre and perhaps more fitting word choice.

As in "A narrow Fellow in the Grass," therefore, an important note in Dickinson's perception of nature is that of caution. Whether she states the conflict between her attempts to perceive and the ghost of nature that refuses to be "simplified" through her perception, whether she dramatizes her speaker within a threatening landscape, attempting to "hide" the hopeless inadequacy of her identity, or whether she employs a finely honed wit as a competent defense against this hopelessness, the continuing implication is the absolute necessity of a defense; she is constantly jockeying for position. Her nature poems show her in the act of teaching herself to perceive both accurately and safely. Because the world is constantly and threateningly in flux, establishing a mind-world continuum requires of the perceiving mind an extraordinary agility and wariness. It will therefore be helpful to examine in detail the kinds of artistic constructs Dickinson develops in order to enhance her perceptual engagement with the world. A great deal has been written about her dramatic personal strategies—her reclusiveness and her intense, obliquely maintained relationships—but the ways in which she employs these conscious maneuvers (almost always constructively) in her modes of poetic expression have been less thoroughly scrutinized. Her employment of poetic personae, her frequent and complex uses of irony, certain significant image patterns which recur throughout her work—all may be related fruitfully to her continual struggle toward a clear-sighted, uncompromised perspective upon the world around her, a perspective crucial to her poetic quest and to her obsessive concern with the reality and mystery of death.

This detailed examination of Dickinson's various perceptual strategies and their relationship to her concern with death will occupy the bulk of this study, but before leaving Dickinson's nature poems we should examine her cluster of lyrics dealing with one of her favorites among "Nature's people," the spider. For Dickinson, the spider's activity best represented both the strategy and the achievement of the artist—and significantly, an artist attempting to work within a cruel natural context.[41] Her five poems about the spider are pertinent in understanding her perception because they describe the necessary stance an artist must take against the outer world, a way in which he in fact may master that world, at least temporarily; the poems describe the spider as an artist with an achieved, self-sufficing identity which permits him an accomplishment typically Romantic in its emphasis on the organic expression of self, a heroic questing for beauty which is externalized through art. The spider represents a mature, transforming stage in Dickinson's perceptual quest because he may self-confidently work "at Night"—the time of absolute terror for many of Dickinson's protagonists—and even "without a Light": and his achievement is a "supreme" one, the absolute self-sufficiency of art. The comparison between the spider's activity and Dickinson's poetic quest is made explicit in her identification with him—"Neglected Son of Genius / I take thee by the Hand—" (P 1275)—and in the central poem of this group she symbolizes the value of artistic endeavor within her larger, always preeminent concerns of death and immortality:

A Spider sewed at Night
Without a Light
Upon an Arc of White.

If Ruff it was of Dame
Or Shroud of Gnome
Himself himself inform.

Of Immortality
His Strategy
Was Physiognomy.
(P 1138)

It should be stressed that in this poem—which focuses upon the spider's quest for immortality rather than his art as an end in itself—the "Strategy" is not synonymous with an achievement of immortality. Rather, the poem implies, the spider's mode of questing has the most potential value and meaning possible, given his conditions: the spider works undaunted within a void of "Night" and in its sureness of purpose combined with its enigmatic character (a combination which reminds us of Dickinson herself) keeps its own counsel as the art is created. "Physiognomy" not only refers to the spider's body and its special equipment, but also to its willingness to pit that body against the void. Thus we have Dickinson as the physical icon in her white robes, the "myth" who certainly informed only herself of her deepest purposes, and the Dickinson canon, the body of poetry, which represents one of the best strategies for immortality one can imagine. In the spider Dickinson found her natural symbol for the highly perceptive poet who, through having accomplished various strategies of perspective and focus, transmutes perception into a self-sufficing poetics, perhaps the best hedge against death itself. She knew that "Physiognomy" in both senses was her primary weapon against meaningless life and a final extinction, and she employed it to the furthest possible extent. Richard B. Sewall suggests a close identification in Dickinson's mind between the spider's activity in this poem and her own work: "Ostensibly [the poem] is about a spider; but she worked at night, too, and often, it seems, with little or no light, a reason (it has been suggested) to account for the fact that sometimes her lines went right off the page. . . . Her 'strategy' by this time (about 1869) was her poetry."[42]

If "A Spider sewed at Night" only hints at success for the spider's strategy, another poem asserts definite failure, though the failure is qualified:

> The Spider holds a Silver Ball
> In unperceived Hands—
> And dancing softly to Himself
> His Yarn of Pearl—unwinds—
>
> He plies from Nought to Nought
> In unsubstantial Trade—
> Supplants our Tapestries with His—
> In half the period—
>
> An Hour to rear supreme
> His Continents of Light—
> Then dangle from the Housewife's Broom—
> His Boundaries—forgot—
> (P 605)

Though the spider's hands are "unperceived," his possession of the "Silver Ball" suggests that within him is an artistic potential that is concentrated, valuable, and ripe for expressive achievement; again the importance of his enigmatic secrecy and self-sufficiency is stressed. The spider's "Yarn of Pearl"—Dickinson's beautiful pun for the poetic fiction—is in this poem unwound across an expanse of "Nought" which like the "Night" of the previous poem symbolizes the void, or meaninglessness, which the spider seems to defeat so easily. Yet, although actively "plying" against this void, his activity is "unsubstantial," a hint of the fallacy his strategy represents, and the foreshadowing of the death of his achievement which comes so rudely in the final lines. The spider's "Boundaries—forgot" recalls the early poem quoted above, in which Dickinson lies beneath the earth and is known only to "Beetles." An interesting variant which Dickinson lists for "Boundaries" is "Sophistries," which makes the situation even more hopeless: the art was only a kind of whistling in the dark after all, of no true value to anyone. The spider's art is like the "old—old sophistries of June" (P 130) in Dickinson's poem about Indian summer, which appears only as a "mistake" that certainly has no effect upon the encroaching death of winter. Yet the poem is not completely nihilistic: the spider's "Continents of Light" are triumphant, "supreme," even if the victory does last only "An Hour." As Dickinson says elsewhere, "The fairest Home I ever knew / Was founded in an Hour" by "a spider" (P 1423)—indicating again that the spider is a symbol for the dweller in possibility whose chief occupation is gathering paradise. Thus the relationship of this cluster of poems to Dickinson's religious and artistic quest is clear—the artistic quest, again, being a type of the religious quest (Dickinson's ultimate goals are never far from her mind). The poem implies also that artistic endeavor is valuable for its own sake—if only as therapy, perhaps—and that momentary triumphs of personal vision, even if they do not ensure immortality, are better than no triumphs at all.

Dickinson's spider poems must ultimately be viewed, however, as "yarns of pearl" in themselves, fictions which dramatize only the more serene moments of an artist whose omnivorous perception and resolute honesty would not long abide serenity. Her various strategies for perception were indispensable, but it became clear that no single stance remained satisfactory in a world of flux and time. Because perceptual conditions shifted constantly, she constantly adjusted her stance as perceiver, and the complexity of these adjustments continued to enrich her art.

3 Confident Despair

Dickinson's poetic quest is synonymous with an idealized progress toward certain knowledge, but because she lives in a world which is less than ideal, that progress is constantly frustrated. Therefore she suffers, doubts, regroups, and continues on with deepened, occasionally bitter insight. She becomes a poet of experience. Throughout the vicissitudes of quest, however, a few primary symbols represent some unchanging elements and conditions of the quest as a whole. The most important of these symbols are related to visual perception:[1] the "night" discussed above in connection with the "bark" poems, which is the symbol of her benighted, "fallen" perception, or spiritual blindness; "noon" and the sun, which represent absolute visionary glory, fulfillment of quest, the eradication of any division between perceiver and perceived; and physical eyesight itself, which must mediate between these two absolutes and align the real and temporal with an envisioned ideal, immortality. But the relationships among night, noon, and perception are dynamic and in constant flux; truth can only be glimpsed obliquely. "The Truth must dazzle gradually / Or every man be blind" (P 1129)—that is, true vision involves the ability to perceive relationships, to comprehend "noon" in terms of the night which is the human condition, the only condition Dickinson knows firsthand and thus the only one she trusts.

Poetic vision, therefore, is not a transcendental oneness with noon, a facile appropriation of the object of spiritual longing into the frame of a mere perceptual moment (though Dickinson did experience such moments, labeling them "ecstatic instants") but rather a multi-faceted endeavor toward gaining perspective upon that object, a perspective which absolutely necessitated *distance*. Again, "Perception of an object costs / Precise the Object's loss," and the acknowledgment of distance immediately creates a new necessity: to measure that distance. Thus the concept of ratio in Dickinson's quest is crucial, since all elements must be seen in their right relations to one another before the poet can have an accurate angle of vision upon the object of quest. And since a universe in flux is one of the givens, establishing these ratios is a never-ending process—thus the "unfinished" and inconclusive quality of Dickinson's canon as a whole and of Romantic long poems in general.

But if the quest cannot be completed, or even organized into a single coherent thrust, individual moments of vision—attainments of true perspective—can be recorded, shaped into discrete poetic wholes. Dickinson's poems have often been called "fragments" which make up a large, loosely related whole, but actually the opposite is true: the canon itself is a fragment while individual poems manage to attain completeness. This is the paradox of a quest which requires numberless strategies, the sum of which—if the number were finite—would succeed in producing complete vision, and thus the poet's union with it in the act of envisioning, the fulfillment of quest. We have already indicated Dickinson's awareness that her poetic strategies were all-important in her attempt to perceive accurately and to measure the value of her perception. In the poetic act of establishing ratios between perception and its object's loss, between artistic gain and personal deprivation, she finds her identity and the role of her own "physiognomy" in the quest for immortality. In order to place herself—a poet working "at night"—in an appropriate relationship to "noon," the object of quest, it was necessary to experiment constantly with visionary perspectives in her poems; thus the poems are often fictions whose personae argue for various of these perspectives. Some of these personae utter profound truths, but often the fictions subtly qualify the speakers' claims; sometimes the personae are still naive, in the state of innocence—and their naiveté is obvious, rather pathetic; and on occasion the speakers simply make fools of themselves. Almost every Dickinson commentator quotes her remark to Higginson about her poetic personae, but it cannot be repeated too frequently: "When I state myself, as the Representative of the Verse—it does not mean—me—but a supposed person" (L 268).[2] This is an uncharacteristically clear statement of artistic intent, and one which indicates Dickinson's awareness that Higginson tended to read her poems simplistically. The error continues to be repeated: "I never saw a Moor," for instance, is still usually read as representing Dickinson's credo, her moment of unshakable faith. To understand the complexity of Dickinson's quest is to become sensitive to her various, often cunning uses of personae and also to an inadequately recognized Dickinson technique: dramatic irony.

The subject of Dickinson's personae could itself involve a book-length study,[3] and here we can only indicate the ways in which she used her lyric "I" toward the goal of establishing visionary perspectives. Again, a poet whose condition is "night," who is a member of those "races nurtured in the dark," must constantly measure the distance between herself and noon in order to discover viable poetic stances. She therefore creates a variety of fictions whose personae represent differing postures and attitudes toward the quest itself: some speakers are cowardly, self-deluding; others are merely complacent; while still others make bold claims for the speaker's own perception and intelligence, her need to scrutinize carefully perceptual relationships—measuring distances, establishing ratios between perceptual gains and losses—and thus her ability to hold her own against some quite formidable antagonists. All of the poems discussed below center upon the key perceptual relationship between physical eyesight and the symbolic sun, or noon, of perceptual fulfillment, the poet's condition being a "night" of spiritual blindness and her quest being to rise toward a dawn of her own making. Unlike the "bark" poems discussed earlier, which allow fantastic intervention from above, a rather jejune wish-fulfillment, the mature quest poems center upon the self and its resources. They also display mature artistry in their subtle uses of personae and dramatic irony.

This group of poems dealing with the problems of perception itself is large, testifying to the importance to Dickinson of visionary perspective. The poems range between two extremes: from advocating the renunciation of perception to claiming for perception the major role in the poetic quest. As one might expect, it is in poems dealing with that first extreme—renouncing sight, having one's eye "put out"—that Dickinson finds the technique of dramatic irony useful. The following poem, for example, seems to focus upon the danger of an incautious perception of nature (though the implied "danger" is a curious one: unbearable joy), but it finally serves as a decisive qualification—in one sense a contradiction—of Emerson's transcendental impulse:

Before I got my eye put out
I liked as well to see—
As other Creatures, that have Eyes
And know no other way—

But were it told to me—Today—
That I might have the sky
For mine—I tell you that my Heart
Would split, for size of me—

The Meadows—mine—
The Mountains—mine—
All Forests—Stintless Stars—
As much of Noon as I could take
Between my finite eyes—

The Motions of The Dipping Birds—
The Morning's Amber Road—
For mine—to look at when I liked—
The News would strike me dead—

So safer Guess—with just my soul
Upon the Window pane—
Where other Creatures put their eyes—
Incautious—of the Sun—
(P 327)

The poem contrasts two kinds of perception—visual and intuitive—and
contains ambiguities deliberately left unresolved by the last stanza. The shock
of the first line, which makes us feel the speaker's terrible deprivation, is eased
by her hint that it is actually the "other Creatures" who are deprived: they
"have Eyes / And know no other way" to perceive, are somehow limited—so
the speaker's calm, logical tone implies—in their possession of what she herself has lost. The basic ambiguity of the poem established, Dickinson devotes
the three middle stanzas to the visionary apprehension of nature which the
speaker has relinquished, but the sensation of breathless excitement conveyed
by these stanzas only increases the tension begun in the opening lines, and
what are meant to be notes of caution, in fact the moral of the story—"I tell
you that my Heart / Would split, for size of me" and "The News would strike
me dead"—only underscore the validity of this potential joy. For this Dickinson persona to give up the chance for "As much of Noon as I could take /
Between my finite eyes" does not help answer the riddle of the first stanza but
only makes it more complex. The speaker in fact seems self-deluded: she has
hinted at the "other way" of perceiving but has only conveyed the excitement
of the way she has lost. After the three lively, "visionary" stanzas, she returns
to the wistful tone of stanza one, reasserting a comparison between herself
and the other creatures:

So safer Guess—with just my soul
Upon the Window pane—
                [*no stanza break*]

> Where other Creatures put their eyes—
> Incautious—of the Sun—

What seems a logical deduction is no deduction at all, since the speaker has so beautifully convinced us that she is wrong.

Thus the poem is a potent satire, an attack upon complacency—always a cardinal sin for Dickinson[4]—and perhaps against empty assertions of spiritual vision made by other poets. The speaker's "safety" has little value, as her unconscious jealousy of the other creatures makes clear. Other critics of this poem, though recognizing the visionary experience in the three middle stanzas, have ignored the poem's unusual ironic frame and have seemed to accept the speaker's argument at face value. E. Miller Budick writes of the poem's middle section: "These stanzas are an exquisitely wrought, graphically mimetic model of the competition between physical and spiritual perception. They unabashedly glory in the pictorial delights of the creation, but they leave painfully uncertain which mode of perception, the eyes or the soul, bestow this sensuous-spiritual feast upon the perceiver." Yet the poem's rhetoric insists that the speaker is denying herself the feast, summoning up the pictorial delights only through the memory of physical seeing; and this does reduce her vision, as Budick acknowledges, from "her originally panoramic perception into discrete and unsynthesizable fragments."[5] Ruth Miller equates the speaker with Dickinson herself, believing that the poem is about "the poet and her soul. . . . Her eyes were put out by the Sun, by her degreeless Noon, by her sudden intuition of a truth so overpowering it shattered her physical sense and replaced that dull way of seeing Nature, that ordinary way ignorant creatures must content themselves with, replaced conventional sight with spiritual vision."[6] But have the speaker's eyes been "put out by the Sun"? Rather it seems that she has put them out herself—that is, resolved to ignore her visual perception, rather than be like other creatures who are "Incautious—of the sun." Her act was a cowardly precaution, nor is there anything in the poem to support Miller's claim for the speaker's "sudden intuition of a truth so overpowering it shattered her physical sense." In fact the speaker is avoiding perceptual truth, attempting to deprecate its value; the middle stanzas, describing what the speaker has renounced, hardly describe "a dull way of seeing Nature," nor do they recall anything resembling "conventional sight." It is rather the "spiritual vision" which is dull and conventional, perhaps a blind attempt to follow in the footsteps of Transcendentalist leaders. Richard B. Sewall, in discussing this poem, says that "for the supremely sensitive soul, mere observation becomes possession and man and nature are one,"[7] but one should also add that the speaker, though sensitive, is supremely cautious as well, and in fact "observes" nothing. It should be noted, too, that Dickinson sent this poem to Higginson in the summer of 1862, having warned him in her preceding letter not to confuse Dickinson the poet with her personae.

One may be tempted toward a biographical reading of the poem because it deals with a renunciation, but Dickinson clearly finds this one abhorrent.[8] Beneath the speaker's extreme and ludicrous precaution of having her eye put out as a defense against perception, however, does lurk Dickinson's very real fear of losing her own sight. Although John Cody reads the poem as being merely about physical blindness, his suggestion that her eye troubles of the 1860s prompted the dramatic situation in the poem may well be correct, and his discussion of her eye disease is illuminating.[9] Knowing Dickinson's anxiety over her own eyes, however, should cast additional doubt upon the assertions of the poem's speaker. When in Cambridge for eye treatments in November of 1864, she employed a telling image in writing to her sister Lavinia: "I have been sick so long I do not know the Sun" (L 296). The speculations of recent biographers that Dickinson's famous "terror" of which she wrote to Higginson may have been a fear that she was going blind seem quite reasonable;[10] clearly, her eyesight was the last thing Dickinson was prepared to renounce.

"Before I got my eye put out" uses dramatic irony to indicate the speciousness of Transcendental arguments for an undifferentiated, indiscriminate, non-perceptual communion between the soul and nature. Dickinson remarked wryly of Emerson: "With the Kingdom of Heaven on his knee, could Mr. Emerson hesitate?" (L 353). Yet here again Dickinson was more closely akin to Emerson than she realized, for he also repeatedly stressed the importance of physical seeing. (Dickinson's satiric thrusts at Transcendental simple-mindedness are often more appropriately directed at his cult-like followers than at Emerson himself.) He insisted that "The eye is the best of artists," and once noted: "I feel that nothing can befall me in life—no disgrace, no calamity, (*leaving me my eyes*), which nature cannot repair."[11] In this passage from *Nature*, he seems to speak specifically of Dickinson's speaker in "Before I got my eye put out": "To speak truly, few adult persons can see nature. Most persons do not see the sun. At least they have a very superficial seeing."[12] Dickinson herself seems to chastise her speaker in another poem which also deals with the crucial difference between guessing and seeing:

Who saw no Sunrise cannot say
The Countenance 'twould be.
      [*no stanza break*]

Who guess at seeing, guess at loss
Of the Ability.

The Emigrant of Light, it is
Afflicted for the Day.
The Blindness that beheld and blest—
And could not find it's Eye.
(P 1018)

Like Emerson, Dickinson knew that facile communion produced a false
and sterile kind of ecstasy based in self-delusion; although it is sometimes
"lighter—to be Blind" (P 761), as she wearily puns in a poem about psychic
exhaustion, it is not illuminating and it is certainly not productive. But "Before I got my eye put out" does more than simply ridicule an immature stance.
Though the poem's speaker misinterprets her fear of complete ecstasy, unconsciously instructing the reader that her solution is a mistaken one, her impulse
holds an element of widom which other Dickinson speakers seize upon and
develop more constructively. Perceptual fulfillment can indeed be "incautious" if the perceiver loses perspective, fails to measure ecstasy against a
human condition which generates despair. This notion informs another poem
whose argument is again extreme, advocating "the putting out of eyes":

Renunciation—is a piercing Virtue—
The letting go
A Presence—for an Expectation—
Not now—
The putting out of Eyes—
Just Sunrise—
Lest Day—
Day's Great Progenitor—
Outvie. . . .
(P 745)

This is one of Dickinson's many "definition" poems and presents no
dramatic situation at all; it therefore freely uses symbolic language and is not
concerned with any actual, particularized dilemma. Unlike "Before I got my
eye put out," the poem does not advocate the total renunciation of perception,
only the renunciation of a perceptual "Day" whose common glare blinds us
to the *value* of perception by causing a loss of perspective. The second half of
the poem works out the dialectic established through the wholly symbolic
language in the preceding lines:

> Renunciation—is the Choosing
> Against itself—
> Itself to justify
> Unto itself—
> When larger function—
> Make that appear
> Smaller—that Covered Vision—Here—

The poem has been attacked as obscure, "badly crabbed," but when the rhetorical structure of the poem is perceived, it can be seen that the lines have a stunning clarity and completeness.[13] The poem argues for a distrust of perception ("the putting out of Eyes") only when perception becomes a limited and rather prideful "Covered Vision," one which has no awareness of its preeminent "larger function." Jean McClure Mudge writes that "the 'Vision' which is covered in this life refers to the first 'itself,' whose claims are blind and incomplete because they are limited to a view from 'Here,' that is, this world as opposed to eternity."[14] To lose perspective is to lose everything. And in the interesting variant Dickinson gives for "Covered"—"sated"—the poem offers yet another warning against complacency.

It is important to understand that "Before I got my eye put out" and "Renunciation—is a piercing Virtue," which may appear similar at first glance, use entirely different poetic modes in arguing the danger of perception and have differing emphases: the first ironically controverts its own position and thus focuses upon a certain kind of erroneous stance, while the second subtly insists upon genuinely necessary qualifications of the visionary act. The complexity of Dickinson's ideas and her ability to communicate precisely through intricate poetic arguments are amply evidenced by such poems. Both of the poems could conceivably be read as neurotic in tone or self-defeating in outlook if their context were misunderstood and if the serious urgency of Dickinson's aims were not recognized.

For the perceiving consciousness to maintain awareness of the "larger function" is crucial to Dickinson's ultimate goals. In one poem she desires "A Landscape—not so great / To suffocate the Eye" (P 495), again fearing that the covered or sated vision might become an end in itself. The renunciation of facile victories is "piercing" because this dogged honesty intensifies experiential pain, the continual frustration of quest: in a telling analogy she says that "To learn the Transport by the Pain— / As Blind Men learn the sun" is a "Sovereign Anguish" (P 167). She is always aware of the status which accompanies her unwillingness to compromise, but the "learning" process is nonetheless painful and requires an acknowledgment of spiritual blindness. Another poem states the relationship between her status and her intensified darkness:

> Had I not seen the Sun
> I could have borne the shade
> But Light a newer Wilderness
> My Wilderness has made—
> (P 1233)

Since she cannot continually "see" the sun, prolong the "ecstatic instants" of vision, she must blindly "learn" it, accommodating her quest to the condition of darkness:

> We grow accustomed to the Dark—
> When Light is put away—
> As when the Neighbor holds the Lamp
> To witness her Goodbye—
>
> A Moment—We uncertain step
> For newness of the night—
> Then—fit our Vision to the Dark—
> And meet the Road—erect. . . .
> (P 419)

"The light of poetic perception," writes Inder Nath Kher, "does not provide an easy escape from the darkness of existence; it simply lends man the courage or vision to put up with existence as such. . . ."[15] And this condition of darkness, of course, is also the condition of mortality: ultimately Dickinson's concept of perceptual values is intimately connected with her meditations upon death. A poem ostensibly about the passing of summer deals with this issue, focusing again upon a visionary perspective which results in "Etherial Gain." The summer puts up her "Hands of Haze"

> . . . to hide her parting Grace
> From our unfitted eyes.
>
> My loss, by sickness—Was it Loss?
> Or that Etherial Gain
> One earns by measuring the Grave—
> Then—measuring the Sun—
> (P 574)

She needs to "measure" and establish ratios, to measure everything against the grave, but the poem also makes a statement about her perceptual stance. To see the sun through a "Haze," an awareness of imperfect human perception and of death, is to "earn" a spiritual insight; transport is achieved through a measured, necessary loss. Also implied here is the speaker's unworthiness; because the speaker feels herself "unfitted," a controlling motif in Dickinson's quest, as David Porter has shown, is that of aspiration: "In general . . . the disposition of Emily Dickinson's mind is between the poles of the *now* and the *hoped for,* between actuality and ideality. The act of the speaker's mind in her poetry is one of aspiration, of attempting to effect a bridge between the two poles."[16]

Rhetorical emphasis upon the speaker's "unfitted eyes" is recurrent in many poems. "An ignorance a Sunset / Confer upon the Eye—" she insists (P 5 5 2), characterizing the perceptual act not as a furtherance of quest but as a necessary humbling: "Omnipotence' inspection / Of Our inferior face." Perception is humbling, but nonetheless an oblique glimpse of God and thus encouraging as well. Another poem about sunset states the ethereal gain:

> Like Mighty Foot Lights—burned the Red
> At Bases of the Trees—
> The far Theatricals of Day
> Exhibiting—to These—
>
> 'Twas Universe—that did applaud—
> While Chiefest—of the Crowd—
> Enabled by his Royal Dress—
> Myself distinguished God—
> (P 595)

Her unfitted eyes are here "enabled" by the "Mighty Foot Lights," bulletins from immortality which the poet can read and interpret. Thus she deduces, in a remarkably compressed two-line poem:

> Not "Revelation"—'tis—that waits—
> But our unfurnished eyes—

The poem appears in a letter to Higginson (L 2 8o), and she introduces the lines by saying that they express her idea that "the 'Supernatural,' was only the Natural, disclosed—." In a very early poem she states with youthful exuberance an idealization of this perceptual disclosure (but notice, even here, the qualifying "ifs" which frame the poem):

> If pain for peace prepares
> Lo, what "Augustan" years
> Our feet await!

If springs from winter rise,
Can the Anemones
Be reckoned up?

If night stands first—*then* noon
To gird us for the sun,
What gaze!

When from a thousand skies
On our *developed* eyes
Noons blaze!
(P 63)

Despite the skeptical "ifs," the tone of the poem is joyous; it is remarkable for an early poem in its synthesis of so many symbols and ideas Dickinson continues to develop in her later poetry. Most important, it reveals an awareness of the relationship between night and noon, of the necessity that one be "girded" for the sun, and that genuine fulfillment can come only through "*developed* eyes." The poem is thus celebratory, picturing a fulfillment that is truly earned.

In many poems the word "heaven" is synonymous with "noon," and when Dickinson employs more specifically religious language the interiority of her quest becomes most evident:

Heaven is so far of the Mind
That were the Mind dissolved—
The Site—of it—by Architect
Could not again be proved—

'Tis vast—as our Capacity—
As fair—as our idea—
To Him of adequate desire
No further 'tis, than Here—
(P 370)

"As a psychological state," Albert Gelpi remarks of this poem, " 'Heaven' is the furthest dimension of selfhood,"[17] and elsewhere Dickinson frequently defines—or admits she cannot define—heaven in terms of her own interpretive and expressive power. Even when these poems honestly fail of "definition" and admit the inexpressibility of spiritual fulfillment, they do not fall back upon preexisting religious concepts.[18] In poems like " 'Heaven' has different Signs—to me" (P 575) and " 'Heaven'—is what I cannot reach!" (P 239), this fulfillment (the old concept placed in quotation marks, suggesting the need for redefinition) is pictured wholly in terms of selfhood and the self's ability to interpret natural "Signs." But these signs, as we have seen, more often confuse than clarify the poet's perception, and therefore her expressive power is likewise stymied. "I found the words to every thought / I ever had—but One" (P 581), and that one is defined as "the Sun," or "Noon," of fulfillment. Her attitude toward this singular failure ranges from the mystical contentment of "The Tint I cannot take—is best—" (P 627) to the brittle, sardonic outrage of "Out of sight? What of that?" (P 703), but even the first poem ends by anticipating a time when "the Cheated Eye / Shuts arrogantly—in the Grave— / Another way—to see—." Whatever the tone, Dickinson's poems constantly turn on perception as the strenuous, often fruitless, but nonetheless indispensable means toward fulfillment.

To reach "Heaven," then, one must have "adequate desire," and in other poems Dickinson again employs irony and limited personae—those without such desire—to undercut conventional notions of the religious quest. In the following well-known poem, another of Dickinson's wistful, obtuse speakers blithely denies the value of perception:

> I never saw a Moor—
> I never saw the Sea—
> Yet know I how the Heather looks
> And what a Billow be.
>
> I never spoke with God
> Nor visited in Heaven—
> Yet certain am I of the spot
> As if the Checks were given—
> (P 1052)

Unlike "Heaven is so far of the Mind," which presents a sophisticated concept of a paradise within, this poem baldly states explicit faith in an external, localized heaven, a place as phenomenally real, the poem implies, as the moors or the sea; but this faith is based upon nothing but specious logic. The argument of the poem turns upon what seems a kind of childish common sense, but in fact the analogies of stanza one are not applied to the speaker's faith in a valid way. Although she never saw a moor or the sea, we assume that she is nonetheless certain that they exist through other kinds of proof—perhaps the evidence of paintings or photographs, written descriptions, or the eyewitness accounts of others. Only through these means could the speaker "know how the Heather looks / And what a Billow be."

Thus far the poem at least makes sense, even if its content seems suspiciously shallow. But with stanza two the poem makes a radical shift; this stanza claims to make an argument that is analogous to the earlier statements, even though the terms of the comparison are crucially different (a fact the speaker ignores). Lines 5 and 6, "I never spoke with God / Nor visited in Heaven—," are indeed analogous to the corresponding two lines of the first stanza, but with line 7 the speaker claims a "certainty" which does not logically follow from her argument about the heather and the sea. While there are definite means through which she might have made "certain" of those phenomena, we are left to wonder *how* the speaker has learned about the existence of heaven. Her blithely dispensing with the "how" of religious quest marks her as immature and untrustworthy; and because the syllogism attempted by the poem is invalid, the speaker's argument collapses. But, as is often the case with a person who is intellectually shallow (Dickinson's psychology here is acute), she seems all the more certain of her argument for having failed to prove it: her childish, insouciant tone, revealed through the lilting singsong of the metrics, implies that she lacks "adequate desire" to fulfill a religious quest of such import, and she certainly lacks all the sophisticated intelligence which other Dickinson speakers bring to bear upon this all-serious subject. All this, added to the speaker's assurance not only that heaven exists, but that she is "certain . . . of the spot," comprises a stance so exaggerated that Dickinson's ironic intent becomes clear.[19]

Comparison with other poems dealing with precisely this subject—the location of heaven—is helpful in placing such poems in perspective. Like "Heaven is so far of the Mind," the following poem indicates that heaven is not "a place," and in a tone which makes it an appropriate reply to the speaker of "I never saw a Moor":

> We pray—to Heaven—
> We prate—of Heaven—
> Relate—when Neighbors die—
> At what o'clock to Heaven—they fled—
> Who saw them—Wherefore fly?
>
> Is Heaven a Place—a Sky—a Tree?
> Location's narrow way is for Ourselves—
> Unto the Dead
> There's no Geography—
>
> But State—Endowal—Focus—
> Where—Omnipresence—fly?
> (P 489)

One may "prate of Heaven" and reach a kind of bland self-assurance, but the serious quester in search of "State—Endowal—Focus" must be prepared continually to adjust her own "focus" as she proceeds through her "newer wilderness" in search of ethereal gains. It is not revelation that waits: omnipresence cannot "fly," and the concept of distance, of quest itself, is an artificial but necessary aid to human understanding: "Location's narrow way is for Ourselves—." Another poem retorts even more bluntly to anyone who is so confident of heaven that she is "certain . . . of the spot":

> The Fact that Earth is Heaven—
> Whether Heaven is Heaven or not
> Is not an Affadavit
> Of that specific Spot. . . .
> (P 1408)

The burden of establishing a link with "Omnipresence" falls not upon faith but upon human perception, which must constantly adjust its focus, never relax into certainty; otherwise, like the speaker of "I never saw a Moor," one can mistake the narrow, artificial concept for the complex reality.

The noon of spiritual fulfillment is omnipresent, and to achieve it one must have "developed," sophisticated eyes. But since human perception, no matter how shrewdly developed, can achieve only instants of vision, oblique glimpses of immortality, the inevitable state of the human quester is despair. For Dickinson, however, this despair contains the key to its own transcendence, precisely because the energy of her quest is so unflagging, and her understanding of its conditions and limitations so thoroughly clear-sighted. As the poems examined above should indicate, the human night and the spiritual noon have their multi-valenced relationship through the mediation of perception and through the creation of poetic stances which enhance perceptual effectiveness. The following poem is a clear statement of the central emotional stance underlying these delicate mediations:

> Had I presumed to hope—
> The loss had been to Me
> A Value—for the Greatness' Sake—
> As Giants—gone away—
>
> Had I presumed to gain
> A Favor so remote—
> The failure but confirm the Grace
> In further Infinite—

'Tis failure—not of Hope—
But Confident Despair—
Advancing on Celestial Lists—
With faint—Terrestrial power—

'Tis Honor—though I die—
For That no Man obtain
Till He be justified by Death—
This—is the Second Gain—
(P 522)

This poem, heretofore ignored by Dickinson's critics, is nevertheless one of her most ambitious: it charts the poet's quest from those presumptuous hopes of a naive quester to the "confident despair" which is the poet's mature stance; and, like Dickinson's entire canon, it points toward death as the crux of all meaning and relationship. The poem also contains an intense and beautiful pride, claiming the "honor" inherent in a quest that can achieve no sustained fulfillment; this honor is itself sustaining and helps maintain the difficult stance of confident despair. The speaker who feels herself "Advancing on Celestial Lists— / With faint—Terrestrial power—" knows that no certainty or true justification can exist on this side of death; but, if she despairs at the "faintness" of her own vision, she nonetheless remains confident in its relationship to the noon of her pictured fulfillment. Confidence in the reality of grace, despair at its incalculable distance—here the central paradox of Dickinson's poetic insight, that perception of an object requires its loss, is stated poignantly in terms of her religious quest as a whole. Only through the effort of her poetic strategies could she alleviate that loss, developing with particular shrewdness a vision of her own questing self and an awareness of the deprivations and the honors of her position.

Though fully aware of her status as a quest poet, Dickinson is also aware of her limitations and her vulnerability. She makes difficult, agonizing progress from the exuberant naiveté of the innocent perceiver to the confident despair of her mature stance—a stance which, because of the acknowledged frustrations of her natural condition, might seem to represent an impasse. But there is another Dickinson. In many poems she seems to eschew human seeing—and often human life itself—in favor of another mode of perception, one which has brought some critics to discuss her work in the context of mystical tradition. When we come to a poem which begins, "What I see not, I better see" (P 939), we may expect an ironic development, a corrective to mindless complacency in the vein of "I never saw a Moor"; but viewing her canon as a whole, and examining the large number of poems concerned with the poet's "soul"—Dickinson's word for the internalized questing self during moments of visionary apprehension—one may see that her quest was tempered and made sublime by her continual awareness, even in despair, of another realm which she perceived through intuition rather than eyesight. As a poet she gives full and accurate rhetorical emphasis to this intuitive seeing, and her experience of this mode of perception brings her to articulate an intensely private and highly individuated faith.

Moments of spiritual dominion do not, however, represent a mere respite from the quester's uphill journey; rather they become, in Dickinson's complex rhetoric, an integral element of that journey and its continuing effort. During those numinous, elevating moments "When we stand on the tops of Things—" (P 242), the soul is able to add her insights to the experiential store of the poet's mortal self, which experiences despair as well as ecstasy. In the following two stanzas, Dickinson emphasizes the work and the loneliness of quest in a way that suggests for us a pertinent definition of "the soul":

Effort—is the sole condition—
Patience of Itself—
Patience of opposing forces—
And intact Belief—

Looking on—is the Department
Of it's Audience—
But transaction—is assisted
By no Countenance—
(P 750)

In describing "Effort" as "the sole condition," Dickinson makes her pun work in three ways: "sole" has its literal meaning of "solitary"; it suggests that effort is the "only" condition worth aspiring to; and, most important, it implies that effort is the primary condition of the soul. (Dickinson puns, too, on "Countenance": the soul has no real audience as it pursues its solitary goal, and the quest is made even lonelier because it is not countenanced by religious orthodoxy or even, for all the poet knows, by God.) By giving her "soul" its proper emphasis in the poems, however, Dickinson does not proclaim herself a mystical poet or attempt to sidestep her commitment to empirical verification; these poems deal, quite simply, with apprehensions outside the natural realm, and through their rhetorical emphases attempt to retain a dimension of their epiphanic, revelatory experience for reinvestment in the "Daily mind" (P 1323) whose access to that dimension is normally denied. In many Dickinson poems, Joanne Feit Diehl writes, "the self perceives nature as an adversary and seeks to go beyond it into an anti- or post-naturalistic environment, pursuing questions in a self-dominated sphere that rejects the province of a communal, natural life."[1] Dickinson's soul, "pursuing questions in a self-dominated sphere," must eventually return to a life dominated by other, possibly inimical forces, but not until she has wrested from her soul's experience its due reward.

A number of Dickinson's critics have regarded the soul as conceptually anomalous in the poet's work, a formidable presence whose intuitions are fugitive, surprising, and cruelly short-lived. Albert Gelpi remarks: "The psyche could—if only for fragile moments—hold heaven, and, for as long as those moments lasted, the ache of love and the ecstasy of death were transfigured into an experience in which the individual, body and soul, sex and spirit, masculine and feminine, met completion."[2] This union of the psyche and its heaven produced, moreover, not ineffable rapture but, as David Porter suggests, an insistence on Dickinson's part that such experience be translated into the terms of a consciousness whose condition is not unity but self-division, not heaven but a hopeless exile from grace. Porter writes: "That instinctual and most evasive of Dickinson's perceptions is what the existentialist critic Marcel Raymond means by fugitive spiritual reality and a presentiment of the nebulous, irrational opacity that subsists beyond knowledge. The raising of that experience to consciousness, so audaciously undertaken by Dickinson, is one of the chief elements that produces repeated surprise in the reading of her poetry. . . ."[3] These surprises, however, are neither random nor gratuitous; they represent Dickinson's conscious technique for rendering an experience so exalting that the quester, temporarily, assumes her guise as "the soul" and makes of the experience what she can. To ignore these fugitive spiritual apprehensions would be as foolhardy as to ignore her actual sense-perceptions. As she warns herself in one poem, "Apprehensions—are God's introductions— / To be hallowed—accordingly—" (P 797).

In an early notebook, Walt Whitman wrote: "I cannot understand the Mystery, but I am always conscious of myself as two—my soul and I; and I reckon it is the same with all men and women."[4] Dickinson also felt this division, equating the "I" with consciousness: "Of Consciousness, her awful Mate / The Soul cannot be rid—" (P 894). Dickinson forces that antagonism to bear fruit, however, by showing the self's ascension from consciousness into soul as only part of a continual, oscillating journey; for such an experience-centered poet as Dickinson, in fact, the journey back "down" into consciousness might seem the most crucial segment of the process. Her emphasis on the soul's perceptual adventure derives in part, of course, from her Puritan heritage,[5] but is also anticipated—once again—in Emerson's essays. In *Nature,* for example, Emerson discusses three major "aspects of Beauty," outlining a progression which can serve as a paradigm for Dickinson's own journey toward the absolute. His first aspect involves empirical perception, "the simple perception of natural forms," and he notes that "The health of the eye seems to demand a horizon. We are never tired, so long as we can see far enough." Perceptions outside the realm of the eye are Emerson's second aspect, which he calls "The presence of a . . . spiritual element." And his third aspect reminds us of Dickinson's own frequently stated goals: "The intellect searches out the absolute order of things as they stand in the mind of God, and without the colors of affection."[6] Elsewhere Emerson stresses, also, the importance of what Dickinson called the "Granitic Base" (P 789) of identity: the flux of existence, he writes, "could never become sensible to us but by contrast to some principle of fixture or stability in the soul."[7] When he describes, in "The American Scholar," the determined and firmly empirical attitude of an "ambitious soul," he draws an accurate portrait of Dickinson's quester in her most exalted moments: "The ambitious soul sits down before each refractory fact; one after another reduces all strange constitutions, all new powers, to their class and their law, and goes on forever to animate the last fiber of organization, the outskirts of nature, by insight."[8]

The insights of Dickinson's soul, again, become incorporated into the larger quest of her whole self, of which the soul is only a rhetorically isolated part. Dickinson, in Martin Bickman's words, "charts symbolically [a] journey from limited awareness to a center of consciousness that radiates out into the entire psychic realm."[9] Poems describing this spiritual nourishment do not contradict her stance of confident despair, nor do they represent fulfillment of quest. Rather they broaden the oscillating spiral of her experience so that experiential strife—the darkest, lowest moments of her rising cycle of aware-ness—can be seen within the context of ineffable joy, producing a more ac-curate picture of the extreme richness of existence, the magnificent complexity of consciousness itself. M. H. Abrams writes of the typical Romantic spiral:

> The self-moving circle . . . rotates along a third, a vertical dimension, to close where it had begun, but on a higher plane of value. It thus fuses the idea of the circular return with the idea of linear progress, to describe a distinctive figure of Romantic thought and imagination—the ascending circle, or spiral. . . . According to this view, the reunion or synthesis which follows after any division into contraries constitutes a "third thing," which is higher than the original unity because it preserves the distinction which it has overcome.[10]

This concept is remarkably accurate when applied to Dickinson's own quest. Remembering Robert Weisbuch's concept of her "mind-world continuum," we may add a third element—spiritual apprehension—which thrusts the po-etic quest upward, out of nature and self. The circle of the continuum be-comes in fact spiral, leading the poet upward through experience toward knowledge.

In his *The Varieties of Religious Experience,* William James noted four characteristics of mystical experience: ineffability, noetic quality, transiency, passivity. The first three of these are often part of Dickinson's own intuitional experience, but passivity seldom is. James writes: "The mystic feels as if his own will were in abeyance, and indeed sometimes as if he were grasped and held by a superior power."[11] It should be clear that since the word "mysti-cism" connotes such passivity and identity-loss, it does not accurately de-scribe Dickinson's poetry of intuitive seeing; exalted as she is in such poems, she has no wish to lose her identity in God, but rather asserts a godlike status for herself. When she envisions herself as a "soul," her exaltation normally derives not from any supernal power but rather from her own power of suffering and endurance, her role as "Queen of Calvary." As Richard Chase remarks, Dickinson's poetry has "one major theme, one symbolic act, one incandescent center of meaning. Expressed in the most general terms, this theme is the achievement of status through crucial experiences."[12] Louise Bogan, asserting that Dickinson is a mystical poet, notes that "the progress of the mystic toward illumination, and of the poet toward the full depth and richness of his insight . . . are much alike. Both work from the world of reality, toward the realm of Essence. . . ."[13] Dickinson's claim to high status in a world of essence must, however, be read in the context of her pain-ridden "confessional" poetry, her articulation of suffering and personal identity which gives crucial ballast to her "soul's" moments of vision and exultation. For Dickinson insight is earned, never gratuitous. Seldom inclined to an inert mysticism, she insists upon her exalted status, the attainment of which has made her intuitional perception valid. Armed with this confidence, she enjoys spiritual visions which continue to encourage and validate her quest.

Andrew Greeley, in his *Ecstasy as Knowledge*, states a truth about the mystical way more precisely applicable to Dickinson: "Every form of human knowledge has its own joys of fulfillment and satisfaction. Mystical rapture is merely the joy that comes from this particular form of contact with Reality."[14] Even more pertinently, William Johnston describes a mysticism which is a kind of "vertical thinking, a process in which the mind goes silently down into its own center, revealing cavernous depths ordinarily latent and untouched by the train of images and concepts that pass across the surface of the mind. It is that mysticism in which one descends to the 'still point' or to the ground of the soul, thus finding a type of knowledge that is supraconceptual and therefore ineffable. . . ."[15] Emerson, describing the "idealist" who attains this still point of selfhood, notes the dramatic change in the self's perceptual vantage point: the soul now sees "the procession of facts you call the world, as flowing perpetually outward from an invisible, unsounded center in himself, center alike of him and of them, and necessitating him to regard all things as having a subjective or relative existence, relative to that aforesaid Unknown Center of him."[16] Even such triumphs of identity, however, are hounded by the poet's sense that in these "cavernous depths" of the soul lurks a self-knowledge that is less enlightening than horrifying, and that the plumbing to her own "unsounded center" brings not mystical joy but an ultimate, existential solitude:

The Loneliness One dare not sound—
And would as soon surmise
As in it's Grave go plumbing
To ascertain the size—

The Loneliness whose worst alarm
Is lest itself should see—
And perish from before itself
For just a scrutiny—

The Horror not to be surveyed—
But skirted in the Dark—
With Consciousness suspended—
And Being under Lock—

I fear me this—is Loneliness—
The Maker of the soul
It's Caverns and it's Corridors
Illuminate—or seal—
(P 777)

Consciousness cannot be "suspended" for long, however; the soul's intuitive seeing, braving all caverns and corridors in its search for what is "deepest hid," is always accompanied by the divisive specter of daily consciousness,
which yearns toward separation rather than synthesis:

Of Consciousness, her awful Mate
The Soul cannot be rid—
As easy the secreting her
Behind the Eyes of God.

The deepest hid is sighted first
And scant to Him the Crowd—
What triple Lenses burn upon
The Escapade from God—
(P 894)

The perceptual quest, an "Escapade from God," involves the debilitating self-
consciousness of a triple scrutiny, and the poem describes, rather too ellipti-
cally, a Chinese-box theory of perception: "the Eyes of God" represent an all-
encompassing perception, a circumference whose reality is synonymous with
spiritual truth; the soul's intuitive perception seeks to grasp this truth by moving radically inward, to what is "deepest hid" in the poet's unsounded center;

and at the furthest remove from truth is the relatively small and powerless perceiving consciousness, nonetheless an awful mate because by clinging to the soul, it prevents the soul's union with spiritual truth. The triple lenses cannot join together, therefore, and the entire process is viewed, as so often in Dickinson, as a cruel "Escapade," a joke played at human expense.

Because of the spiritually debilitating aspect of consciousness, Dickinson is usually content to claim "etherial gains" through her perception of natural phenomena, making cautious inferences and claiming at times to "distinguish God." Some poems focus not upon natural inference but upon a direct intuitive confrontation with spiritual reality; here, however, it is the failed attempt to express, and thus learn from, this confrontation which often dictates the poem's rhetoric:

> The Love a Life can show Below
> Is but a filament, I know,
> Of that diviner thing
> That faints upon the face of Noon—
> And smites the Tinder in the Sun—
> And hinders Gabriel's Wing—
>
> 'Tis this—in Music—hints and sways—
> And far abroad on Summer days—
> Distils uncertain pain—
> 'Tis this enamors in the East—
> And tints the Transit in the West
> With harrowing Iodine—
>
> 'Tis this—invites—appals—endows—
> Flits—glimmers—proves—dissolves—
> Returns—suggests—convicts—enchants—
> Then—flings in Paradise—
> (P 673)

This poem, straining beyond the visible to something ineffable that is perceived by the poet's spirit, stresses that the "diviner thing" is inconstant: it "Flits—glimmers—proves—dissolves—." The extraordinary final stanza conveys a poignant fascination with that inconstancy as well as the poet's frustration in her attempt to capture it in language, while the triumphant last line eschews natural comparison altogether in the end result of supernal vision, beyond which experience might seem incommunicable, "mystical." But Dickinson is on equal terms with her visions, as other poems will make clear.

Two poems about sunset show a marked difference from the sunset poems discussed earlier which used natural splendor as an agent of inference. The first is deceptively simple in tone:

> The Mountains stood in Haze—
> The Valleys stopped below
> And went or waited as they liked
> The River and the Sky.
>
> At leisure was the Sun—
> His interests of Fire
> A little from remark withdrawn—
> The Twilight spoke the Spire,
>
> So soft upon the Scene
> The Act of evening fell
> We felt how neighborly a Thing
> Was the Invisible.
> (P 1278)

The first two stanzas exemplify Dickinson's remarkable descriptive powers, but the final stanza does not really follow from them; rather the poet makes an imaginative leap toward the abstract "Act of evening" and the poet's closeness with the "Invisible." The first two stanzas set mood rather than provide inference, and this mood—that of a villager's awe—generates the intuitive "feeling" of the final two lines. Another poem, equally complex, is didactic as well, and partakes of a new and exalted tone; clearly, the speaker is Dickinson's soul.

> The Lilac is an ancient shrub
> But ancienter than that
> The Firmamental Lilac
> Upon the Hill tonight—
> The Sun subsiding on his Course
> Bequeathes this final Plant
> To Contemplation—not to Touch—
> The Flower of Occident.
> Of one Corolla is the West—
> The Calyx is the Earth—
> The Capsules burnished Seeds the Stars—
> The Scientist of Faith
> His research has but just begun—
>   [*no stanza break*]

Above his synthesis
The Flora unimpeachable
To Time's Analysis—
"Eye hath not seen" may possibly
Be current with the Blind
But let not Revelation
By theses be detained—
(P 1241)

The sublime arrogance of the last four lines shows Dickinson in possession of her intuitive vision; her eyes are "furnished." The "Firmamental Lilac" is unavailable to the "Scientist of Faith," who judges and infers within the laws of time and nature. But the poet herself is giving us not another representative sunset, but her posture of oneness with the spiritual essence such a sunset represents. She is communicating to the spiritually blind through a natural metaphor which they can understand, and she makes no effort to hide her condescension.

Dickinson's soul has humbler moments, but they are relatively few. In the following poem the spiritual onslaught does seem gratuitous, the speaker wholly passive:

Did Our Best Moment last—
'Twould supersede the Heaven—
A few—and they by Risk—procure—
So this Sort—are not given—

Except as stimulants—in
Cases of Despair—
Or Stupor—The Reserve—
These Heavenly Moments are—

A Grant of the Divine—
That Certain as it Comes—
Withdraws—and leaves the dazzled Soul
In her unfurnished Rooms—
(P 393)

The final line recalls her brief poem, "Not 'Revelation' 'tis, that waits / But our unfurnished eyes," and describes a return to blindness. But it should be noticed that the word "I" is entirely missing here, a striking omission in any Dickinson poem; thus the poem describes an experience shared by many, important and valid but not on the exalted plane of Dickinson's mythic, lonely quester. It is an example of Dickinson's didacticism, her assertion of spiritual realities through the creation of a comprehensible poetic "definition." Another poem has a similar function:

The Soul's distinct connection
With immortality
Is best disclosed by Danger
Or quick Calamity—

As Lightning on a Landscape
Exhibits Sheets of Place—
Not yet suspected—but for Flash—
And Click—and Suddenness.
(P 974)

Here the perception is lightning-quick, an ineffable experience made concrete through analogy; again Dickinson is teaching, offering the fruits of her own quest experience. It is crucial to notice here the linking of "danger" to the lightning flash of numinous perception: the soul has not yet ascended into its own spiritual landscape because that landscape is still essentially unknown, foreign. As Dickinson wrote to Higginson: "These sudden intimacies with Immortality, are expanse—not Peace—as Lightning at our feet, instills a foreign Landscape" (L 641).

But ultimately the soul does come into its own, and several poems of spiritual intuition present dramatically her evolving myth in its exclusive splendor. This stage of her quest is egocentric in the best sense, conveying both the rapture and the authority of her continuing upward spiral. Dickinson, having sounded "The Loneliness One dare not sound," now reaps the rewards of her courage and persistence. She had noted that "The Maker of the soul / It's Caverns and it's Corridors / Illuminate—or seal," and the maker here is not God but the stubbornly progressing self. This idea of the self-made soul, as it were, surely reflects Dickinson's belief in Emersonian self-reliance, but perhaps the most striking analogue to her concept is that of a British Romantic predecessor. In a famous letter to his brother and sister-in-law, John Keats had written of the soul in terms of the temporal world, stressing identity, perception, evolving selfhood (through the effort of quest), and the value of a personalized vision of immortality:

Call the world if you Please "The vale of Soul-making" Then you will find out the use of the world (I am speaking now in the highest terms for human nature admitting it to be immortal which I will here take for granted for the purpose of showing a thought which has struck me concerning it) I say *"Soul making"* Soul as distinguished from an Intelligence—There may be intelligences or sparks of the divinity in millions—but they are not Souls ~~the~~ till they acquire identities, till each one is personally itself. I[n]telligences are atoms of perception—they know and they see and they are pure, in short they are God—How then are Souls to be made? How then are these sparks which are God to have identity given them—so as ever to possess a bliss peculiar to each ones individual existence? How, but by the medium of a world like this?[17]

Dickinson, like Keats in this passage, discovers that the use of the world lies in its role as a "medium" for the soul's evolution, its coalescing of "atoms of perception" into the bliss of a unified vision. One poem locates the beginning of this process, the exciting moment when the quester's isolation begins to bear the fruit of spiritual apprehension:[18]

> Conscious am I in my Chamber,
> Of a shapeless friend—
> He doth not attest by Posture—
> Nor Confirm—by Word—
>
> Neither Place—need I present Him—
> Fitter Courtesy
> Hospitable intuition
> Of His Company—
>
> Presence—is His furthest license—
> Neither He to Me
> Nor Myself to Him—by Accent—
> Forfeit Probity—
>
> Weariness of Him, were quainter
> Than Monotony
> Knew a Particle—of Space's
> Vast Society—
>
> Neither if He visit Other—
> Do He dwell—or Nay—know I—
> But Instinct esteem Him
> Immortality—
> (P 679)

Especially intriguing here is the speaker's unwillingness to "Forfeit Probity";

a more facile mysticism would bring emotion into play, but here perception is sober, cautious, making no claims to knowledge outside the central "instinct" that she is not alone.

Another pair of related poems, one describing the intuitional experience and the second commenting on it, focuses sharply on the issue of perception itself. What is this spiritual "instinct," and what are its uses? The first poem, rather mysterious in tone and in certain of its references, uses the metaphor of a dream for the state of spiritual seeing:

> What I see not, I better see—
> Through Faith—my Hazel Eye
> Has Periods of shutting—
> But, No lid has Memory—
>
> For frequent, all my sense obscured
> I equally behold
> As someone held a light unto
> The Features so beloved—
>
> And I arise—and in my Dream—
> Do Thee distinguished Grace—
> Till jealous Daylight interrupt—
> And mar thy perfectness—
> (P 939)

The "jealous daylight" is synonymous with the common "Day" of "Renunciation—is a piercing Virtue," which allows only a "Covered Vision"; and the dream's "perfectness" recalls the central poem, "Perception of an object costs / Precise the Object's loss," in which perception "upbraids" the perfectness which must situate at such a distance from the perceiver. The object of the poem's "Faith" and the identity of "Thee" in line 10 remain mysterious,[19] but whether the poem describes human or spiritual longing, this perceptual "Best Moment" is surely intuitive and fleeting. A similar poem comments on this central spiritual problem, the perception of essences:

> Best Things dwell out of Sight
> The Pearl—the Just—Our Thought.
>
> Most shun the Public Air
> Legitimate, and Rare—
>
> The Capsule of the Wind
> The Capsule of the Mind

Exhibit here, as doth a Burr—
Germ's Germ be where?
(P 998)

Dickinson insists that phenomenal "exhibition" implies spiritual essence, that temporal nature is a sign of immortality. As in "The Love a Life can show Below," she is once again straining beyond the visible, and characteristically she ends with a question rather than an answer.

Though "faith" has a relatively subordinate role in the drama of Dickinson's evolving soul, she sometimes does assert that "I better see— / Through Faith," an idea which the following poem places specifically in the context of perceptual quest:

Faith—is the Pierless Bridge
Supporting what We see
Unto the Scene that We do not—
Too slender for the eye

It bears the Soul as bold
As it were rocked in Steel
With Arms of Steel at either side—
It joins—behind the Vail

To what, could We presume
The Bridge would cease to be
To Our far, vascillating Feet
A first Nescessity.
(P 915)

While consciousness diffuses the soul's concentration upon essence, faith protects the soul with "Arms of Steel," representing a kind of invisible lifeline between the soul and whatever exists "behind the Vail." Dickinson's pun upon "Pierless" indicates that faith, if embraced, is without peer as a means of spiritual contentment. We know that the poet's own "far, vascillating Feet" have undertaken a more rigorous journey and require a more substantive reward than one for whom faith provides such contentment; but Dickinson nonetheless acknowledges faith as a "first nescessity," even if it does not play the major role in her own particularly active, egocentric form of religious seeking.

In her magnificent cluster of poems dealing with the soul's isolated drama, Dickinson creates a fiction which suspends all doubts; the authority of the exalted self is unquestioned. In these poems Dickinson's stance is that of the quest poet whose wrestling with experience has earned moments of uncompromised vision. These moments are made objective through the elaboration of the fictional persona, the soul, whose status cannot be measured in earthly terms.[20] The central poem of the group articulates clearly this status and its meaning:

> The Soul's Superior instants
> Occur to Her—alone—
> When friend—and Earth's occasion
> Have infinite withdrawn—
>
> Or She—Herself—ascended
> To too remote a Hight
> For lower Recognition
> Than Her Omnipotent—
>
> This Mortal Abolition
> Is seldom—but as fair
> As Apparition—subject
> To Autocratic Air—
>
> Eternity's disclosure
> To favorites—a few—
> Of the Colossal substance
> Of Immortality[21]
> (P 306)

The speaker and her perception of spiritual reality meet on equal terms, like independent monarchs; graciously the soul "abolishes" what is mortal, and eternity "discloses" its rarefied substance. The relationship is thus reciprocal, cordial, the two identities clearly focused and discrete. Not surprisingly, other poems of the group describe the superior instants as social calls of the most exalted kind—"The Soul that hath a Guest / Doth seldom go abroad" (P 674)—and one poem even states a kind of spiritual etiquette:

> The Soul should always stand ajar
> That if the Heaven inquire
> He will not be obliged to wait
> Or shy of troubling Her
>
> Depart, before the Host have slid
> The Bolt unto the Door—
> To search for the accomplished Guest,
> Her Visitor, no more—
> (P 1055)

The reference to the soul's "accomplished Guest" may be described as a decorous understatement, and one infers that the host is deserving of such a guest, accomplished in her own right; as another poem has it, "The Soul selects her own Society" (P 303), possesses a "divine Majority" of her own. This is Dickinson's peculiar brand of mystical joy, one which insists upon her own independent status as perceiver, having by her own effort closed the distance between perception and its yearning for the "perfectness" of vision.

Dickinson thus records the triumphs as well as the failures of her perceptual quest, her fictional personae in their various stances and voices assuming mythic stature. Through the "I" of her poems she provides an exemplary quest and dramatizes all its necessary strategies, giving accurate emphasis to pain and ecstasy, failure and success, and attempting to delineate their relationships. In one poem, very Emersonian in cast, she seems to encourage the reader toward his own achievement of vision. Despite the exultant, even "transcendental" tone of the poem, she ends with a piece of practical advice:

> You'll know it—as you know 'tis Noon—
> By Glory—
> As you do the Sun—
> By Glory—
> As you will in Heaven—
> Know God the Father—and the Son.
>
> By intuition, Mightiest Things
> Assert themselves—and not by terms—
> "I'm Midnight"—need the Midnight say—
> "I'm Sunrise"—-Need the Majesty?
>
> Omnipotence—had not a Tongue—
> His lisp—is Lightning—and the Sun—
> His Conversation—with the Sea—
> "How shall you know"?
> Consult your Eye!
> (P 420)

The relationship between the "Eye" and the "intuition" by which "Mightiest Things / Assert themselves" is taken for granted here, implying a natural progression from sensual to spiritual perception. Also implied is Dickinson's own role as shamanistic poet / medium ("as One returned, I feel, / Odd secrets of the line to tell!" [P 160]), determined to extend her own soul's experiences to others. All she knows, in such exalted moments, are "Bulletins all Day / From Immortality" (P 827), and in her poems she translates these "Bulletins" into human terms.

Despite Dickinson's privileged sense of spiritual intuition, however, she doubts and despairs more frequently than she boasts of her superiority. The soul is only one of her voices, and the soul herself notes that such assurance comes but seldom.[22] Although her spiritual intuitions are genuine, she gives them only the emphasis they deserve. The empirical, fact-finding process of quest cannot end with the attainment of "Superior instants" because instants do not last. "Mortal abolition" is thus followed by the reacceptance of mortality and its limited perceptual terms, the "divine Majority" giving way to a "timid life of evidence." The following poem recognizes bitterly that spiritual "glory" is of limited value until one has encountered the final test of death:

> Their Hight in Heaven comforts not—
> Their Glory—nought to me—
> 'Twas best imperfect—as it was—
> I'm finite—I cant see—
>
> The House of Supposition—
> The Glimmering Frontier that
> skirts the Acres of Perhaps—
> To Me—shows insecure—
>
> The wealth I had—contented me—
> If 'twas a meaner size—
> Then I had counted it until
> It pleased my narrow Eyes—
>
> Better than larger values—
> That show however true—
> This timid life of Evidence
> Keeps pleading—"I don't know."
> (P 696)

Ultimately the "errand" of Dickinson's narrowed eye was its confrontation with death, and she examined this crucial confrontation with an imaginative energy unequaled by any other poet. This distinctive focus of her quest, however, necessitates an examination of the elaborate system of values which evolved from her poetic strategies. Although I have emphasized thus far the developing identity of Dickinson's questing self, it should be clear that her appraisal of surrounding phenomena and the wide range of her emotional responses concerned her deeply in the unremitting search for relevance. She measured all relationships carefully, often characterizing her perceptual transactions in terms of mathematical equations, profit and loss. In the world of space and time, the quester's work along the continual spiral toward death involved three important concerns: to establish ratios constantly between the condition of despair and the promise of fulfillment; to measure the effects of transience; and to estimate the values of essence. Her awareness of the uncertainties—the variables—of existential life caused her to perceive with narrowed eyes but also to know that only her perception brought the value of her quest into focus, moment by moment.

Part Two
Broken Mathematics:
Ratio, Transience, Essence

I had a daily Bliss
I half indifferent viewed
Till sudden I perceived it stir—
It grew as I pursued

Till when around a Hight
It wasted from my sight
Increased beyond my utmost scope
I learned to estimate—

P 1057

Would it be prudent to subject
an apparitional interview to
a grosser test?

L 558

5 *Delight Is as the Flight*

Dickinson's mature quester, having identified her attitude toward natural life as one of "confident despair," focuses her abundant energies upon an exhaustive analysis of human perceptual values. From her acknowledgment of the distance between perceiver and perceived, and her awareness that this distance gives any perception its value, she evolves one of her central poetic ideas: she insists that the value of the perceived object is directly proportionate to its distance from the perceiver. For the purposes of Dickinson's religious quest, to know that perception of an object costs precisely its loss is not enough, for the element of time places this relationship in constant flux: thus the concept of a flexible ratio, implying movement and change through the temporal dimension, can measure the value of perception within any human context. And, since natural existence and its conditions are important only within the "larger function" of her quest for spiritual knowledge, Dickinson offers the empirical truth of these "measurements" (having proved their validity in her poems) as a metaphor for spiritual reality.

Dickinson would have agreed with Emerson that "The axioms of physics translate into the laws of ethics," and that scientific propositions "have a much more extensive and universal sense when applied to human life, than when confined to technical use."[1] Dickinson uses the language of empirical verification, with unique intensity, to describe the impalpable relationships between perceiver and object, and to suggest their spiritual implications. In working out her own "mathematics," she consistently employs both the premises and the vocabularies of human systems of measurement. Thus her poems become "axioms," "experiments"; she attempts to "estimate" perceptual values, to arrive at valid "equations." In addition, she uses metaphors of temporal values—riches, prizes, gems—to convey the ultimate value of perceptual "possession" once its ratio to the corresponding distance (the object's actual loss) has been established. These metaphors of fixed systems and values, used to express relationships that cannot be fixed, create a meaningful paradox; for this paradox is itself a metaphor for human perceptual limitations, the poet's acknowledgment that final answers are unattainable. The poet thus evolves a system with a built-in skepticism, but one which does not deny the value of the quester's efforts or the achievement of temporary gains. She shares Emerson's spirit when he insists that his efforts do not "settle anything as true or false. I unsettle all things. No facts are to me sacred; none are profane. I simply experiment, an endless seeker. . . ."[2] It will be seen that Dickinson's central idea of ratio, by its very precision, in fact brings her to an awareness of her inadequate perceptual faculties, the ultimate "value" of spiritual fulfillment being so great that its distance is incalculable.[3]

Once again the poet's earliest work shows one of her most characteristic themes developed with remarkable sophistication and complexity. Just as she was conscious, in the "bark" poems discussed above, of the basic conditions of her quest and its inevitable frustrations, in other early poems she is also aware of the central paradox inherent in her mode of perception and therefore of the value of these frustrations in themselves. "Success is counted sweetest / By those who ne'er succeed," she wrote about 1859 (P 67); at the very outset she understood that her sorest need produced clearest perceptual "definition," and her unusual choice of the verb "to count" indicates her determined effort to measure the gain produced by her deprivation, stating a ratio which justifies her way of thought and, by extension, her entire way of life. Although the word "ratio" appears only three times in the poet's work— twice in poems of 1859, once again in 1861—the idea it expresses is nevertheless present in scores of other poems of the early period; nor does she abandon the concept in later work, but rather deepens its meaning by relating it to various aspects of her quest experience, especially her experience of life's transience and of the essential perceptual gains she has realized.

A full presentation of Dickinson's "ratio" first appears in one her most distinguished early poems:

As by the dead we love to sit,
Become so wondrous dear—
As for the lost we grapple
Tho' all the rest are here—

In broken mathematics
We estimate our prize
[*no stanza break*]

Vast—in it's fading ratio
To our penurious eyes!
(P 88)

Much critical argument has centered upon this poem, and particular disagreement has arisen over the meaning of the "fading ratio" in line 7.[4] A
number of misreadings, in fact, have resulted from a failure to recognize the
poem's rhetorical structure. The crucial "as" in lines 1 and 3 indicates what
Robert Weisbuch has called "the analogical collection," which "develops by
a series of perceptions or stories. . . . Each scene is illustratory, and our attention is finally drawn away from its specific content to the *general principle*
which relates it to other scenes. Concept subordinates examples. . . ."[5] The
second stanza of "As by the dead we love to sit," following upon the two
analogies, states the truth which the analogies have illustrated. Thus the poem
is about a peculiar emotional response to loss, any loss; and it also states a
formula which indicates the heightened value of any perception as the perception's object fades from our sight or possession. What is lost becomes a "prize,"
its value becoming more "vast" as its distance increases. The terms of the
"fading ratio" are explicitly stated as being the "prize" and "our penurious
eyes"—this ratio has nothing to do with what is not lost. Line 4, containing
the only reference to "all the rest" who are not lost, merely emphasizes the
intensity of our emotional response to loss itself: "the rest" have nothing to
do with stanza two, however, or even with the general principle offered by
the poem as a whole.

The adjective "fading" does not modify "ratio" in the conventional way:
"fading ratio" means a ratio which becomes evident through the *distance*—
the fading, the dying away—of what is lost. Dickinson's two other uses of the
word "ratio" support this definition. In "For each extatic instant" (P 125) the
"keen and quivering ratio" is a similarly compressed locution (again, the adjectives do not literally modify the noun "ratio"); and in a poem of about
1861 Dickinson asserts that "Delight is as the flight / Or in the Ratio of it"
(P 257), again insisting that distance enhances value. In a later poem she
describes daylight as "Fairer through Fading," the word "fading" having the
same meaning as in the poem under consideration. Thus, given the paradox
in Dickinson's theory of perception, the imaginative argument of "As by the
dead we love to sit" makes perfect sense, its mathematical metaphor both
expressing a truth about human perceptual values and—through an oxymo-
ron, "broken mathematics"—making a point of its own inadequacy.

Dickinson's second poem detailing her concept of "ratio," though not dealing directly with perception, nonetheless states a view of experiential loss which is analogous to that of the first poem; here she uses metaphors of monetary value in addition to the mathematics metaphor:

> For each extatic instant
> We must an anguish pay
> In keen and quivering ratio
> To the extasy.
>
> For each beloved hour
> Sharp pittances of years—
> Bitter contested farthings—
> And Coffers heaped with Tears!
> (P 125)

Dickinson's first editors gave this poem an appropriately ironic title: "Compensation." Once again the possession of a genuine "prize," ecstasy, requires an amount of deprivation ("anguish") directly proportionate to the value of the prize, and again Dickinson does not satirize this relationship; the unfairness of its proportions is only suggested by the word "bitter." The focus of the poem is rather upon defining the ratio itself, the poet's attempt to state accurately the relationship between value and loss.[6] The "keen and quivering ratio" indicates the exquisite sharpness of the speaker's perception, one which has resulted in a formula that helps, at least, to define her deprived position. In her anguish the poet can see clearly, and in the second stanza, using the imagery of farthings and coffers, she indicates her awareness of the relationship between emotional prizes and deprivations.

The third and most complete statement of Dickinson's ratio focuses upon perception as the source of experiential value. Here the quintessential perception, heightened through transience and an acute consciousness of loss, is symbolized in a brief narrative which describes the quester's passage into the state of experience:

> Delight is as the flight—
> Or in the Ratio of it,
> As the Schools would say—
> The Rainbow's way—
> A Skein
> Flung colored, after Rain,
> Would suit as bright,
>   [no stanza break]

Except that flight
Were Aliment—

"If it would last"
I asked the East,
When that Bent Stripe
Struck up my childish
Firmament—
And I, for glee,
Took Rainbows, as the common way,
And empty Skies
The Eccentricity—

And so with Lives—
And so with Butterflies—
Seen magic—through the fright—
That they will cheat the sight—
And Dower latitudes far on—
Some sudden morn—
Our portion—in the fashion—
Done—
(P 257)

Once again Dickinson's rhetorical structure clarifies her meaning. Stanza one states the general concept, "Delight is as the flight," and expresses a distrust of transcendent "vision": "A Skein / Flung colored, after Rain" symbolizes the diminished value of such a possession, as compared with the actual transient splendor of the rainbow itself.[7] Thus the perceiver's "Aliment" is not the vision but its flight from her perception. The ratio between vision and transience thus asserted, and concrete examples given of their corresponding values, stanza two provides evidence in the form of a brief analogical narrative (and the poem begins to achieve a remarkable coherence through the relevant continuation and expansion of the rainbow metaphor). The speaker notes that as a naive perceiver she had enjoyed the rainbow with a pure childish "glee"—an emotion, the poem implies, which is bland and immature because such a perceiver has no consciousness of loss. In this limited awareness rainbows are merely the "common way," inadequately valued. Stanza three, by contrast, then elaborates upon the perceptual enhancement of a mature stance, and relates the poem's central image to all facets of perception: rainbows, butterflies, life itself, all are "Seen magic—through the fright— / That they will cheat the sight." The magic of heightened perception can be attained only through the keen and frightful recognition that it cannot last.

Many of Dickinson's later poems reiterate her central concept of perceptual value, often providing further elucidation by focusing upon various dramatic contexts and perceptual relationships. The following poem employs a vocabulary reminiscent of "Delight is as the flight," but here the poet emphasizes the element of space rather than time; the pain of distance is analogous to that of transience, however, since both serve to increase "delight":

> Delight—becomes pictorial—
> When viewed through Pain—
> More fair—because impossible
> That any gain—
>
> The Mountain—at a given distance—
> In Amber—lies—
> Approached—the Amber flits—a little—
> And That's—the Skies—
> (P 572)

This poem employs a typical analogical structure: theoretical statement followed by an illustrative analogy. In stanza one perception is "fair" because the union of perceiver and object is impossible—a familiar Dickinson idea; and such a "gain," as she asserts in other poems, is at any rate a negligible one, only a spurious "glee" based in immaturity and self-delusion. In the second stanza she "proves" her theoretical statement through an example, one which indicates that she is conducting a kind of experiment involving definite measurement. When viewed from a "given" distance, the mountain lies in amber: a magical, poetic perception. But like a mirage the amber vanishes as the perceiver attempts to approach it, and the final two lines, dryly ironic in tone, suggest again that empty skies are not really the eccentricity; in this life they are the common reality and a negligible perceptual possession.[8] Dickinson's central theory is thus stated and proved in a poetic experiment of under three dozen words.

Once Dickinson has defined the ratio of visionary intensity to the fading of its object and plotted various degrees of this central relationship, she takes the idea to its furthest extreme in her quest for the "perfectness" of vision. Although she "upbraids a perfectness / That situates so far" from her possession, this upbraiding is only her frustrated human reaction; the search for truth and beauty (both implicit in Dickinson's recurrent word, "perfectness") requires a full acceptance of experiential realities. In another poem structured through analogy Dickinson again asserts the truth of her central theory, here locating what she calls elsewhere "the extatic limit / Of unobtained Delight" (P 1209). By extending her visionary ratio to this limit, Dickinson realizes that the highest perceptual ecstasy comes just as the object is vanishing from sight:

> Fairer through Fading—as the Day
> Into the Darkness dips away—
> Half her Complexion of the Sun—
> Hindering—Haunting—Perishing—
>
> Rallies Her Glow, like a dying Friend—
> Teazing with glittering Amend—
> Only to aggravate the Dark
> Through an expiring—perfect—look—
> (P 938)

Here the theory is stated in only three words, followed by the "as" which begins the poet's illustrative analogy. Appropriately she compares the last moment of daylight to "a dying Friend," foreshadowing death as her ultimate subject for dealing comprehensively with perception and her visionary quest. In this poem what scant daylight remains seems to the poet a "glittering Amend" when compared to the encroaching darkness, almost a rescinding of the light's anticipated disappearance; but the light is only teasing her with its heightened intensity. The perceiver's great recompense is the "expiring—perfect—look" of this very last moment of daylight, and yet ecstatic perception is followed instantly by total deprivation. And again the poem suggests that completion comes only through death.

Dickinson applies these poetic insights to widely varying human situations, frequently dramatizing her theory and once again employing poetic personae. Her most important application is toward the central myth of her own highly individuated quester: the cloistered, white-robed poet whose intensity of feeling—interpersonal perception—caused her to shun actual encounters. Actually to "see" a beloved face was a dangerous fulfillment for various complex reasons. In a very real way this isolated quester had to view significant persons as if they *were* dead, at least dead to her; then she could endow them with a mythic status of her own, a status which seemed appropriate to her intense feeling. Mere reality could not match such intensity, and meeting the object of her devotion face to face caused a dramatic decrease in the "enchantment" of her affections. In describing this aspect of Dickinson's perceptual theory, of course, critical and biographical discussion are very nearly one; a brief poem which states in terms of a human relationship her central concept of perceptual values seems in fact to have been intended as a personal message to one of Dickinson's close friends, Kate Scott Anthon:[9]

> We shun because we prize her Face
> Lest sight's ineffable disgrace
> Our Adoration stain
> (P 1429)

The lines are perhaps a rationalization of the poet's neurosis; certainly they express an amazingly selfish outlook on human relationships, since the beloved is valuable only as a "prize" of the poet's imagination (and they serve as a poignant affirmation of Yeats's dictum that perfection of an artist's work precludes the perfection of his life). Nevertheless the lines are an accurate statement of Dickinson's extreme position and are entirely consistent with her ideas about perception as a whole. Once again she is estimating her prize by a broken mathematics: her penurious eyes, through shunning Anthon, understand the vastness of the prize itself. The ineffable disgrace of sight must be prevented through renunciation of the beloved object, and the resulting distance produces the desired "perfectness" of vision.

Another poem states a rationale for the quester's reclusiveness from an opposite point of view: she emphasizes that her own value likewise increases in the eyes of others because she shrouds herself in mystery. Perception without obliqueness and frustration would be almost worthless:

> A Charm invests a face
> Imperfectly beheld—
> The Lady dare not lift her Vail
> For fear it be dispelled—
>
> But peers beyond her mesh—
> And wishes—and denies—
> Lest Interview—annul a want
> That Image—satisfies—
> (P 421)

For Dickinson, "satisfaction" is an undesirable condition: "Satisfaction—is the Agent / Of Satiety" (P 1036), and satiety means nothing less than a stalled quest.

Characteristically she dramatizes her reclusive, deprived persona within situations which illustrate the kinds of gains she can realize through her rejection of fulfillment. The most frequent metaphor in these poems is that of monetary value, again implying her inability to measure the ratio of actual loss to perceptual gain.[10] Cynthia Chaliff, discussing the frequent economic metaphors in Dickinson's work, writes that the poet "has in fact introjected the capitalistic system and has made it a part of her own psychological dynamics."[11] Thus while the poem "Fairer through Fading" described the "perfect" perception one may achieve at the moment when deprivation is imminent, poems such as the following dramatize this paradox as the quester's guiding principle, her way of life:

> Because 'twas Riches I could own,
> Myself had earned it—Me,
> I knew the Dollars by their names—
> It feels like Poverty
>
> An Earldom out of sight to hold,
> An Income in the Air,
> Possession—has a sweeter chink
> Unto a Miser's Ear—
> (P 1093)

The speaker has earned her riches because she "could own" them but has chosen, in fact, to possess nothing. This only "feels like Poverty," however. Although her earldom, her riches, are "out of sight," they are no less real than the secret riches of a miser; and like a miser, she has a sharpened appreciation of the "possessions" she chooses to renounce in favor of these hoarded invisible gains.

Dickinson's central metaphor of mathematics subsumes the major symbols through which she contrasts perceptual values: earthly riches and the state of poverty, food and the state of hunger. Her mathematics is her abstract, universally applicable system for relating the temporal to the potentialities of the eternal, a system which is surely "broken" in its inability to prove her speculations, but one which nevertheless permits a richly abundant source of valid inferences, as well as acute, even provable observations on existential life itself—a life which can often seem to be its own reward, despite its anguish. By the process of her mathematics she arrives at her poems, her "experiments," through which she tries to solve various hard dilemmas—words, of course, becoming the equivalent of numerical exponents. David Porter writes that "The poet's language pleased itself in the way mathematics does, without much concern for the other, prosaic, self-consuming function of mimesis,"[12] but deemphasizes the poet's self-conception as a problem solver who must constantly "cipher at the Sign / And make much blunder" (P 1099), who is always "Low at my problem bending" (P 69). Her language existed not merely to please itself, but sought constantly to gauge the conditions of, and attempt to solve, a profound spiritual dilemma.

In several poems of her maturity, Dickinson uses the vocabulary of mathematics to describe the adjustments of perspective necessary to the quester who earns her progress into the state of experience, citing both the value and the limitations of her experiments. The following poem embodies the familiar theme of value heightened through its remoteness, and finally suggests her method of coping with this anguished insight:

> I had a daily Bliss
> I half indifferent viewed
> Till sudden I perceived it stir—
> It grew as I pursued
>
> Till when around a Hight
> It wasted from my sight
> Increased beyond my utmost scope
> I learned to estimate—[13]
> (P 1057)

In the state of innocence she possessed a "daily Bliss"—like a Wordsworthian child, living near the fountainhead of immortality—but could not appreciate its value. The process of maturing involved the loss of this bliss, a loss which is characteristically described in terms of a ratio: the more she pursued her lost prize, the more its value increased. Ultimately the loss was complete, the bliss going completely out of her sight, and by now its value had increased beyond her ability to measure in earthly terms. What did she learn from this painful experience? "I learned to estimate"—that is, she learned that through her poetry she could experiment, speculate, make cautious inferences. A broken mathematics is better than none.

Another poem states the new, intriguing problem resulting from this crucial lesson learned by the deprived quester: because she has learned to estimate, to employ her own system in exploring the vast range of human experience, she finds that the temporal dimension is itself so magnificently complex that it could "engross" all her time and talents, her very being. Here again she hints at the danger of a "covered vision": but whereas in "Renunciation—is a piercing virtue—" this limited outlook is due to easy fulfillment and complacency, here she fears that it may result from the "vastness" of the enriched, more complex life she has chosen as poet:

> Time feels so vast that were it not
> For an Eternity—
> I fear me this Circumference
> Engross my Finity—
>
> To His exclusion, who prepare
> By Processes of Size
> For the Stupendous Vision
> Of His Diameters—
> (P 802)

But the poem stands as the answer to its own fears: the second stanza indicates Dickinson's persistent hope that "this world is not conclusion," that her learning experience, her mathematics itself, is only a "process of size" preparing her for a stupendous vision, an absolute perceptual fulfillment which is, for Dickinson, seeing God. It is possible, after all, to "blunder" in conceptualizing eternity as hopelessly distant by then believing in the concept, forgetting that "Heaven is . . . of the mind":

> The Blunder is in estimate
> Eternity is there
> We say as of a Station
> Meanwhile he is so near
> He joins me in my Ramble
> Divides abode with me
> No Friend have I that so persists
> As this Eternity
> (P 1684)

If the poet's "friend" here seems literally to hound her, she still knows that within her own emotional response to her present life is a new kind of bliss which transcends the expressive capabilities of her mathematics and serves as a "sign" of eternity:

> If I could tell how glad I was
> I should not be so glad—
> But when I cannot make the Force
> Nor mould it into Word
> [*no stanza break*]

> I know it is a sign
> That new Dilemma be
> From mathematics further off
> Than from Eternity—
> (P 1668)

Always she returns to the ultimate "dilemma," the "riddle" through which "at the last— / Sagacity, must go" (P 501). She has the paradoxical insight that "One and One—are One" (P 769) and seems to exult in the knowledge that her mathematics are broken, since they will be mended at some future time when "Algebra is easier" (P 600) and when her various, disparate perceptions will resolve into "One"—a unity of life and death, time and eternity. Now she can peceive her present dilemma, however, only through having articulated her experience of the "processes of size" and seen the shape, the pre-eminent *gestalt*, suggested by these processes. Through humanly possible knowledge she can gauge the size of the unknowable, even to the extent of sensing in moments of blissful inarticulateness the sudden nearness of eternity—in ratio to the sudden remoteness and inefficacy of her earthly means of measurement and denotation. It is through such experimenting that the quester earns her soul's superior instants, her exalted status. It is also the means by which she intuits in her pattern of experience the crux of all meaning and relationship, and thus the chief subject and focus of her poetry: death.

Dickinson's stress upon the value of experience, and the need to explore exhaustively all relationships in human perception, is once again made clear. Although she frequently makes eloquent complaint against the seeming indifference of God and nature to the dilemmas of human consciousness, these again are in the voices of vulnerable, suffering personae who may be seen to represent ordinary humanity, as well as the experiencing self of the poet.[14] But in her identity as a quest poet who profits by experience, she uses her mathematics to gauge the morality of a universe whose laws are themselves beyond her understanding, and she occasionally arrives at a surprising conclusion: there is a kind of justice after all. In the following poem she envisions human beings as "cypherers" groping through darkness toward certain answers, and God as a kind of benign, fair-minded schoolmaster:

> 'Tis One by One—the Father counts—
> And then a Tract between
> Set Cypherless—to teach the Eye
> The Value of it's Ten—

Until the peevish Student
Acquire the Quick of Skill—
Then Numerals are dowered back—
Adorning all the Rule—

'Tis mostly Slate and Pencil—
And Darkness on the School
Distracts the Children's fingers—
Still the Eternal Rule

Regards least Cypherer alike
With Leader of the Band—
And every separate Urchin's Sum—
Is fashioned for his hand—
(P 545)

In the first stanza Dickinson focuses sharply on perception as the symbol of all value: in order to "teach the Eye" to appreciate what it can perceive (the Father's gifts, which he counts out "one by one"), he leaves innumerable gray areas, aspects of reality which are "Set Cypherless" and cannot be measured. Through this deprivation and doubt, this "Darkness on the School," the hand of divine justice may nonetheless be perceived: ordinary people (least cypherers) are considered as equals to the most exalted and serious quester (the leader of the band—surely Dickinson has herself in mind); and yet, also justly, each is given a perceptual gift ("Sum") measured in an appropriate ratio to his own ability. As Emerson put the idea, using an even homelier metaphor, "In the transmission of the heavenly waters, every hose fits every hydrant."[15] In Dickinson, however, one must also infer that each person receives a corresponding burden of suffering and loss, since these elements intensify perceptual acuteness.[16] In another poem, Dickinson again uses the third person to talk about herself. Here she writes from the point of view of a family member or close friend:

Had we known the Ton she bore
We had helped the terror
But she straighter walked for Freight
So be her's the error—
(P 1124)

But the persona of this poem misunderstands the quester's heroic solitary coping as an "error"; elsewhere Dickinson corrects such a notion:

> Power is only Pain—
> Stranded, thro' Discipline,
> Till Weights—will hang—
> Give Balm—to Giants—
> And they'll wilt, like Men—
> Give Himmaleh—
> They'll Carry—Him!
> (P 252)

Through these many considerations of loss, doubt, and suffering weighed against corresponding attainments of vision, strength, and exalted status— all proved through assertions of definable ratios, thus making sense of what may seem, to one less acute, both chaotic and unjust—Dickinson justifies her own hard-won position as quest poet. She likewise defends both God and the universe, making human sense out of unknowable relationships. Because "The stimulus of Loss makes most Possession mean" (L 364)—her pun on "mean" is surely deliberate—her deprived, solitary state makes perfect sense as well: she is a miser enjoying the sweet chink of her own heightened bliss. The following well-known lines do not express, as Thomas H. Johnson claims, a "mood of jubilation,"[17] but rather a joy both sobered and rarefied by the fact of loss:

> Oh Sumptuous moment
> Slower go
> That I may gloat on thee—
> 'Twill never be the same to starve
> Now I abundance see—
>
> Which was to famish, then or now—
> The difference of Day
> Ask him unto the Gallows led—
> With morning in the sky
> (P 1125)

Characteristically, Dickinson focuses not upon the gloating momentary satisfaction but upon the increased value of future starvation: " 'Twill never be the same to starve" because her perception of fulfillment will be all the keener; she will see her "ecstatic instant" with new and furnished eyes, like the condemned prisoner glimpsing a morning sun which is about to vanish forever from his perception. This is "Annihilation—plated fresh / With Immortality"

(P 705), a way of perceiving which for Dickinson makes human life an enchantment.

A pair of related poems, both written in Dickinson's maturity, elaborates upon this idea that satisfaction precludes an "enchanted" perception: both argue the necessity for deprivation in this life, warning against premature "satiety."

> Satisfaction—is the Agent
> Of Satiety—
> Want—a quiet Comissary
> For Infinity.
>
> To possess, is past the instant
> We achieve the Joy—
> Immortality contented
> Were Anomaly.
> (P 1036)

Moreover, "Want" contains an awareness of the extreme tenuousness of earthly joys, a knowledge that joy is always vanishing, always in danger; and this awareness itself deepens the "Sum" of any visionary achievement:

> Expectation—is Contentment—
> Gain—Satiety—
> But Satiety—Conviction
> Of Nescessity
>
> Of an Austere trait in Pleasure—
> Good, without alarm
> Is a too established Fortune—
> Danger—deepens Sum—
> (P 807)

As she wrote in a letter to T. W. Higginson, "The Risks of Immortality are perhaps its' charm—A secure Delight suffers in enchantment . . . even in Our Lord's 'that they be with me where I am,' I taste interrogation" (L 353). It is through her fascination with insecure delight, her awareness that "Remoteness is the founder of sweetness" (L 388), that Dickinson gradually, "a pittance at a time," earns her "Superiority to Fate": only in this way can "The Soul with strict economy / Subsist till Paradise" (P 1081).

It is clear, therefore, that Dickinson's elaborate perceptual mathematics must serve the "larger function" of her poetic vision: the quest for knowledge, for earthly evidence of immortality. Although many of the poems discussed above stress that the discernible ratio between deprivation and visionary gain enhances the value of experience itself, few are without the suggestion that the pre-eminent value of loss is its role as a "Comissary / For Infinity." Many other poems, not surprisingly, employ religious language in applying Dickinson's mathematics to this ultimate quest, often using the familiar subsidiary metaphors of money and food for the purposes of analogy. A pair of important early poems deals explicitly with "Heaven" in terms of human skepticism. The first of these emphasizes the necessary pain of loss:

> I should have been too glad, I see—
> Too lifted—for the scant degree
> Of Life's penurious Round—
> My little Circuit would have shamed
> This new Circumference—have blamed—
> The homelier time behind.
>
> I should have been too saved—I see—
> Too rescued—Fear too dim to me
> That I could spell the Prayer
> I knew so perfect—yesterday—
> That Scalding One—Sabacthini—
> Recited fluent—here—
>
> Earth would have been too much—I see—
> And Heaven—not enough for me—
> I should have had the Joy—
> Without the Fear—to justify—
> The Palm—without the Calvary—
> So Savior—Crucify—
>
> Defeat whets Victory—they say—
> The Reefs in Old Gethsemane
> Endear the Shore beyond—
> 'Tis Beggars—Banquets best define—
> 'Tis Thirsting—vitalizes Wine—
> Faith bleats to understand—
> (P 313)

The poet speaks of an unnamed earthly fulfillment, now lost, which she realizes would have given her too much joy; the "penurious Round" of ordinary life cannot honestly sustain such joy. Moreover, she would have lacked the justifying fear that doubt or want provide, and the depth of perception created by that fear.[18] Without loss she would have been "too saved," "too rescued"—phrases which recall the "too established Fortune" of "Expectation—is Contentment." The poem, unusually long for Dickinson and imbued with a tone of weary resignation to suffering, makes extremely painful reading: its voice seems largely overwhelmed by the suffering itself, and can only faintly assert the heightened insight her loss has produced. This particular state of mind—that of the temporarily enervated, disconsolate quester—is suggested in a letter of 1876: "It is true that the unknown is the largest need of the intellect, though for it, no one thinks to thank God . . ." (L 471). Nonetheless it is through her harrowing experience of loss, doubt, and pain—her private "Calvary"—and her sudden stark confrontation with the unknown which she must chart in isolation, that she is spurred onward to higher knowledge. Dickinson employs the analogical collection to clarify her new position, increased doubt defining the need and whetting the desire for knowledge:

> Defeat whets Victory—they say—
> The Reefs in Old Gethsemane
> Endear the Shore beyond—
> 'Tis Beggars—Banquets best define—
> 'Tis Thirsting—vitalizes Wine—
> Faith bleats to understand—

But it is this confused and bleating faith—rather than a "contented" one—that will struggle to achieve greater understanding.

A less anguished but equally keen awareness is expressed in a poem which employs similar imagery, again ending on a note of doubt:

> As Watchers hang upon the East,
> As Beggars revel at a feast
> By savory Fancy spread—
> As brooks in deserts babble sweet
> On ear too far for the delight,
> Heaven beguiles the tired.
>
> As that same watcher, when the East
> Opens the lid of Amethyst
> And lets the morning go—
> That Beggar, when an honored Guest,
> Those thirsty lips to flagons pressed,
> Heaven to us, if true.
> (P 121)

The first stanza describes the deprivations of this life and the "beguiling" possibility of fulfillment—the idea of fulfillment—which provides the "tired" quester with her own austere refreshment; the second stanza posits fulfillment itself, completing the analogies of stanza one, but the qualifying "if true" gives the poem its final ambiguity.[19]

In exploring the relevance of Dickinson's mathematics to her ultimate religious quest, it should here be noted that the remarkable proliferation of analogical structures in Dickinson's poems is itself an indication of this relevance.[20] Robert Weisbuch, discussing her "analogical poetics," rightly notes that "the essential quality of Dickinson's verse is its compressed inclusiveness" and that this inclusiveness is achieved through a habitual method: "The essence of the method is analogy, and analogy becomes a way of poetic life."[21] It should be further remarked that Dickinson's analogies are almost always concerned to suggest one particular relationship: that between the laws of a realm the poet has experienced and those of a posited spiritual realm. Dickinson does not insist upon the validity of this inferential method, and almost always—as in the above poem—a qualifying note of doubt reiterates her awareness that the mathematics of human perceptual measurement are essentially "broken"; her analogies, however precise, are nonetheless tentative, exploratory, restless. In 1839, Emerson had written in his journal: "I cannot accept without qualification the most indisputable of your axioms. I see that they are *not quite* true,"[22] and Dickinson applies this skepticism to her own deductions as well as to received ideas. But the unknown is the greatest need of the intellect, and she can still make intellectual progress through her scrupulous "estimations," her analogy-making which serves to measure the unknown against the conditions of the known. Meanwhile she continues to assert that the tension created by her analogies—so rich in implication, but finally inconclusive—has a vitalizing effect upon the "Grace" of whatever vision is validly achieved:

A Tooth upon Our Peace
The Peace cannot deface—
Then Wherefore be the Tooth?
To vitalize the Grace—
(P 459)

The central paradox of Dickinson's thought—her awareness that the ratio of actual loss to visionary gain formed the controlling, measurable condition of existential life—ultimately energized her thought itself, made her quest vital and meaningful.[23] Thus the austerity and toughness of her thinking, the "strict economy" of her mode of experiencing life and therefore of her poetic mode. Perception, the basis of human confrontation with reality and of consciousness itself, is the exhaustively analyzed matrix whose patterns of meaning, expressed through her poetic method of analogy, extend into all conceivable confrontations between self and other. "Perception of an object costs / Precise the Object's loss," and having examined Dickinson's concept of ratio, her persistent development of her own mathematics, one may perhaps emphasize the word "precise." To the last, Dickinson is a verbal mathematician; she is determined to establish precisely the results that *can* be established and at least to "estimate" those that cannot. The many forms of loss—the absence of a serene religious faith, her emotional deprivations, the constant worrying presence of death—only provided what she called "fortitude" (a word that has appropriately religious connotations), an internal stamina that was nourished by the progress of the religious quest itself. She states the process, not surprisingly, in terms of measurement and degree:

> Lest this be Heaven indeed
> An Obstacle is given
> That always guages a Degree
> Between Ourself and Heaven.
> (P 1043)

Understanding and accepting this paradoxical relationship between obstacles and progress brought her to recognize the proper mode and finally the extent of her achievement. This strange pattern of her quest, based in the relationship between her acknowledgment of experiential reality and her fervent religious longings, thus provided its own encouragement:

> To undertake is to achieve
> Be Undertaking blent
> With fortitude of obstacle
> And toward encouragement
>
> That fine Suspicion, Natures must
> Permitted to revere
> Departed Standards and the few
> Criterion Sources here
> (P 1070)

She expressed this need for "fortitude of obstacle" in many poems: "If What we Could—were what we would— / Criterion—be small— / It is the Ultimate of Talk— / The Impotence to Tell—" (P 407); "There is no Diligence like that / That knows not an Until—" (P 779); "hunger—does not cease— / But diligence—is sharper— / Proportioned to the Chance—" (P 904). And the encouragement provided by the process of quest, by her own fortitude, continued to generate the idealism necessary to her main effort. As she wrote in a letter of 1878, "To make even Heaven more heavenly, is within the aim of us all" (L 572).

But, as Robert Weisbuch notes, Dickinson is a poet who will not even submit "to any one world of her own hopeful making. She will not stop thinking."[24] The necessity for continued thinking, as will be seen, is related to Dickinson's acute consciousness of time: the fact of transience creates one of her most agonizing dilemmas. Her poetry is not a series of answers but an ongoing experiment, its conditions fluctuating as her perceptions submit to the rigors of her mathematics or refuse submission to any of her human powers, leaving her only with a bewildered, fascinated awareness of eternity. It is when she discovers a dilemma "From mathematics further off / Than from Eternity" that she "cannot make the Force / Nor mould it into Word" (P 1668).[25] Though this impotence provides a "gladness" of its own, it is not the characteristic Dickinson joy which results from the consciousness of her own solid achievements and her growing status an quest poet.

" 'Heaven'—is what I cannot reach," she announces grimly in one poem (P 239), but through her ceaseless reaching she contradicts this voice of despairing irony; always she pits her own formidable energies against the temptation of nihilism. Dickinson will not stop thinking because she *cannot;* the lack of rest is a condition of this world:

> Experiment escorts us last—
> His pungent company
> Will not allow an Axiom
> An Opportunity
> (P 1770)

In one poem she described the natural world as "This whole Experiment of Green" (P 1333), her choice of the phrase "whole Experiment" confirmed in the act of writing the poem itself: she vacillated among no fewer than thirteen variants before settling upon the phrase that fitted her sense of the tenuousness of a world seized by a single—and perhaps unreliable—perceiving mind. Her large-scale experiment escorted her, at last, to the crucial brink of death, but her obsession with "the White Exploit"—which was either the final end of seeing or the door to stupendous vision—did not preclude her fascination with the limited world of life. This fascination brought into focus two crucial elements of her experiential ratio: the flux of her experience, its transience, which could make all her verbal mathematics seem invalid, and the defined essences of her ethereal gains, which ultimately gave the entire struggle its relevance and meaning.

6 The Arithmetic of Time

The agonizing fact of transience is a familiar theme in Dickinson's poetry and is persistently mentioned in the poet's letters as well. Like other subjects which obsessed her, especially death, she looked at the mystery of time from every conceivable angle and discussed it in many tones of voice, seeming by turns sardonic or despairing or resigned. Several of Dickinson's letters, all written within a single year, are unusual in the way they comment upon the relentless passing of time. "Since I wrote you last," she says to a close friend, "the summer is past and gone, and autumn with the sere and yellow leaf is already upon us. I never knew the time to pass so swiftly, it seems to me, as the past summer. I really think someone must have oiled his chariot wheels, for I don't recollect of hearing him pass, and I am sure I should if something had not prevented his chariot wheels from creaking as usual" (L 8). Although she does not define this "something," what clearly bothers her is that change has taken place and yet has eluded her perception; the tone, however, is one of wry acceptance, the metaphor of the chariot's wheels cleverly apt. In another letter to this same friend, Dickinson is less cheerful: "The ceaseless flight of the seasons is to me a very solemn thought. . . . Let us strive together to part with time more reluctantly, to watch the pinions of the fleeting moment until they are dim in the distance . . ." (L 13). And in yet another letter she questions her friend, with obvious discomfort: "Have you altered any since I have seen you [?] Isn't it a funny question for one friend to ask another" (L 7). Dickinson might well have worried that her correspondent, Abiah Root, would consider unusual this reiterated concern with transience and change, for all the passages quoted above are from letters that mostly contain clever, cheerful nonsense, and were written when Dickinson was only fifteen. But especially unusual is the way they foreshadow, with stunning accuracy, the chief anxieties over time which would torment the mature poet.

Like her poems which establish ratios, Dickinson's poems dealing with

transience are concerned to make sense of painful experience without resort-
ing to self-delusion. In her adolescent letters she wants to locate the specific
moment of change, but the moment eludes her—"someone must have oiled
his chariot wheels, for I don't recollect of hearing him pass"—and the result
is that Dickinson suddenly finds herself in another, changed world without
having had the opportunity to make sense of this change through her conscious perception. Her resulting anxiety causes her to insist that she and Abiah
must "watch the pinions of the fleeting moment until they are dim in the
distance," for perhaps through meticulous observation the moment of change
may be located and her sense of meaningless flux palliated through conscious
understanding. Dickinson's mature poems about transience thus partake of
her "mathematics" in general, her overpowering need to create systemic patterns which illustrate a meaningful coherence in human life. Her work repeatedly echoes the question Emerson had asked in 1842: "Must every
experience—those that promised to be dearest and most penetrative,—only
kiss my cheek like the wind and pass away?"[1] Comparing her entrapment
within time to being "Without an oar" on a constantly moving stream, she
asks:

> What Skipper would
> Incur the Risk
> What Buccaneer would ride
> Without a surety from the Wind
> Or schedule of the Tide—
> (P 1656)

Having inherited no "schedules," she tried to write her own; just as her concept of ratio helped her adjust to the intensity and certainty of loss, her poems
centering upon transient moments allow her to articulate with great precision
her highly sensitized perception, even if she cannot uncover the mysterious
nature of time itself. For the purposes of ultimate answers, of course, her
mathematics is still broken; but in dealing with transience she hallows the
mystery itself with an attitude of scrupulous tenderness, and the result is a
handful of the most beautiful poems she ever wrote.

Returning to the adolescent letters to Abiah Root, one sees that even at
fifteen Dickinson speaks of transience in terms of a natural drama, "the ceaseless flight of the seasons." Seasonal change always haunted Dickinson. In
1866, for example, she wrote to Elizabeth Holland: "You mentioned spring's
delaying—I blamed her for the opposite. I would eat evanescence slowly"
(L 318). This constant emotional impulse in Dickinson to seize the moment,

to create within it a kind of Edenic stasis, is of course humanly natural and inevitably doomed; Dickinson knew this, but as always her human longings fed her mythmaking imagination, and the passing of seasons—a figure which fulfilled the need of that imagination for a reliable cycle, a system—becomes in her poetry the analogue for the ceaselessly changing drama of the human condition. Since for Dickinson the climax of the human drama (as for her poetic quest) is the moment of death, it is not surprising that she fixes almost exclusively upon a single, highly symbolic seasonal change: the passing of summer into fall. By attempting to locate the moment of summer's passing— since summer, like noon, is often a symbol of human fulfillment—she is examining not only the mystery of time but that of death as well, of our central dilemma as natural beings endowed with merely natural perception. Ultimately all Dickinson's anxieties relate to death, the crucial experience through which her quest might be resolved.

Although Dickinson's fascination with seasonal change helped allay her despair when she confronted the constant flux of experience, the seasons falling always into a logical cycle of progression, death, and renewal, she nonetheless despaired anew—as in her youthful letters—at her inability to assimilate entirely this progression into her perception. Three poems of her maturity, all of them describing the movement of summer into fall, focus sharply upon what is imperceptible in the effects of passing time. "How Human Nature dotes," she remarked in a late poem, "On what it cant detect" (P 1417); though she could refer to time as "the thief ingredient" (L 359), nonetheless her complex, nearly ineffable response to the mystery of natural process was far from bitter: in these poems, two of them among her very finest, her voice assumes a reverential, even sacramental tone. Though attempting to fix the passing moment and to measure the effects of transience upon her perception, she is also acceding to the largeness and beauty of natural mysteries. The first of these three poems is the most explicit in its use of religious language and its tone of deepening awe:

> Further in Summer than the Birds
> Pathetic from the Grass
> A minor Nation celebrates
> It's unobtrusive Mass.
>
> No Ordinance be seen
> So gradual the Grace
> A pensive Custom it becomes
> Enlarging Loneliness.

Antiquest felt at Noon
When August burning low
Arise this spectral Canticle
Repose to typify

Remit as yet no Grace
No Furrow on the Glow
Yet a Druidic Difference
Enhances Nature now
(P 1068)

The most sensitive individual response to this poem is still that of Yvor Winters, writing in 1938: "In [this] poem, we are shown the essential cleavage between man, as represented by the author-reader, and nature, as represented by the insects in the late summer grass; the subject is the plight of man, the willing and freely-moving entity, in a universe in which he is by virtue of his essential qualities a foreigner. The intense nostalgia of the poem is the nostalgia of man for the mode of being which he perceives imperfectly and in which he cannot share."[2] Winters concludes by noting the "intense strangeness" of the poem, and adds: "The poem . . . is probably one of her five or six greatest, and is one of the most deeply moving and most unforgettable poems in my own experience; I have the feeling of having lived in its immediate presence for many years."[3] Such a felt response is itself moving, and Winters points accurately to the poem's source of emotional power: its intense nostalgia for what is imperceptibly passing away, a height of summer which represents to the poet's imagination a "mode of being," a fulfillment in which she cannot share because of inevitable process, continual movement through time. "No Ordinance be seen / So gradual the Grace," but though the ordinance is unperceived it is nonetheless present in the poet's generous imagination: Dickinson does not impose a ritual configuration upon temporal flux in order to control it or deny its power, but rather exalts the transient moment by endowing it with sacramental form. Paul J. Ferlazzo writes that here Dickinson "sustains an articulated awareness of the inscrutable. The poem does not offer a lesson or an answer but simply an insightful grasp of the mystery of existence."[4] The poignant loneliness mentioned in the poem is "Antiquest felt at Noon," the time of fulfillment, and the sound of the crickets "typifies" repose; the poet is both in and out of time, lonely in her human estrangement yet rested in her sense of a natural typology keenly perceived, undisturbed by human anxieties or perceptual distortion. It is this repose, the poem implies, not forgetting the lessons of experience yet freed by an accepting faith in reality as perceived, which can "enhance" the natural condition. The poem finally expresses a quiet joy in the reality of this enhancement.

At one point in its composition the poem had three additional stanzas; it remains uncertain whether they existed in early drafts and were later discarded, or whether they were added later.[5] The stanzas were placed between stanzas two and three of the received text:

> 'Tis audibler at dusk
> When day's attempt is done
> And nature nothing waits to do
> But terminate in tune;

> Nor difference it knows
> Of cadence or of pause
> But simultaneous as sound
> The service emphasize;

> Nor know I when it cease,
> At candle it is here;
> When sunrise is, that is it not.
> Than this, I know no more.[6]

Although these stanzas are in every respect inferior to those of the final version, they nonetheless provide valuable clarification of the poet's intent. The first stanza, noting that the crickets' "mass" is "audibler at dusk," provides an interesting analogue in its linking of heightened perception and coming darkness: the drama of seasonal change is related to the daily drama of sunset, and both serve as types of death. The second stanza amplifies the basic theme of the poet's inability to perceive change, and goes even further by emphasizing the unselfconsciousness of the natural sacrament itself: it is innocent of cadence, of pause, and "simultaneous as sound" it partakes of its own repose and ineffable mode of being. The third stanza finally focuses upon the speaker; she knows no more than that the sacrament has begun by dusk and ended by morning, the quick magical change occurring in the interval and eluding her entirely. Again the tone is of an awed acceptance of this process.

The second of these poems begins by asserting the imperceptible quality of this seasonal change, and again views the lapse of summer not as perfidy but as an awesome, sacramental event:

As imperceptibly as Grief
The Summer lapsed away—
Too imperceptible at last
To seem like Perfidy—
A Quietness distilled
As Twilight long begun,
Or Nature spending with herself
Sequestered Afternoon—
The Dusk drew earlier in—
The Morning foreign shone—
A courteous, yet harrowing Grace,
As Guest, that would be gone—
And thus, without a Wing
Or service of a Keel
Our Summer made her light escape
Into the Beautiful.
(P 1540)

In her brilliant description of the late summer's light as "A courteous, yet harrowing Grace, / As Guest, that would be gone," Dickinson suggests many of the themes inherent in her concept of ecstatic experience: that it is a privileged grace, with religious significance for the perceiver; that it is an exalted transaction between a deserving human host and a spiritual guest; that its most harrowing and valuable moment occurs as the grace is departing, making her light escape into the beautiful. The speaker's tone is not one of deprivation, however, but of someone who has soberly witnessed and understood an event which is at the heart of reality itself:[7] a transient grace cannot be measured, cannot be preserved in its essence except through the poet's creative perception, which must deal with the most painful aspects of reality. The event having been sensitively perceived, the speaker's emotional response having been delineated in precise detail, she then makes of her inability to fix the passing moment a kind of transcendence: her quest for knowledge and fulfillment is sobered but also furthered by such poems which, through acknowledging the mystery and loss of what is transient, nonetheless celebrate the perceived moment in its spiritual significance.[8] Not surprisingly, this poem also had several additional stanzas before being cut to its present form (Dickinson often wrote uncharacteristically long poems when attempting to "fix" some perception whose essential nature eluded her). Again these extra stanzas are inferior to those retained—in this case we know they were in an early draft and later deleted—but nonetheless are impressive in their feeling for the "somberness" of the moment, imagining all of nature responding to summer's passing. Here the added stanzas come after stanza two of the final version:

Sobriety inhered
Though gaudy influence
The Maple lent unto the Road
And graphic Consequence

Invested sombre place—
As suddenly be worn
By sober Individual
A Homogeneous Gown.

Departed was the Bird—
And scarcely had the Hill—
A flower to help His straightened face
In stress of Burial—

The Winds came closer up—
The Cricket spoke so clear
Presumption was—His Ancestors
Inherited the Floor—[9]

The first two of these discarded stanzas are particularly impressive—the rhetorical structure, the diction, the bold and stately rhythms are all perfectly appropriate to Dickinson's theme. The opening statement, "Sobriety inhered," presents the crucial fact of change, but the next seven lines exalt its natural manifestations in bold, oracular tones; the language and rhythm partake of the Miltonic sublime mode (perhaps by way of Keats) in these five lines especially:

Sobriety inhered
Though gaudy influence
The Maple lent unto the Road
And graphic Consequence

Invested sombre place—

The inherent sobriety of the changed landscape thus creates a beauty of its own; the poet's language is charged with her conflict in feeling this new, austere beauty and yet mourning the loss of summer, which has escaped into that Edenic stasis—embodied appropriately in the abstract phrase, "the

Beautiful"—while the speaker must remain in the world of process, in the new and ever-darkening season.

The third poem dealing with the passing of summer, though not in the rank of the two just discussed, is nevertheless a distinguished and ambitious meditation upon the meaning of transience to one in search of spiritual knowledge. Typically, human perception is crucial to this search: the moment of seasonal change is when "the eye begins it's avarice."

> Summer begins to have the look
> Peruser of enchanting Book
> Reluctantly but sure perceives
> A gain upon the backward leaves
>
> Autumn begins to be inferred
> By millinery of the cloud
> Or deeper color in the shawl
> That wraps the everlasting hill
>
> The eye begins it's avarice
> A meditation chastens speech
> Some Dyer of a distant tree
> Resumes his gaudy industry
>
> Conclusion is the course of All
> At *most* to be perennial
> And then elude stability
> Recalls to immortality—
> (P 1682)

The structure of this poem illustrates with special clarity the pattern of Dickinson's thought when she is attempting to draw inferences about immortality from natural phenomena. Her first concern is always to see clearly, and then to evoke her emotional response to change: the first stanza describes summer, "an enchanting Book" drawing almost imperceptibly to a close; the second stanza describes the signs of approaching autumn—an altered look to the clouds, a new coloring to the landscape. In stanza three, once it is clear that the moment of transition is upon her, the speaker notes that the "eye begins it's avarice" and "a meditation chastens speech"—as in the poem itself, of course, whose tone is meditative, receptive to the natural rite. The poet calls the changing colors of the leaves a "resumption," pointing to the cyclical, systematic quality of natural change. And in the final stanza she makes her theoretical statement derived from her perception of summer's transience:

> Conclusion is the course of All
> At *most* to be perennial
> And then elude stability
> Recalls to immortality—

Here she reasserts the inevitable brokenness of any mathematics, any system—even a natural system like the predictable recurrence of the seasons. One can hope "At *most* to be perennial," but in the end our human destiny is to elude the "stability" of any fixed pattern; and this recalls the speaker to the thought of immortality since she clearly understands that "Conclusion is the course of All." As she notes in another poem about summer, "Forever is deciduous— / Except to those who die" (P 1422). It is clear once again that Dickinson's search for knowledge leads her ultimately to death. In the three poems just examined there is in fact a pattern of movement characteristic of Dickinson's thought as a whole: her sympathetic imagination, exalting what is transient in nature and making inferences relevant to her own being, brings her inevitably to eschatological speculation and desire. The eye's avarice for what can be seen is matched by her spirit's yearning for what death might reveal.

Other poems likewise focus upon what is imperceptible in natural acts which herald change and mark the passage of time. Mysterious, impalpable natural phenomena—light, frost, the wind—are examined in the attempt to fix their evanescent beauty, but also in meditations upon their validity as natural signs. In one famous poem she notes that "There's a certain Slant of light, / Winter Afternoons" which is perceived by the poet as an "imperial affliction," a "Heavenly Hurt" which inexplicably causes an "internal difference" within her. This light comes and goes without pattern, but it brings a heightened awareness of mortality, a peculiar blend of certainty and terror:

> When it comes, the Landscape listens—
> Shadows—hold their breath—
> When it goes, 'tis like the Distance
> On the look of Death—
> (P 258)

Conversely, the light of another season brings the poet serenity and contentment, assuming in her mind the status of another natural sacrament:

> A Light exists in Spring
> Not present on the Year
> At any other period—
> When March is scarcely here

A Color stands abroad
On Solitary Fields
That Science cannot overtake
But Human Nature feels.

It waits upon the Lawn,
It shows the furthest Tree
Upon the furthest Slope you know
It almost speaks to you.

Then as Horizons step
Or Noons report away
Without the Formula of sound
It passes and we stay—

A quality of loss
Affecting our Content
As Trade had suddenly encroached
Upon a Sacrament.
(P 812)

"Science cannot overtake" this light, it cannot be measured; but it can be understood intuitively, through feeling. Elizabeth F. Perlmutter, in her discussion of the "existential sentence" as a rhetorical fixture in Dickinson's poetry, remarks that "The light is not distinguished in the first stanza from all other kinds of light; it is a unique, singular phenomenon in itself, as the indefinite noun phrase in the existential sentence implies. . . . Both 'waits' and 'shows' suggest the game of hide-and-seek, where the light moves elusively, from place to place, illuminating 'Lawn' and 'Tree' as locations, governing the perception of the landscape, yet never fully revealing itself to the searching mind that wishes to 'overtake' or understand the true nature of the light."[10] And yet the poignance of this "sacrament" lies in its very transience ("It passes and we stay"), the memory of its beauty mingled with a new "quality of loss." For Dickinson, of course, this loss is mitigated through the poetry itself, through her having captured the transient moment and her intense response. As she wrote to T. W. Higginson, when "a sudden light on Orchards, or a new fashion in the wind troubled my attention—I felt a palsy, here—the Verses just relieve—" (L 265).

Like the passing seasons and certain qualities of winter light, another natural phenomenon served Dickinson as an intimation of death, and its mysterious workings could make her feel "palsied" once again. The rapidity, elusiveness, and deathliness of the frost are evoked in two of her poems, the first describing the frost's evanescent beauty, the second using it as an analogue for deeper mysteries:

A Visitor in Marl—
Who influences Flowers—
Till they are orderly as Busts—
And Elegant—as Glass—

Who visits in the Night—
And just before the Sun—
Concludes his glistening interview—
Caresses—and is gone—

But whom his fingers touched—
And where his feet have run—
And whatsoever Mouth he kissed—
Is as it had not been—
(P 391)

Here the frost is cast into the typically ambiguous role of a social caller; Dickinson's restrained diction—describing the way the frost "influences" flowers, making them "orderly," "elegant," and leaving with a last "caress"— shows an ironic detachment toward a phenomenon both beautiful and destructive. The second poem lacks this verbal artistry, but its theme is ultimately more serious:

The Frost was never seen—
If met, too rapid passed,
Or in too unsubstantial Term—
The Flowers notice first

A Stranger hovering round
A Symptom of alarm
In Villages remotely set
But search effaces him

Till some retrieveless Night
Our Vigilance at waste
The Garden gets the only shot
That never could be traced.

Unproved is much we know—
Unknown the worst we fear—
[no stanza break]

Of Strangers is the Earth the Inn
Of Secrets is the Air—

To analyze perhaps
A Philip would prefer
But Labor vaster than myself
I find it to infer.
(P 1202)

The first three stanzas, describing the way frost eludes perception, even a determined "Vigilance," serve to present the frost as an object of meditation; the last two stanzas are the philosophical speculations which have resulted from this meditation. Here the poet specifically denies her ability to draw valid inference from a natural sign; nor can she assume the posture of a fact-minded Philip, who bluntly asked Christ to make God the Father visible to him, since she acknowledges that "Of Strangers is the Earth the Inn / Of Secrets is the Air." Although, unlike Coleridge in "Frost at Midnight," Dickinson will not assume that the "secret ministry" of frost is a sign of harmonious reciprocity between man and nature, neither will she make it the sign of a cruel natural extinction. In her poem she evokes the mystery without explaining it; she knows that nature is a "haunted house" whose ghost cannot be "simplified" (P 1400). Another poem on a favorite Dickinson subject, the sunset, similarly lacks explanation, ending on a note of perceptual confusion:

These held their Wick above the West—
Till when the Red declined—
Or how the Amber aided it—
Defied to be defined—

Then waned without disparagement
In a dissembling Hue
That would not let the Eye decide
Did it abide or no—
(P 1390)

Anything in nature so transient and inexplicable must be acknowledged, even when its ability to elude perception create anxiety and disorientation, and effectually breaks any perceiver's "mathematics" or pattern-making. Dickinson progresses in her quest not only through achieving knowledge, but also by realizing what she cannot know.

But even her honest achievements, as she well understood, could them-

selves be transient, and certain of her quest narratives focus upon the fleeting-
ness of her "ethereal gains." The first stanza of poem 359, "I gained it so,"
emphasizes the intense difficulty of her quest, the amount of sheer effort required to gain her measure of "Bliss":

> I gained it so—
> By Climbing slow—
> By Catching at the Twigs that grow
> Between the Bliss—and me—
> It hung so high
> As well the Sky
> Attempt by Strategy—

The stanza contains an apparent contradiction which indicates the enormity
of her achievement: her ethereal gain (the gain remains unspecified, but "bliss"
usually refers to the possession of a spiritual insight into life) was at such a
distance that to attempt the sky "by Strategy" seems the fitting analogue to
her effort. Yet we know, from the poet's opening statement "I gained it so,"
that she has succeeded in this seemingly impossible task. The poem's second
stanza then focuses upon the precariousness of her possession, her intense
consciousness that if "an hour" can raise her to a superior status, it can just
as easily return her to poverty:

> I said I gained it—
> This—was all—
> Look, how I clutch it
> Lest it fall—
> And I a Pauper go—
> Unfitted by an instant's Grace
> For the Contented—Beggar's face
> I wore—an hour ago—

Thus the poem is one of many in which Dickinson warns herself of the treacherous conditions of her quest, its cyclical rather than linear progress, and of
her subjection to the friable and essentially patternless dimension of time,
continually thwarting her attempts to establish patterns of meaning in her
experience. Consciousness of her subjection often produces despair, a sense
of being "stranded then / In our Economy." This poem concludes:

> Our Estimates a Scheme—
> Our Ultimates a Sham—
>   [*no stanza break*]

We let go all of Time without
Arithmetic of him—
(P 1184)

Yet Dickinson never gives up her "arithmetic" for long. The anxiety underlying her awareness of transience is balanced, for example, by the argument of another poem in which the poet transforms a daily event in her life—waking to the familiar landscape outside her bedroom window—into a meditation upon what is permanent in her world, what is transient, and their relative values.[11] Again she focuses upon seasonal change and upon the inability of her perception to partake imaginatively of evanescent phenomena, even though she knows the landscape intimately:

The Angle of a Landscape—
That every time I wake—
Between my Curtain and the Wall
Upon an ample Crack—

Like a Venetian—waiting—
Accosts my open eye—
Is just a Bough of Apples—
Held slanting, in the Sky—

The Pattern of a Chimney—
The Forehead of a Hill—
Sometimes—a Vane's Forefinger—
But that's—Occasional—

The Seasons—shift—my Picture—
Upon my Emerald Bough,
I wake—to find no—Emeralds—
Then Diamonds—which the Snow

From Polar Caskets—fetched me—
The Chimney—and the Hill—
And just the Steeple's finger—
These—never stir at all—
(P 375)

The several precisely placed compositional elements of the poem heighten its drama: the situation is vividly presented with its configuration of a passive perceiver waking continually to the same vision—apple tree bough, chimney, weather vane, and the backdrop of the hills. The time of the poem's action—

the moment of the speaker's waking—is likewise significant, since her sleeping represents the benighted aspect of perception, which remains unaware that change is taking place, and since her daily look out the window is a fixed perceptual rite opposed dramatically to the shifting of what she sees. Dickinson emphasizes her passivity: the landscape "Accosts my open eye" and "The Seasons—shift—my Picture" while she stands by helplessly. Yet the very transience of what she sees enhances its worth, and characteristically she translates perceptual value into the language of material, measurable wealth: the springtime boughs of the trees are "emeralds," while the winter snowfall seems like "Diamonds" from "Polar Caskets."[12] The concluding stanza, listing the things which are permanent—the chimney, the hill, the steeple—seems prosaic by comparison, its final line "These—never stir at all" forming a disappointing anti-climax: the poet finds enchantment in what is continually vanishing.

If Dickinson's poems about transience seem to contradict one another—some of them emphasizing the value of enchantment and mystery, others complaining that continual flux prevents any coherent perception of the world—this is because she writes both as a human sufferer and as a poet of experience, one who feels acutely what is painful in life but who recognizes that this pain furthers her poetic quest for knowledge.[13] As in her adolescent letters, she continued throughout life to maintain a sense of humor about the subjects that bothered her most. In a letter of 1878 she writes:

> Hours—have Wings—
> Riches—have Wings—
> Wings are a mournful perquisite—
> A Society for the Suppression of Wings
>   would protect us all.
> (L 550)

And to a retiring Amherst professor, she remarks philosophically during the last year of her life: "To know you better as you flee, may be our recompense" (L 989). If she could adjust to the "mournful perquisite" of wings in her personal life, turning the impermanence of hours, riches, and friends to advantage through her ability to know them better, she could incorporate this insight poetically into her theory of perception:

> By a departing light
> We see acuter, quite,
> [no stanza break]

Than by a wick that stays.
There's something in the flight
That clarifies the sight
And decks the rays
(P 1714)

Her characteristic ratio is implied once again: the more fleeting her perception, the greater its distinctness. Dickinson sent a consolatory poem to T. W. Higginson after the death of his daughter, suggesting that "The Face in evanescence lain / Is more distinct than our's" and calling his loss a "Detriment divine" (P 1490). A poem with a similar theme employs the familiar imagery of earthly values to indicate the worth of transient experience:

Uncertain lease—developes lustre
On Time
Uncertain Grasp, appreciation
Of Sum—

The shorter Fate—is oftener the chiefest
Because
Inheritors upon a tenure
Prize—
(P 857)

It is time's "Uncertain lease" that gives the lustre to what prizes the poet does achieve, the transience and formlessness of experience actually intensifying poetic gains. It is through Dickinson's consideration of essence, in fact, using the attendant imagery of riches, prizes, and jewels, that she defines these gains in terms of her difficult quest conditions.

In the poem "The Angle of a Landscape," the valued perceptions were of transient phenomena—the "emeralds" of the tree boughs, the "diamonds" of the snowfall. These, for Dickinson, were the true poems, absolute perceptual gifts presented to the passive, impotent perceiver. Her need to define the essential gains of her poetic quest evolved directly from her experience of transience; for, as she wrote in another poem, "True Poems flee" (P 1472). By continuing with her broken mathematics, establishing ratios and profiting from the fact of transience, she came to see the distilled essences of her perception, again conveyed through metaphors of measurement and valuation, as the ultimate fruits of her labor.

7 A Pearl of Great Price

The original impetus of Dickinson's poetic quest as a whole—both her search for religious certainty and her struggle to find meaning in earthly existence—seems to have been an early, deeply felt sense of loss. A number of her earliest poems describe what she has lost as something infinitely precious, an essential possession that can never be replaced:

I had a guinea golden—
I lost it in the sand—
And tho' the sum was simple
And pounds were in the land—
Still, had it such a value
Unto my frugal eye—
That when I could not find it—
I sat me down to sigh.
(P 23)

In a similar poem, she describes the loss as her "priceless Hay," and notes that her attitude toward life has changed dramatically: "from a thriving Farmer— / A Cynic, I became" (P 178). The loss, moreover, is a deeply personal one, something inconsequential to others but of paramount importance to her:

A Rich man—might not notice it—
Yet—to my frugal Eye,
Of more Esteem than Ducats—
Oh find it—Sir—for me!
(P 181)

And in the poem which is perhaps the most distinguished early variation on this theme, she introduces the image of a priceless gem, which will become in later poems a frequent symbol for this unnamed loss. She indicates that the loss came about through her failure to recognize the gem's value:

> I held a Jewel in my fingers—
> And went to sleep—
> The day was warm, and winds were prosy—
> I said "'Twill keep"—
>
> I woke—and chid my honest fingers,
> The Gem was gone—
> And now, an Amethyst remembrance
> Is all I own—
> (P 245)

In all these poems, several elements remain constant: before losing the essential possession the speaker was honest, thriving, and "simple," while afterward she became cynical and miserly; it is her "frugal eye" which enables her to understand, in the state of experience, what she has lost; and the possession itself, for which the early poems offer such a variety of images, is never precisely defined. One of the complexities of the poet's quest is thus made clear from the start: she does not know exactly what she is looking for or where to find it, or even how to properly conduct the search.

It was this sense of hopeless drifting that prompted her to symbolize life in many early poems as a chaotic sea and herself as a frail bark barely managing to keep afloat. Some of the hallmarks of her progressing quest, however, are an increasing sense of inner security and self-identity, a growing confidence in her own powers, and a developing ability to define the essential spiritual gains which she has begun to realize. The quest is thus self-nourishing: increased confidence produces more definite ethereal gains, which in turn continually add to the quester's confidence itself, eventually bringing her to assert her exalted status and her soul's "distinct connection" with immortality. Early poems about the frail bark and threatening sea give way to poems emphasizing her ability to steer a complex, effective course through experience and to create human sense out of chaos through her perceptual mathematics, her ratios and measurements and valuations; and the early poems describing her sense of undefined emptiness give way to poems which assert her ability to fill that emptiness with the gains produced by her own efforts. She finds that the story of her developing identity, her progress from what she once called her "barefoot rank" toward a truly monarchial status, requires a fitting poetic symbol, and she finds this symbol—it is not too much to say, perhaps, that it becomes the symbolic center of her poetry—in the image of the pearl. In her maturity, comfortable with the image and its significations, she uses it to talk about her feminine identity, about her role as poet, about poetry itself. The history of this image in Dickinson's work, and of the particular identity it symbolizes, forces the reader to view the mature Dickinson's isolation not in terms of her loneliness and pain, but as an indication of her rarity, her poetic self-confidence, and her firm sense of her own identity as a quest-heroine.

This issue of Dickinson's poetic development, or lack thereof, has been a controversial one, partly because of the difficulty in positively dating most of the manuscripts and partly because the form of Dickinson's canon, her hundreds of brief, discrete, free-floating and independent lyrics left to posterity unedited and unarranged, seems to defy critical searching for a discernible shapeliness and cohesion, an orderly artistic progress. Although I have disagreed with David Porter's rather exasperated conclusion that Dickinson's work represents "utter miscellaneousness," "an art without progress,"[1] the opposite view expressed by William R. Sherwood is perhaps too confident in referring to "definite periods" in the poet's career: "a period of questioning in which she tried and failed to find conclusive evidence of [an] immortal estate . . . ; a period where, in resentment and defiance fierce to the point of heresy, she chose and indeed created (doing both quite without his permission) her own god, the Reverend Charles Wadsworth . . . ; a period of despair, in every sense of this word she herself chose so carefully; and, finally, a period in which all her wrongs were righted. . . ."[2] Such a neat patterning ignores the presence of contradictory attitudes expressed in poems of any definable "period," the coexistence throughout Dickinson's work of ecstasy and despair, spiritual fulfillment and existential terror, passionate love and equally passionate resentment of nature, God, and the workings of her own consciousness. My own approach to Dickinson's work, though roughly chronological, is not intended to suggest any unwavering development from one position to another; even regarding Dickinson's identity, the subject whose treatment shows the most noticeable curve of development, there are early poems which display confidence and self-esteem just as there are late poems which describe psychological disorientation and a sense of worthlessness. Moreover, as I have repeatedly stressed, all of Dickinson's major thematic concerns are present, in a highly developed form, in her earliest surviving work. I have found, however, that the poetry shows a steadily increasing sense of the poet's ability to deal with experiential loss and to guide the progress of her quest efficiently; and that the difficulty of establishing *general* patterns of development has been exaggerated by many of Dickinson's critics. Nor is it necessary to depend upon Thomas H. Johnson's dating of manuscripts to "prove" a given theory of development; rather, the evolution of the quester's identity throughout the canon can generally be seen to bear out the chronological arrangement given by the Variorum.

In a recent essay, Roland Hagenbüchle outlines "three main phases of her poetry, the early phase lasting to 1861, the middle phase from 1862 to 1869, and the late phase from 1870 onwards,"[3] a pattern which conforms to my own understanding of the quester's progress: the early phase representing the tortured awareness of loss and disorientation described, for instance, in the "bark" poems; the middle phase, containing most of her major work, describing psychological upheaval, religious crisis, and the emergence of a purged, queenly identity symbolized by the "pearl" of her art and selfhood; and the late phase, representing a kind of emotional and artistic plateau from which the quester-poet, still struggling toward further knowledge but relatively serene in her achieved status and self-realization as artist, further clarifies and extends the insights of the turbulent middle phase. Although these phases may also be seen to conform to known biographical episodes in Dickinson's life—especially her mysterious crisis of 1861–62—it should be stressed that our understanding of the poetry does not depend upon (though it may gain from) knowledge of such parallels. The poet's mythmaking is highly deliberate, and the heroine of her quest-narrative appropriately separable from the person of Emily Dickinson.

Though Dickinson's work hardly displays the stylistic evolution of a Yeats or a Sylvia Plath, neither is it true, again in David Porter's words, that the poetry never changed: "Its form, its language ploys, its unarranged mosaic of glimpses did not alter, did not evolve."[4] Although Dickinson did, of course, remain amazingly faithful to her chosen hymnal form, there are nonetheless marked *tonal* differences among poems of the three phases, and clusters of imagery (as in the "bride" poems, the "spider" poems, the "pearl" poems) which define specific areas of concern pertinent to the quester's development at a given stage. The tonal uniqueness of the early phase, for instance, is most distinct. In poems of 1861and earlier the speaker's manner is rather hectically effusive, displaying the anxious disorientation so many of the poems describe. The poems of this phase contain a definable collection of attitudes: a self-consciously sentimental wonder at the mysteries of nature and time; a shrill and self-pitying awareness of loss; a yearning for death as an end to the speaker's uncertainty and pain. In this youthful intensity, italics and exclamation points abound. Of the 213 poems estimated by Thomas H. Johnson to have been written in 1861 or before, fully 75 percent contain at least one exclamation point; by 1864, a year in which 173 poems were written, this figure has fallen to less than 7 percent. The relatively rapid change in tone over a three-year period corresponds to the depiction in the poetry of anxiety and exuberance giving way to crisis and finally to a sobered, often despairing manner appropriate to one who has survived the ultimate psychological and spiritual terror.

The poems of the middle phase have likewise a remarkable integrity of manner, representing Dickinson's period of great creativity and showing especially an absorption in her newly emerged identity (almost all the "bride" and "pearl" poems, for instance, date from this period). In the summer of 1862, the year in which Thomas H. Johnson estimates that Dickinson wrote an astounding 366 poems, she remarked in a letter to Samuel Bowles: "I grope fast, with my fingers, for all out of my sight I own—to get it nearer—" (L 266). Here Dickinson surely refers to her writing (as well as to her emphasis upon perception), and supports the notion that this was indeed the time of her most feverish creativity. Poems of the late period, by contrast, are both more varied and more relaxed: gone is the intent concentration upon certain image-clusters; gone is the brooding concern with the darker areas of the psyche. Though the later poems are consistent with Dickinson's lifelong skepticism, her tone is one of resignation—not desperation—toward continuing religious doubt. Her attitude is that of the self-confident artist who continues to exercise her well-developed powers and continues to find "amazing sense" (P 448) in her perception of the world, but who is also aware that "Experiment escorts us last" (P 1770) and no longer seems resentful that the poetic consciousness cannot resolve the deeper mysteries of existence.

A number of recent critics have pointed to various indications of Dickinson's development, and their comments are borne out by specific stances and remarks included in the poems themselves. Martin Bickman comments: "In Emily Dickinson's poetry . . . the images of death, sacred marriage, and rebirth become the basic symbolic enactments in the drama of a mind moving toward individuation. The movement is neither linear nor direct, but the poems can be arranged to correspond to what is both a basic ritual pattern and the sequence of psychic development."[5] Once Dickinson has undergone the terrible disorientation described in the early poems, her "search for location," as discussed by David C. Estes, reaches its apogee during her most creative years: "Such references appear more frequently during the early 1860's, her most active period, than during any other period and are an important means of communicating her perception of the insufficient unity and coherence in life."[6] What she continued to perceive as external disorder, however, was balanced by the emphasis—especially in poems after 1862—upon her own "psychic development." The rhetoric of these poems nearly always contrasts her present status against an earlier, less formidable self. The following poem, for instance, uses the familiar synecdoche of the poet's feet for the progressing quester:

> I find my feet have further Goals—
> I smile upon the Aims
> That felt so ample—Yesterday—
> Today's—have vaster claims—
>
> I do not doubt the self I was
> Was competent to me—
> But something awkward in the fit—
> Proves that—outgrown—I see—
> (P 563)

An uncommonly long narrative poem, beginning "Let Us play Yesterday," is only one example of what becomes a virtual genre for Dickinson after 1862: the reminiscence poem, in which she looks back upon the earlier self, takes stock of her progress, and usually draws some philosophical conclusion about her new freedom and access of power.[7] Using a typical mathematics metaphor, she implies that poetry has been the agent of transformation:

> Easing my famine
> At my Lexicon—
> Logarithm—had I—for Drink—
> 'Twas a dry Wine—

The poem ends with Dickinson's meditation upon her new freedom, the tone a peculiar mingling of exultation and anxiety:

> Can the Lark resume the Shell—
> Easier—for the Sky—
> Would'nt Bonds hurt more
> Than Yesterday?
>
> Would'nt Dungeons sorer grate
> On the Man—free—
> Just long enough to taste—
> Then—doomed new—

God of the Manacle
As of the Free—
Take not my Liberty
Away from Me—
(P 728)

She stresses that her development has been slow, even imperceptible, but no less real for that:

I made slow Riches but my Gain
Was steady as the Sun
And every Night, it numbered more
Than the preceding One

All Days, I did not earn the same
But my perceiveless Gain
Inferred the less by Growing than
The Sum that it had grown.
(P 843)

Another poem reminisces purely through metaphor, but the speaker's accomplished status is nonetheless clear:

The Props assist the House
Until the House is built
And then the Props withdraw
And adequate, erect,
The House support itself
And cease to recollect
The Augur and the Carpenter—
Just such a retrospect
Hath the perfected Life— . . .
(P 1142)

Poems of the late phase show even greater confidence, proclaiming the "ecstatic Nation" (P 1354) of the self, the "indestructible estate" (P 1351) of spiritual identity, and often sounding the theme of heroism:

We never know how high we are
Till we are asked to rise
And then if we are true to plan
Our statures touch the skies—

> The Heroism we recite
> Would be a normal thing
> Did not ourselves the Cubits warp
> For fear to be a King—
> (P 1176)

As another poem has it, "give a Giant room / And you will lodge a Giant / And not a smaller man" (P 1286). And occasionally the quest-heroine can compare herself only to God:

> Art thou the thing I wanted?
> Begone—my Tooth has grown—
> Supply the minor Palate
> That has not starved so long—
> I tell thee while I waited
> The mystery of Food
> Increased till I abjured it
> And dine without Like God—
> (P 1282)

Though Dickinson had been "at first estranged" in life, she notes that she had once desperately sought the shore; in her maturity, however, she has become "acclimated," and "pines no more / For that Peninsula—" (P 1425).

Returning to her middle phase, we should note several poems of the mid-1860s which look back on her early experience of loss and take stock of her progress, at the same time looking forward to the work still lying ahead. In "I had a daily bliss" she concludes her reminiscence of the crucial loss by saying that she now has "learned to estimate" the bliss and to place past losses and present gains in perspective. In another poem, written at about the same time, she looks back on her youthful bereavement with detached sympathy and congratulates herself on her present wisdom. But the poem ends on a characteristic note of doubt:[8]

> A loss of something ever felt I—
> The first that I could recollect
> Bereft I was—of what I knew not
> Too young that any should suspect
>
> A Mourner walked among the children
> I notwithstanding went about
> As one bemoaning a Dominion
> Itself the only Prince cast out—

Elder, Today, a session wiser
And fainter, too, as Wiseness is—
I find myself still softly searching
For my Delinquent Palaces—

And a Suspicion, like a Finger
Touches my Forehead now and then
That I am looking oppositely
For the site of the Kingdom of Heaven—
(P 959)

Dickinson's self-doubt, her "suspicion" that her search might be taking an erroneous course, recurs throughout her work, as if to prevent her pride in her own accomplishments from leading to a "covered vision" and allowing her to think that she has progressed farther than she actually has. But, in emphasizing the poet's concern with pain and frustration and madness, most Dickinson scholars have not recognized that the dominant strain in her mature work—poems written in the great year 1862, and afterward—is one of confident progress, and of a healthy pride in this progress. Her expressions of doubt, as in the above poem, are more often statements of intellectual honesty than confessions of psychological vulnerability or depression. Her early poems, whose despair over the fact of loss frequently mingled with an explicit death-wish, evolved into the later poetry in which despair is fortified by confidence in the quester's integrity and creative power and in which an immature death-wish has been transformed into a willingness to accept death as an objective phenomenon which must be examined exhaustively and with scrupulous honesty. When examining her attitude of "confident despair," therefore, one must give "confident" its proper emphasis. Though plagued by her sense of early and irrevocable loss, she had the ability to create a new, ultimately finer "gain" through self-actualization, the expression of her own identity—an identity which she called, in a typical image of essential strength and hardness, her "Granitic Base" (P 789). In her superb essay on Dickinson, Adrienne Rich remarks upon her own sense of the poet's strength: "Dickinson—viewed by her bemused contemporary Thomas Higginson as 'partially cracked,' by the 20th century as fey or pathological—has increasingly struck me as a practical woman, exercising her gift as she had to, making choices. I have come to imagine her as somehow too strong for her environment, a figure of powerful will, not at all frail or breathless, someone whose personal dimensions would be felt in a household."[9] The extent of these personal dimensions is a frequent theme in Dickinson's work; she is always concerned with the individual's achievement of high status through experience. It is not surprising, therefore, that the poet's consideration of essence, of distilled perceptual gain, is intimately connected with her estimate of herself and her strengthening identity.

Because "Advance is Life's condition" (P 1652), Dickinson accepts the necessity of personal growth and understands the value of moving forward into new stages of development. It was through this forward-looking confidence and acceptance of loss that she could "advance" toward further poetic gains. In the early poetry she searches among a variety of figures to describe her initial loss, while in her mature work she fastens almost exclusively upon the image of the pearl to describe her new, slowly evolving replacement; the image is given two major (and closely related) symbolic values. The pearl represents the refined gain of her earthly existence, her poetic achievement; and it symbolizes her own creative self, her identity as poet. Not surprisingly, the pearl image begins to proliferate in poems of the early 1860s,[10] the years in which Dickinson herself began wearing white.

The study of Dickinson's concern with essence is thus largely a study of imagery; nor should one overlook the extent to which Dickinson made of herself, of her own literal body, an image of the exalted quester whose progress she narrates in her poems. "Dare you see a Soul *at the White Heat?*" she asked in 1862 (P 365). By then her life, even her very clothing, became devoid of external color: she implies that she would no longer let earthly hues, in Shelley's words, "stain the white radiance of eternity," since she had all but removed herself from time and begun to partake imaginatively of eternity for herself. "Not any color will endure / That scrutiny can burn" (P 1671), and the intensity of Dickinson's perception, her daily undisturbed "scrutiny," enabled her to see beyond phenomenal colorations to the white radiance itself, which she symbolized concretely in the pearl as her own valuable essence, her central being. "A solemn thing—it was—I said— / A Woman—white—to be" (P 271), but in this solemn vision of herself she was not seeing the "New England nun" or the virginal renunciatory figure of her legend, but rather a woman accepting the call of her own tremendous gifts. The emphasis should not be placed upon her rejection of any conventional role but upon her acceptance of a radically new and independent identity. By examining her use of the pearl image, one can see the significance she attached to her role as quester and to the distillations of her perception which she achieved in the poetry itself.

The image of the pearl has relevance to Dickinson's life and work in a variety of ways.[11] In one poem she refers to the "perfect pearl" as a symbol of celestial marriage, absolute consecration of the self, but more importantly as a symbol of "A whiter Gift—within," which she also calls a "munificence" (P 493). She is clearly talking about her poetic gifts, which she characteristically places within the context of her religious quest as a whole. And since Dickinson frequently points to suffering as the means of reaching her essential, queenly identity, the pearl—which requires a constant irritant around which to form itself and thus transcend the irritation—is the most apt jewel to express the pattern of her life and achievement. Moreover, the pearl is hidden from view within a tightly secured shell, like Dickinson herself. (In early 1877 she wrote to her friend Mrs. Holland, "This is a stern Winter, and in my Pearl Jail, I think of Sun and Summer as visages unknown" (L 487).) The image also applies to her poems, gradually accumulating in the small cherry bureau until finally discovered by Lavinia Dickinson after the poet's death.[12] All this, added to the color, rarity and value of the pearl, makes evident Dickinson's motives in choosing this particular symbol to explore both essential selfhood and essential value in human existence—both of which, for her, are inextricable from poetry itself.

In examining some of the poems employing the pearl image, it is once again helpful to proceed according to a rough chronology. The earliest examples of the image, not surprisingly, are concerned with the poet's emotional adjustment to her sense of loss, her awareness that the original gem is gone forever. In "Your Riches—taught me—Poverty," the loss is that of a loved one (perhaps Benjamin Newton) and the poem ends on a philosophical note, expressing the familiar Dickinson ratio between loss and increased perceptual acuteness:

> At least, it solaces to know
> That there exists—a Gold—
> Altho' I prove it, just in time
> It's distance—to behold—
>
> It's far—far Treasure to surmise—
> And estimate the Pearl—
> That slipped my simple fingers through—
> While just a Girl at School.
> (P 299)

Characteristically, Dickinson plans to "estimate" the value of what she has lost; but another poem is imbued with the excitement of what she discovers in this process. This poem does not look backward to the lost pearl but forward to one which she can earn—and create—for herself:

> *One Life* of so much Consequence!
> Yet I—for it—would pay—
> My Soul's *entire income*—
> In ceaseless—salary—
>
> *One Pearl*—to me—so signal—
> That I would instant dive—
> Although—I *knew*—to *take* it—
> Would *cost* me—*just a life*!
>
> The Sea is full—I know it!
> That—does not blur *my Gem*!
> It burns—distinct from all the row—
> *Intact*—*in Diadem*!
>
> The life is thick—I know it!
> Yet—not so dense a crowd—
> But *Monarchs*—are *perceptible*—
> Far down the dustiest Road!
> (P 270)

This poem has frequently been misread, the "signal" pearl taken to be a figure for a romantic lover;[13] but Dickinson is surely talking about herself and her own solemn new existence which, she has come to realize, is "of so much Consequence!" When she writes that "*Monarchs*—are *perceptible*— / Far down the dustiest Road," she is glimpsing a future, fulfilled self,[14] and in the poem's third stanza she emphasizes the clarity of her vision, how it "burns—distinct," showing that she can adequately estimate the value of her own developing pearl.

An intriguing pair of poems, both written in 1862, presents a brief narrative through which Dickinson describes her struggle to understand her new identity. The poems contain four basic elements: the sea, symbol for the chaotic experience into which the poet must dive fearlessly in order to extract her pearl; the pearl itself, symbol of the essential value of life which the poet is struggling toward; the Malay native, who represents the poet's naive, innocent self which she must reluctantly leave behind; and, of course, the speaker ("the Earl") of the poems, poised at a transitional moment in her life and trying to make a crucial decision. The first poem emphasizes the speaker's fear of entering experience with full consciousness:

> The Malay—took the Pearl—
> Not—I—the Earl—
> I—feared the Sea—too much
> Unsanctified—to touch—
>
> Praying that I might be
> Worthy—the Destiny—
> The Swarthy fellow swam—
> And bore my Jewel—Home—
>
> Home to the Hut! What lot
> Had I—the Jewel—got—
> Borne on a Dusky Breast—
> I had not deemed a Vest
> Of Amber—fit—
>
> The Negro never knew
> I—wooed it—too—
> To gain, or be undone—
> Alike to Him—One—
> (P 452)

But, despite the speaker's frustration, she still knows that the native's possession is negligible because he cannot comprehend its worth: "To gain, or be undone— / Alike to Him—One—".[15] The poet thus describes the point in her quest when she can estimate her pearl, but still feels "unsanctified" to embrace the new identity it represents: the poem therefore justifies renunciation; she insists that her state of deprivation is what makes her an "Earl," and is far superior to the Malay's easily achieved fulfillment.[16] The second poem is more explicit in pointing to the analogical function of the Malay / pearl imagery:[17]

> Removed from Accident of Loss
> By Accident of Gain
> Befalling not my simple Days—
> Myself had just to earn—
>
> Of Riches—as unconscious
> As is the Brown Malay
> Of Pearls in Eastern Waters,
> Marked His—What Holiday

Would stir his slow conception—
Had he the power to dream
That but the Dower's fraction—
Awaited even—Him—
(P 424)

Again she insists that she had to "earn" her riches by becoming what Melville called a "thought-diver"; although her sense of loss was inexplicable, an "Accident," she realizes that a replacement cannot come by a similar accident: that kind of fulfillment, again, is like that of the Malay who lacks the "power to dream" that the pearl has great value. The speaker has progressed from her "simple Days" into an awareness not only of her riches, but of what she must do to develop them.

Several poems of 1862 make explicit the identification of Dickinson's symbol of quintessential value, the pearl, with her poetic achievement. Her gift for poetry is innate, as she frequently recognizes: "It was given to me by the Gods— / When I was a little Girl"(P 454). But developing her gift is a matter of conscious effort, gained only through "practice" and the skillful deployment of "tactics":

We play at Paste—
Till qualified, for Pearl—
Then, drop the Paste—
And deem ourself a fool—

The Shapes—though—were similar—
And our new Hands
Learned *Gem*-Tactics—
Practicing *Sands*—
(P 320)

As David Porter notes, "The '*Gem*-Tactics,' we may assume, represent the facility with which Emily Dickinson, in her maturing skill, edged her brittle language with a lapidary's precision. 'Pearl' signifies poetic accomplishment arrived at after years of apprenticeship."[18] Another poem stresses the refining function of poetry:

This was a Poet—It is That
Distills amazing sense
From ordinary Meanings— . . .
(P 448)

She insists that "Essential Oils—are wrung" (P 675), the product of the artist's effort to distill meanings into a precise, marmoreal, irreducible form.
Once the artist has reached his maturity, however, he is less a conscious shaper
than, as in the spider poems, someone entirely at ease and almost unconscious
in his creativity, the fulfilled artist whose art is a natural expression of his own
essential being: the spider, "dancing softly to Himself / His Yarn of Pearl—
unwinds—"(P 605). Another poem, through a conversation between the
speaker and her pearl, dramatizes this progress into a unity between the poet
and her gift:

> Shells from the Coast mistaking—
> I cherished them for All—
> Happening in After Ages
> To entertain a Pearl—
>
> Wherefore so late—I murmured—
> My need of Thee—be done—
> Therefore—the Pearl responded—
> My Period begin
> (P 693)

The poet chides the pearl because she feels she no longer has need of it; now,
in "After Ages," she can distinguish pearl, the nacreous essence of poetry,
from mere shells. Her perception, at last, is one with her creative power; they
are united in a happy reciprocal process and she no longer makes perceptual
"mistakes." Her irritation with the pearl is understandable, but the pearl corrects her notion that it has arrived "too late." It has arrived exactly when it
must arrive, with the poet's own mature possession of her powers. In fact, the
pearl *is* her possession of those powers. The age of the pearl is now beginning
because the speaker, in her maturity, is one with her ability to create refined
gems; her believing the pearl to be something external to herself is therefore
only an accident of perception, which the pearl wisely corrects. In this poem
Dickinson thus separates pearl and speaker in order to illustrate that they are
inseparable, a single entity.

　　Dickinson's confidence in her secure identity as poet, achieved at last
through the quester's efforts to perceive accurately and then to distill her
vision into genuine art, brings her an exuberance of spirit in which, once
again, she claims for herself a royal status. In one poem her joy is such that
she hyperbolically claims to care no longer for pearls; her sense that she has

mastered human experience ("the ample sea") brings her to a position of absolute wealth and power:[19]

> 'Tis little I—could care for Pearls—
> Who own the ample sea—
> Or Brooches—when the Emperor—
> With Rubies—pelteth me—
> Or Gold—who am the Prince of Mines—
> Or Diamonds—when have I
> A Diadem to fit a Dome—
> Continual upon me—
> (P 466)

Such moments of fulfilled identity, however—like her soul's "superior instants" of spiritual apprehension—were short-lived, and she never allowed them to blind her to experiential realities. She knew that this was "A Plated Life—diversified / With Gold and Silver Pain" and that " 'tis when / A Value struggle—it exist—" (P 806).

The imagery she uses to speak of her struggle makes clear that her quest was almost wholly internalized: the relationship between her perception and its creative transformation into the pearl of her art and being was so intensely focused that other, external concerns seemed irrelevant. Many of her poems, using the pearl or other imagery indicative of wealth and value, stress the productive interiority of her quest and its tendency to rarefy her poetic gains. One of these poems is particularly interesting because its irony clarifies one's sense that Dickinson had indeed mastered her personal and artistic situation, had made her choices consciously and without regrets:

> She rose to His Requirement—dropt
> The Playthings of Her Life
> To take the honorable Work
> Of Woman, and of Wife—
>
> If ought She missed in Her new Day,
> Of Amplitude, or Awe—
> Or first Prospective—Or the Gold
> In using, wear away,
>
> It lay unmentioned—as the Sea
> Develope Pearl, and Weed,
> But only to Himself—be known
> The Fathoms they abide—
> (P 732)

The poem's distinctly feminist perspective has been missed by many of Dickinson's critics, who have read the poem as a description of joyful marriage. Michael R. Dressman, for instance, writes that the poem presents "a picture of total submission to the omniscient husband as the path to a new maturity," and that "the persona finds fulfillment and security in self-abnegation."[20] But, as Clark Griffith notes about such poems in general, "Far from expressing simple jubilation . . . Emily Dickinson's marriage poetry is a poetry of ambivalences."[21] "She rose to His Requirement" contrasts two kinds of fulfillment: the conventional role "Of Woman, and of Wife," the woman who literally drops everything at the time of her marriage in order to fulfill a man's "Requirement," and a more individualistic role which stresses the inner life. The second stanza, describing the married woman, focuses upon what she must relinquish in her "new Day"—namely, a life of the mind, the opportunities for "Amplitude, or Awe." She must also lose her "first Prospective," the essential individual outlook on life which had been, until her marriage, undisturbed by external requirements, and she risks the "Gold" of her unique personal growth, which must now begin to "wear away." The third stanza suggests a kind of possible salvation for the married woman: the qualities of her mind must lie "unmentioned," but the pearl remaining in the depths may nonetheless be known and secretly preserved, though the husband will not suspect "The Fathoms" of his wife's inner being.[22]

The poem is clearly Dickinson's meditation to herself about the choices in her life: she imagines the compromise a conventional existence would try to force upon her, and further imagines how she might fulfill her duties both to a husband and to her own gifts. Richard Chase has noted that "one of the careers open to [nineteenth-century] women was perpetual childhood,"[23] and Dickinson clearly understood that her rejection of marriage gave her an inferior, childlike status in the eyes of others. In her moments of frustration and self-doubt she could even see herself as inferior, as someone who had inexplicably failed to grow up and accept an adult role;[24] this aspect of her work, in which she seems actually to be viewing herself as a "naughty" little girl, can make pathetic reading. But, as in the poem "I'm nobody—who are you!"—in which, as Adrienne Rich acutely notes, "underlying anger translates itself into archness"[25]—she frequently employed such postures as masks, clearly knowing her own worth and, from behind the mask's seeming innocuousness, satirizing the shallowness of contemporary social expectations. Thus, in the first stanza of the poem quoted above, one may note Dickinson's dryly ironic tone:

> She rose to His Requirement—dropt
> The Playthings of Her Life
> To take the honorable Work
> Of Woman, and of Wife—

To be a conventional woman is "honorable Work," but the woman's life before this work is mere child's play: "The Playthings of Her Life," even poetry, must give way to home and duty.[26] Such a poem makes clear Dickinson's awareness of her choices and how jealously (and justifiably) she guarded her pearl. The possibilities of compromise, hesitantly suggested by the poem's central analogy, represented a risk she was unwilling to take.

Dickinson thought of her own identity, then, as a priceless essence which she valued highly and protected carefully. She was not closed to the idea of personal relationships but simply found very few people, men or women, who were up to her standards: in "His Mind like Fabrics of the East" she again uses a masculine pronoun to talk about herself:

> His Mind like Fabrics of the East
> Displayed to the despair
> Of everyone but here and there
> An humble purchaser—
> For though his price was not of Gold—
> More arduous there is—
> That one should comprehend the worth
> Was all the price there was—
> (P 1446)

She knew that few could "comprehend the worth" of her mind—least of all a leading literary critic, as her dealings with T. W. Higginson showed her. Though such comprehension "Was all the price there was," the price was too stiff for the nineteenth-century American sensibility. Her value was like that of a mine: "A Mine there is no Man would own / But must it be conferred. . . ." She concludes that hers is a "Potosi never to be spent / But hoarded in the mind" (P 1117). And in another poem she speaks of essences as the "Best Things" which must remain "out of sight":

> Best Things dwell out of Sight
> The Pearl—the Just—Our Thought.

Most shun the Public Air
Legitimate, and Rare—

The Capsule of the Wind
The Capsule of the Mind

Exhibit here, as doth a Burr—
Germ's Germ be where?
(P 998)

While the poem "Essential oils are wrung" describes Dickinson's own poetic mode, her "gift of screws," this poem is concerned with a deeper problem. The pearl, symbol of concentrated artistic value (a symbol encompassing both Dickinson's work and the poet herself), dwells out of sight for reasons already indicated: it is being nurtured within a protective shell. The pearl, like the poet's "Thought," is a rarefied essence. The poem goes beyond that claim to speculate upon, as it were, the essence of essence ("Germ's Germ"). "The Capsule of the Mind" does "Exhibit here, as doth a Burr," but Dickinson finally seeks the true, irreducible essence; she asks how the fact of any refined perception, any genuine art, relates to something more basic and unseen. One is brought again and again to the pervasiveness of Dickinson's religious impulse, her desire to strain beyond the visible, the mortal—a concern which brought about her intense preoccupation with death.

Though the final stages of Dickinson's quest must concern us exclusively with death, it should be apparent that the result of Dickinson's mathematics, her constant wrestling with experiential antagonists such as loss and the passing of time in the desire to view them within a larger pattern of meaning, was a state of mind whose confidence began to outweigh its despair. "One Blessing had I than the rest" describes this state of mind, and is a central and underrated Dickinson poem; in an anthology of her work which stressed the development of her quester's identity, the poem might have the honored position of being placed last, providing as it does a synthesis of all the elements which recur throughout her work as major concerns: perception; her preoccupation with measurement ("gauging") and size; the "value" of the individual, striving quester; the possibility of a paradise within; and, above all, a justification of the ratios of earthly loss and artistic gain.

One Blessing had I than the rest
So larger to my Eyes
That I stopped guaging—satisfied—
For this enchanted size—

It was the limit of my Dream—
The focus of my Prayer—
A perfect—paralyzing Bliss—
Contented as Despair—

I knew no more of Want—or Cold—
Phantams both become
For this new Value in the Soul—
Supremest Earthly Sum—

The Heaven below the Heaven above—
Obscured with ruddier Blue—
Life's Latitudes leant over—full—
The Judgment perished—too—

Why Bliss so scantily disburse—
Why Paradise defer—
Why Floods be served to Us—in Bowls—
I speculate no more—
(P 756)

Few of Dickinson's poems combine such largeness of theme with such faultless execution. In order to mine the riches this poem has to offer, one should proceed stanza by stanza and then return to experience the poem as a whole. Each stanza focuses upon a different aspect of the quest, but all disparate elements are resolved dramatically in the confident quester's achievement of a newly sensitized consciousness.[27] The first stanza emphasizes her concern with perceptual measurement:

One Blessing had I than the rest
So larger to my Eyes
That I stopped guaging—satisfied—
For this enchanted size—

At first glance, it might appear that these lines describe a stalled quest, the speaker having decided to "stop guaging" and content herself with a "covered vision." The word "satisfied" has a particularly uncharacteristic ring. But, as the rest of the poem makes clear, Dickinson can stop gauging only because she has been pursuing her mathematics and developing her art through hundreds of other poems; she does not indicate a permanent end to her quest but a level of understanding which she personifies in her own "enchanted size." As Vivian Pollak says of this poem, "The speaker has shrugged off her nervous, prudential measuring. . . . Gauging has been supplanted with an intensity of feeling. . . . This poem goes beyond intellectual skepticism and emotional reserve, shrugging off numerical metaphors in the brilliant second stanza."[28] When one equates Dickinson's "Blessing" in this poem with her pearl, her identity as poet and her achievement, it seems natural that she stop gauging, at least temporarily: the stanza announces simply that she has found herself. She has an "enchanted size," and "size" does not indicate limitation but rather exclusiveness and focus: "Size circumscribes—it has no room / For petty furniture . . ." (P 641). Though it is still true that "Experiment escorts us last" and the quester's work can never end, nevertheless this poem asserts that the poet has found her own "intrinsic size" (P 641), one which is "enchanted" because of her security of identity and purpose.

Now that she has claimed possession of her own fully developed, essential self, the second stanza gives her emotional reaction to her perfected status. It is one of the finest stanzas Dickinson ever wrote:

It was the limit of my Dream—
The focus of my Prayer—
A perfect—paralyzing Bliss—
Contented as Despair—

Her new state was the "limit of my Dream," representing her highest fulfillment in this life; and it was the "focus of my Prayer," since she felt that only through a courageous acceptance of her own identity could she earn whatever grace might exist beyond death. Her emotional response to the "Blessing" is "Bliss"—but rather than an ephemeral "instant," this bliss is undergirded with contentment, a contentment as solid and unshakable as that which attends despair.[29]

In her blissful fulfillment as poet, therefore, it is not surprising that her previous feelings of deprivation should leave her:

I knew no more of Want—or Cold—
Phantasms both become
For this new Value in the Soul—
Supremest Earthly Sum—

She has found herself fully in the pearl of her art, which she recognizes as the "Supremest Earthly Sum," and she has replaced conventional notions of heaven and judgment with the realization of her own paradise within. As she had suggested in "Heaven is so far of the mind," a true and meaningful heaven may be contained within the raptured consciousness of the poet:

The Heaven below the Heaven above—
Obscured with ruddier Blue—
Life's Latitudes leant over—full—
The Judgment perished—too—

The poem's final stanza makes a statement similar to the first, in which she claimed to have "stopped guaging"; here she notes that she will "speculate no more" upon the strange conditions of earthly existence:

Why Bliss so scantily disburse—
Why Paradise defer—
Why Floods be served to Us—in Bowls—
I speculate no more—

These lines do not mean that her quest has come to an end, only that she has understood and accepted the *terms* of the quest, against which she had complained so bitterly in previous poems. She has, in short, made sense of her existence by recognizing the ratios between experiential losses and spiritual values and by understanding, above all, that the *essential* gains wrung from long years of labor do indeed provide a meaningful reward within existence itself. Dickinson does not finally insist (though early poems hinted at this) that on earth all is suffering and any reward remains somewhere in a future unknown. The "granitic base" of any individual's identity—in her case, the "enchanted" one of poet—provides its own deep satisfactions when truly earned.

Dickinson's vision of her own identity, expressed with such great originality in her use of the pearl metaphor, remains inseparable from her ultimate goal of immortality; as the biblical sources of her metaphor make clear, her yearning for the pearl of art partook of a larger yearning for a "new heaven and a new earth." The Book of Revelations, which Dickinson included in a list of her favorite reading,[30] anticipates a time when "the first heaven and the first earth were passed away; and there was no more sea." It goes on to describe the immortal "holy city": "[T]he gates *were* twelve pearls; every several gate was of *one pearl* . . ."(21:1, 21). The emphasis upon unity and integrity reminds us of Dickinson's own pearl, her symbol of her artistic powers and her own highly personal quest to the holy city itself. Another biblical reference to the pearl metaphor comprises an even more striking analogue to Dickinson's own journey. Here the parable equates heaven with a single human being who quests for pearls and emphasizes what the individual must renounce in order to earn a single earthly possession of crucial value:

> Again, the kingdom of heaven is like unto a merchant man,
>   seeking goodly pearls;
> Who, when he had found one pearl of great price, went and
>   sold all that he had, and bought it.
> (Matthew 13:45–46)

It was for the "one pearl of great price"—Dickinson's own poetic canon—that she gave everything. In recompense she had her own sense of self-worth and a private understanding of what she had achieved. Fully developed selfhood was the essential pearl to be found within human life; whether or not there was a further, spiritual reward—an immortal "state" which bore out her mystical apprehensions—was a matter for further speculation.

Part Three

Death:

The Great Romance

Our journey had advanced—
Our feet were almost come
To that odd Fork in Being's Road. . . .
P 360

Death sets a Thing significant
The Eye had hurried by—
P 615

8 A Stealthy Wooing

Dickinson defines the progress of her quest as a "process of size" that might lead her toward "Stupendous Vision"(P 802), a vision which she characteristically places within a religious context: it is the idea of God's "diameters," however—his own incomprehensible size—which breaks her human mathematics and forces her to rely, uneasily, upon moments of intuitive faith. Richard Chase and David Porter, among others, have stressed the extent to which the achievement of personal status on Dickinson's part constitutes a chief hallmark of her poetry. But it is also true that the value of that achievement, for her, had meaning only in ratio to its epistemological frustration; Dickinson's pride in her artistic "pearl" was always counterbalanced by her obsessed awareness of physical death, an awareness which often forced her back into a posture of abject humility because it threatened so powerfully to engulf her individuated self, to reclaim her pearl for the sea of natural extinction. Although Dickinson called death a variety of names—"that Old Imperator," "the White Exploit," "Despot"—her defenses as a master ironist, so effective in dealing with lesser antagonists (such as God the Father) were of little use when she grappled with the possibility that death rendered her existence meaningless. "All but death," she wrote, "can be adjusted," and this particular poem ends on a note of chilling despair: "Death—unto itself— Exception— / Is exempt from Change" (P 749). This idea that death is paradoxically free from the realm of process, containing no seed of a further metamorphosis, represents Dickinson's darkest conception of her own quest effort: in this forbidding eschatology, one which she formulated again and again, death is not a door but a wall, and "stupendous vision" is only a whimsical conceit of her own making.

This anxiety over death recurs throughout her writing, in letters as well as poems, and with such frequency that it must be labelled obsessive. Much critical argument, in fact, has centered upon the "problem" of Dickinson's unremitting concern with death, implying that a highly personal, psychic conflict must be at odds with literary seriousness or relevance. But the simple fact that many of Dickinson's finest poems are about death contradicts such a view. She need not be defended against charges of morbidity, of what one critic has called an "addiction to graveyardism,"[1] for this addiction prompted some of her best work; neither should Dickinson's obsession be rationalized and pronounced "normal," for such rationalization has the flavor of condescension, as if claiming that Dickinson's neurosis must be ignored because she is a great poet. As with so many of Dickinson's peculiarities, her obsession with death is directly related to her creative impulse and achievement; in the death poems her anxiety provides impetus for a startling originality of imagery, tone, and rhetorical stance, as well as for a comprehensive examination of her quest in its largest context. Several critics, most recently David Porter, have seemed unwilling to recognize this relationship between Dickinson's death-obsession and her poetic power. Porter, bound by his thesis that Dickinson is a nineteenth-century modernist, trivializes the death poetry by claiming it is "more a matter of style than of idea" and thereby ignores the great intensity and seriousness of the death poetry as a whole. Death, according to Porter, was "the theme of much popular literature and one she substituted for experience of her own in the outside world. Death was the topic of letters, of gossip, of day-to-day social intercourse. It was what one talked about. . . . She employed death in the way people use the weather as an excuse for communicating."[2] There is ample evidence, I believe, for an opposite view: that Dickinson's concern with death was unremitting and profound, the spur to her highest achievement because it represented both the barrier and potential door to the stupendous vision that was her lifelong quest object.[3]

As a poet, Dickinson is obsessed with death because it is impervious to her perceptual mathematics; it cannot be "adjusted." Of all other conditions of existence she could make a kind of sense—often the sense was painful, but nonetheless she could feel herself controlling experience by creating coherent poetic structures. Only death made no sense, and thus she returned to it again and again, achieving artistic complexity and range through her personal frustration. She once called death a "Circumference without Relief— / Or Estimate—or End—" (P 943); it not only rendered her helpless, since it was beyond her ability to "estimate," but it seemed to render her helpless for all time. The idea of death, therefore, is "all we need of hell" (P 1732): it suspends her in an agony of passing time which seems to hurtle her constantly nearer to extinction.

One of her earliest surviving poems, probably written in 1858, expresses a characteristic concern with death and what may lie beyond it, and also contains many elements typical of her poetic vision as a whole, especially regarding human perception. It is distinct from her mature work, however, in its overt expression of a death wish (much of her early poetry shows a literal infatuation with death), and it indicates that Dickinson's stance of "confident despair" has not yet been achieved. Rather the poem's expression of "faith" seems to mask or forestall a despair that cannot be qualified:

> The feet of people walking home
> With gayer sandals go—
> The Crocus—till she rises
> The Vassal of the snow—
> The lips at Hallelujah
> Long years of practise bore
> Till bye and bye these Bargemen
> Walked singing on the shore.
>
> Pearls are the Diver's farthings
> Extorted from the Sea—
> Pinions—the Seraph's wagon
> Pedestrian once—as we—
> Night is the morning's Canvas
> Larceny—legacy—
> Death, but our rapt attention
> To Immortality.
>
> My figures fail to tell me
> How far the Village lies—
> Whose peasants are the Angels—
> Whose Cantons dot the skies—
> My Classics vail their faces—
> My faith that Dark adores—
> Which from it's solemn abbeys
> Such resurrection pours.
> (P 7)

Here Dickinson's ratio, perversely, states a death wish rather than an affirmation of poetic survival: "The feet of people walking home / With gayer sandals go."[4] In stanza two, the familiar pearl image represents immortality "extorted" from the natural sea, and death is merely "our rapt attention" to this coming salvation. The final stanza, however, focuses upon the poet's doubt, her awareness that her mathematics cannot provide any answers: "My figures fail to tell me / How far the Village lies. . . ." But the speaker's orthodox resolution, seeming to suspend her in a state of happy ignorance, expresses not only her death wish but also the kind of facile contentment Dickinson would later satirize in "I never saw a Moor": her assertion that "My faith that Dark adores" indicates a stance which is not only anti-perception, but anti-poetry as well, since she is blindly adoring an unfathomable darkness, contenting herself not only with the featureless quality of death but also with her own benighted condition. The poem is clearly related to other early poems quoted above, such as "A poor—torn heart—a tattered heart—" (P 78) and "Adrift! A little boat adrift!" (P 30), in which a conventionally imaged heaven of angels and resurrection is presented as a temporary "resolution" of buried anxieties. Robert Weisbuch calls this figure "the reunion fiction" and writes that "As a consolatory fib, the reunion fiction leads away from Dickinson's serious thought."[5] But Dickinson's thought in such poems does not really lack seriousness; it is simply immature. To read through her early work is to see her gradually coming to grips with death as a reality, replacing the conventional fantasy with her own poetic insights.

Another early poem, written about a year later, may be seen to represent an advance in Dickinson's maturity, since it focuses not on what lies beyond death but on the obstacle itself. Again the poet emphasizes perception:

> Our lives are Swiss—
> So still—so Cool—
> Till some odd afternoon
> The Alps neglect their Curtains
> And we look farther on!
>
> *Italy* stands the other side!
> While like a guard between—
> The solemn Alps—
> The siren Alps
> Forever intervene!
> (P 80)

Even this early in her career, Dickinson's metaphorical ingenuity is considerable: in a daring figure, she implies that human life is comparable to the geographical situation of Switzerland, a country which is sheltered but also totally isolated by the natural phenomenon of the Alps; on the other hand, Italy has the symbolic value of a "celestial city"—probably because Rome is the center of Christianity—which the all but unscalable mountains "guard" from human perception. The Alps are "solemn" in their character as massive and impenetrable sentinels; they are "siren" because by the very immensity of the frustration they represent, they spur the speaker's quest to get beyond them (even as she recognizes that they intervene "forever"). Like all of Dickinson's best early work, this poem states her religious dilemma with honesty and precision yet retains a note of youthful zest (the many exclamations are characteristic), a sense of awe before the magnitude of the quest lying ahead. The conviction remains that despite formidable obstacles, there *is* an Italy beyond physical death. In a similar early poem, also equating salvation with perceptual splendor, she draws another significant parallel, one which will become increasingly emphasized in later work: "At last, to be identified! / At last, the lamps upon thy side / The rest of Life to *see!*" (P 174). For Dickinson, fulfillment of her perceptual quest is identical with the ultimate development of her human self, her individuation as poet.

Throughout her life, Dickinson continued to employ a kind of double vision with regard to human destiny: she expanded and deepened the dominant theme of her early work, presenting a view of reality in which the role of faith is indispensable; and she faced repeatedly the opposing possibility of nihilism. It is the tension between these opposing visions which gives her poetry of death its energy and emotional immediacy. Dickinson's canon, viewed as a whole, makes apparent that she leaned more heavily toward the pessimistic viewpoint, in terms of both the quantity and quality of poems dealing with death as the ultimate horror which "nails the eyes" (P 561) of human beings forever. Expressions of a persistent faith did continue, however, and they are all the more moving for being ambiguous and troubled. In the following poem, whose fragmentary quality is perhaps its most telling feature, Dickinson employs her typical language of mathematics to argue that the pain of this life will come to be seen, from the vantage of immortality, as a "fallacy," a figment of the imagination:

> Not so the infinite Relations—Below
> Division is Adhesion's forfeit—On High
> Affliction but a Speculation—And Wo
> A Fallacy, a Figment, We knew—
> (P 1040)

The lines seem a direct, affirmative response to Emerson's assertion in "The Divinity School Address": "What am I? and What is? asks the human spirit with a curiosity new-kindled, but never to be quenched. Behold these outrunning laws, which our imperfect apprehension can see tend this way and that, but not come full circle. Behold these infinite relations, so like, so unlike; many, yet one."[6] In Dickinson's poem the complexities of human life, its "infinite relations," are negated by the viewpoint of heaven; for one "On High," pain is only a "Speculation." Though Dickinson would like to believe in this vision of the future, the poem's expression of faith is leavened by a characteristic bitterness toward the indifference of heaven. The troubled faith which results implies that the quester must have courage, must "dare" to believe, even though fear is her dominant emotion:

> Not seeing, still we know—
> Not knowing, guess—
> Not guessing, smile and hide
> And half caress—
>
> And quake—and turn away,
> Seraphic fear—
> Is Eden's innuendo
> "If you dare"?
> (P 1518)

"Not seeing" is what causes the quester's fear. Another poem has a similar emphasis:

> Unfulfilled to Observation—
> Incomplete—to Eye—
> But to Faith—a Revolution
> In Locality—
>
> Unto Us—the Suns extinguish—
> To our Opposite—
> New Horizons—they embellish—
> Fronting Us—with Night.
> (P 972)

In this poem heaven is "our Opposite," a locality which enjoys a view of "New Horizons" when human beings are rudely fronted with night. Although heaven exists in this poem and is merely "Unfulfilled to Observation," the poem nevertheless contains an implicit rebelliousness and anger at being shut out. In other poems the complaint is more overt: "Why—do they shut Me out of Heaven?" (P 248). Often she found the possibility of nihilism more acceptable than that of a cruel and tyrannical God.

More than any other aspect of her work, Dickinson's confrontation with death illustrates dramatically her tendency toward a rebellious individualism, what Roy Harvey Pearce has called the impulse to be "radically and unflinchingly free."[7] Although she employs biblical tropes and images, her interpretations are frequently ironic and always wholly her own. As Robert Weisbuch observes, "To identify Dickinson's typology of death as Christian-derived in many of its aspects is less important than to identify its spirit as independent."[8] Within a literary context, Dickinson's place within "tradition" is similarly independent. Her meditations upon the physical aspects of death, for instance, represent what is surely the most significant modern extension of the *ars moriendi* tradition which flourished in the Renaissance; and, as Judith Banzer points out, Dickinson's death poetry has particular affinities with that of the metaphysical poets, especially Donne.[9] But Dickinson's interest in dying, unlike Donne's in *The Devotions* or the "Holy Sonnets," is hardly motivated by the conviction that her rebelliousness is an impertinence, or by the need to humble herself through considerations of bodily corruption. Rather she insists upon her own intellectual and imaginative freedom, and it is in this egoism of her poetic stance that she carries the antinomian impulse in American Romanticism to its most radical extent.

In a context particularly relevant to Dickinson, Harold Bloom has commented upon the crucial Romantic displacement of an external, conceptualized authority by the authority of poetic imagination: "The movement of quest-romance, before its internalization by the High Romantics, was from nature to redeemed nature, the sanction of redemption being the gift of some external spiritual authority. The Romantic movement is from nature to the imagination's freedom. . . ."[10] Dickinson's own movement is from an inherited Christian interpretation—the chiliastic vision of "redeemed nature"—to a personal vision of the supremacy of imagination; through the progress of her own quest romance, she follows an intuitive and nonprescriptive road toward imaginative truth, a truth which could involve many contradictory attitudes and impulses. As Bloom remarks elsewhere, for Dickinson this truth resides only in the quester's individuated consciousness which will, he writes, "some day be aware of dying, and will be altogether solitary, autonomous, and unable to communicate its final knowing to others. This final adventure will be a quest indistinguishable from the quester. . . ."[11] Emerson, who like Dickinson stressed identity and individuated perception, nonetheless tried to ignore his own troubled awareness of death as this ultimate event of consciousness. In 1837 he had written in his journal:

The event of death is always astounding; our philosophy never reaches, never possesses it; we are always at the beginning of our catechism; always the definition is yet to be made. What is death?

I see nothing to help beyond observing what the mind's habit is in regard to that crisis. Simply I have nothing to do with it. It is nothing to me. After I have made my will and set my house in order, I shall do in the immediate expectation of death the same things I should do without it.[12]

Emerson's imaginative truth depended upon ignoring death, Dickinson's upon ignoring almost everything else. Claiming that death changes nothing, Emerson could bravely maintain his claims for consciousness. Dickinson, insisting that a consciousness that ceases with death is rendered valueless in life, was forced into a relentless exploration of the feared phenomenon. Though taking opposite stances, both writers illustrate a major Romantic principle: the preeminence of imaginative and artistic freedom.

Dickinson was even capable of questioning the moral value of this freedom itself (the more one reads Dickinson's work, the more her rebelliousness seems the central quality of her mind), but she never misinterprets her dark nights of the soul as a signal that the quest has ended, or ought to end. The following poem is therefore largely rhetorical, a way for Dickinson to externalize her fears by fully developing an idea she cannot really accept. The "prudence" of the last line is a self-defeating one, and the speaker's "dreaming" a way of avoiding a painful reality. The poem may even be read as a tiny critique of the British Romantic tradition of the dream-vision, pointing toward a necessarily starker (in literary terms, both more American and more "modern") confrontation between the poet and her perception of the world. The fear implicit in the poem is nevertheless real enough:

We dream—it is good we are dreaming—
It would hurt us—were we awake—
But since it is playing—kill us,
And we are playing—shriek—

What harm? Men die—externally—
It is a truth—of Blood—
But we—are dying in Drama—
And Drama—is never dead—

Cautious—We jar each other—
And either—open the eyes—
                [*no stanza break*]

Lest the Phantasm—prove the Mistake—
And the livid Surprise

Cool us to Shafts of Granite—
With just an Age—and Name—
And perhaps a phrase in Egyptian—
It's prudenter—to dream—
(P 531)

This poem is about the poet's fear of a stark confrontation between herself and an awareness of death; it argues that a buffer of "dreaming" is necessary to protect the human spirit from a reality that would produce utter despair if faced with full consciousness.[13] The first stanza perhaps suffers from excessive compression, but it is readily understood if one assumes that the pronoun "it," in lines 2 and 3, refers to death. If we were fully awake, therefore, the fact of death would hurt us; but, she continues in line 3, "since [death] is playing," it would kill us. The word "playing" here has a double significance: it anticipates the drama metaphor in stanza two, suggesting that death somehow plays a role within human life; and it embodies Dickinson's frequent complaint that death is a kind of cosmic joke which is played at our expense. Line 4 of the poem—"And we are playing—shriek—" means that as human beings we play the role of death's victim, whether we like it or not; and if we shed our protective dreaming, we will be forced to acknowledge this role and react to its unbearable pain.

Stanza two immediately questions the assumptions of this theme and its images, even as it extends them:

What harm? Men die—externally—
It is a truth—of Blood—
But we—are dying in Drama—
And Drama—is never dead—

How can a simple fact harm us? the poet asks; that "Men die—externally" is a truth of nature, "of Blood." The poet answers her question by returning to the play metaphor, insisting that external death has little significance when compared to the continuing drama of death within her own consciousness. "I suppose there are depths in every Consciousness," she once wrote, "from which we cannot rescue ourselves—to which none can go with us—which represent to us Mortally—the Adventure of Death" (L 555). Death is thus omnipresent because it has become internalized and exists as a constant pressure upon the quester's spirit. In the final two stanzas the speaker insists that

to "open the eyes" and admit death into her poetic vision would be like opening her eyes to Medusa: she would turn to stone. Paradoxically, her despair
would.then cast her into a kind of death-in-life, the "livid Surprise" of death's
play bringing about a spiritual entombment. Therefore, the poem concludes,
"It's prudenter—to dream—".

The rhetoric of this poem is powerful, but it would seem to represent an
impasse for the poet's quest: it implies, finally, that perception must be selective, that to face the tragic possibility is to enter a state of death-in-life and to
lapse into silence. For Dickinson, however, with her peculiar emphasis on
perceptual confrontation, dreaming is not a metaphor for imaginative freedom but for cowardly evasion,[14] even though she could speculate that such
evasion was "prudent," the only course which would not destroy her spirit.
In a well-known poem she also views the relationship between her quest
object (the unnamed "He," referring in this poem to God) and the possibly
permanent obstacle of death, focusing upon visual perception as the means
toward "Bliss":

> I know that He exists.
> Somewhere—in Silence—
> He has hid his rare life
> From our gross eyes.
>
> 'Tis an instant's play.
> 'Tis a fond Ambush—
> Just to make Bliss
> Earn her own surprise!
>
> But—should the play
> Prove piercing earnest—
> Should the glee—glaze—
> In Death's—stiff—stare—
>
> Would not the fun
> Look too expensive!
> Would not the jest—
> Have crawled too far!
> (P 338)

The first stanza states the familiar position of a settled faith in the unseen
(our merely natural vision is "gross" and incapable of perceiving the "rare
life" of God), while the second stanza goes a step further by asserting once
again the poet's theory of ratio: "Bliss" must "Earn her own surprise," or

otherwise the value of seeing God would not be properly appreciated. Our progress toward death is thus only an "instant's play," a kind of joke whose underlying intentions are beneficent. Thus far the poem resembles much of Dickinson's earliest work, and an earlier poem might indeed have ended here. But this poem continues, changing direction abruptly as the poet speculates upon the possibility of simple extinction. In this vision of death, the play becomes "piercing earnest"; the drama has abruptly shifted from comedy to tragedy.[15] Not surprisingly, Dickinson pictures the tragic moment as a chilling confrontation between the perceiver and death: "Should the glee—glaze— / In Death's—stiff—stare. . . ." In a poem written about a year earlier she had pictured death as a "Face of Steel" with a "metallic grin": "The Cordiality of Death— / Who drills his Welcome in" (P 286). It was only a short step from these speculations to a final admitting of the tragic possibility.

Dickinson's frequent and curious personification of death as a romantic lover, most famously in the poem "Because I could not stop for Death," is meaningfully related both to her emphasis upon a perceptual confrontation with death and to the progress of her own quest romance.[16] By picturing death as a potential suitor the poet is able, paradoxically, to keep him at a distance, to remain critical and safely detached even as she is hopelessly involved. In these poems the relationship between the poet and death is "civil" (P 712), "cordial" (P 286); it involves a "stealthy Wooing" which is "Conducted first / By pallid innuendoes / And dim approach" (P 1445). At times it is not entirely clear who is doing the courting.[17] By establishing this uneasy, tense relationship, however, Dickinson gives herself a position as someone equal to death, someone with her own sources of power and leverage. Just as constraining romantic conventions are society's way of regulating the sexual drive, Dickinson's casting death in the role of romantic lover puts him, at least temporarily, on his best behavior. In this way Dickinson buys time, staves off despair, and is enabled to perceive him comprehensively, in all his manifestations.[18] But the "romance" between Dickinson and death has another, more literary connotation, for she never forgets that the quest romance embodied in her poetry can find completion only when the relationship between herself and death is consummated. As she notes in the following undated fragment, this ultimate romance of life's meaning is "foreclosed," and only those who are dead possess the "secret" which is the poet's quest object:

> We do not think enough of the Dead as exhilarants—they are not dissuaders but Lures—Keepers of that great Romance still to us foreclosed—while coveting their wisdom we lament their silence. Grace is

still a secret. That they have existed none can take away. That they still exist is a trust so daring we thank thee that thou hast hid these things from us and hast revealed them to them. The power and the glory are the post mortuary gifts. (PF 50)

When Dickinson is able to view the dead as "exhilarants," or "lures," she possesses her full imaginative freedom as poet; her perceptions need not be blunted by the protective aura of a dream vision. Precisely because her faith implies a genuine power and glory as the "post mortuary gifts," her earthly perception must be completely undistorted and deal exclusively with *reality*. If the rewards of quest are to be absolutely fulfilling, then the progress of quest must be an absolutely honest and undeviated perceptual course. This viewpoint, of course, does little to mitigate the horror of death; it simply frees the poet to confront it directly. The poetic energy generated by this confrontation and the ultimate horrible "otherness" of death give remarkable tension to the poem quoted below, a poem which is perhaps Dickinson's central early poem about death. Its chief importance is that it announces that the evasions, fantasies, and wishful thinking of her earlier work are at an end, and that at last her imagination is free:

'Tis so appalling—it exhilirates—
So over Horror, it half Captivates—
The Soul stares after it, secure—
To know the worst, leaves no dread more—

To scan a Ghost, is faint—
But grappling, conquers it—
How easy, Torment, now—
Suspense kept sawing so—

The Truth, is Bald, and Cold—
But that will hold—
If any are not sure—
We show them—prayer—
But we, who know,
Stop hoping, now—

Looking at Death, is Dying—
Just let go the Breath—
And not the pillow at your Cheek
So Slumbereth—

> Others, Can wrestle—
> Your's, is done—
> And so of Wo, bleak dreaded—come,
> It sets the Fright at liberty—
> And Terror's free—
> Gay, Ghastly, Holiday!
> (p 281)

The speaker is one whose consciousness has fully accepted the reality of death, and the poem describes both her appalled reaction and the more permanent reaction of exhilaration.[19] As Emerson had noted in his journal, "It is awful to look into the mind of man and see how free we are,"[20] his "awful" expressing an ambivalence similar to Dickinson's. Her speaker is exhilarated, however, because her unproductive "Suspense" is over; she knows the worst. Because she no longer needs to "grapple," to "wrestle," she can devote all her energies to a close, almost clinical observation of death as a means of furthering her quest. No longer immured within a dream-state, she discovers the liberating effect of death upon her imagination:

> It sets the Fright at liberty—
> And Terror's free—
> Gay, Ghastly, Holiday!

And because "Looking at Death, is Dying," the chief work of her quest becomes a comprehensive perceptual involvement with death, a theme that was both gay and ghastly, the focus of her best hopes and her most haunting fears.

9 Compound Vision

Dickinson's chief concern in her death poetry is to explore the possible effects of death upon human perception, since in Dickinson's mind the ability to perceive selectively is the most cherished aspect of human identity: almost every significant poem in this large group, therefore, is in some way concerned with either the quality of perception or the transformed identity of the perceiver. Because Dickinson's imaginative freedom allowed her to entertain the opposing possibilities of personal immortality and extinction, her poetry does not develop from one viewpoint to another, but rather oscillates repeatedly between the two positions, speculating upon the wide variety of effects the experience of death may have upon perception. Most critics who have dealt extensively with her death poetry have chosen to divide it, for purposes of clarity, into several major groupings: poems dealing with speakers who witness an actual death; poems describing the speaker's own death; and nondramatic poems which attempt to state a general truth about death and its effect upon the human spirit.[1] This kind of categorization, however, tends to distort the imaginative design of Dickinson's death poetry as a whole, since the major polarities to be recognized are not those of the poet's technical approach, but rather those of her progressing epistemological quest. It should therefore prove more faithful to the cast of Dickinson's mind if her death poetry is discussed within two rather loose and nonprescriptive frameworks: that suggested by recurrent image patterns she employs to suggest highly various relationships between perception and death; and that of her continually repeated movement from speculative and hopeful ignorance, in which she posits the perceptual fruits of immortality, to the despairing knowledge of experience, through which she is impelled to formulate a vision of perceptual extinction.

Whether Dickinson's view of death in any given poem is hopeful or despairing, and whether she chooses to dramatize the experience of death

(another person's or her own) or to issue more general, "bardic" pronounce-
ments, the major images she employs are those of perception itself—chiefly
the human eye—and images of light. In Dickinson's typical progress from a
hopeful stance to the more pervasive despairing one,[2] she associates light with
immortality and the absence of light with both the limitations of human perception and the absolute end of perception in death. Her use of the eye image
is similarly consistent: whether she is discussing the "unfurnished eyes"
(P 685) of the natural condition or the "superior eyes" (P 993) of an immortal
state, she always conceives of perception as a *relationship* between the visual
organs and the presence or absence of an objective illumination. The fulfillment of her quest through the attainment of personal immortality, therefore,
does not involve a metamorphosis into a type of other, unknowable existence—Dickinson rarely seeks a mystical loss of selfhood, however ecstatic—
but rather the highest imaginative enhancement of her human identity. When
she writes of receiving "Bulletins all day—from Immortality," therefore, she
is describing enhanced perceptual moments and positing a stasis of such enhancement as "Heaven."

In many poems she projects in explicit terms the reality of this stasis,
presenting the experience of death only to insist upon its function as the doorway to visionary fulfillment. In poem 1039, "I heard, as if I had no Ear," she
employs her most typical images in describing the moment of this fulfillment:

> I saw, as if my Eye were on
> Another, till a Thing
> And now I know 'twas Light, because
> It fitted them, came in.

In another poem she contrasts the fading light of a natural sunset with her
new apprehension of immortal light, a permanent noon:

> The Sun kept setting—setting—still
> No Hue of Afternoon—
> Upon the Village I perceived—
> From House to House 'twas Noon—

The poem ends with the assertion that death is a benevolent process, one that
is devoid of fear because the knowledge it brings is the knowledge of spiritual
life:

> How well I knew the Light before—
> I could see it now—
> *[no stanza break]*

'Tis Dying—I am doing—but
I'm not afraid to know—
(P 692)

These poems of unmixed optimism, however, are relatively few. Even
when Dickinson does insist that visionary fulfillment lies beyond death, she
frequently balances this optimistic view with a rather grim picture of death
itself. In this formulation, death is a purgatorial experience, and fulfillment is
preceded by a sharp sense of what she is losing—the familiar comforts of
human perceptions, "Human faces." In the following poem, the process of
death is dramatized within the context of Dickinson's typological sea, here
representing the threat of extinction, the disorienting chaos of experience,
and finally the eternal "mystic mooring" whose discovery she described in a
very early poem as "the errand of the eye":

Three times—we parted—Breath—and I—
Three times—He would not go—
But strove to stir the lifeless Fan
The Waters—strove to stay.

Three Times—the Billows threw me up—
Then caught me—like a Ball—
Then made Blue faces in my face—
And pushed away a sail

That crawled Leagues off—I liked to see—
For thinking—while I die—
How pleasant to behold a Thing
Where Human faces—be—
(P 598)

Here the speaker is totally vulnerable as she is tossed by the "Billows" of
eternity, and her perceptions are seized by their malevolent "Blue faces" (perhaps the corollary in eternity to the "blue uncertain stumbling Buzz" of the
fly in "I heard a Fly buzz—when I died"—which describes an unpleasant
perception on the temporal side of death). The speaker seems threatened and
helpless, and when she finally fixes her vision upon "A sail . . . where Human
faces—be," this single comforting object has been "pushed away" and is already "Leagues off"; thus far she seems at the mercy of malign forces, so that
the final two lines—"Then Sunrise kissed my Chrysalis— / And I stood up—
and lived"—seem incongruent with the preceding stanzas. Dickinson's fascination with immortality as an unending source of light is nevertheless a per-

sistent one. In poem 1053, for example, where she assents to the romantic "proposal" of death with an "answer of the Eyes," she ends by stating a relationship between her eyesight and a "fastened" source of light as the final destination of her quest journey: "Sunrise stopped upon the place / And fastened it in Dawn."

When Dickinson writes from the vantage point of her limited human perception, she is often similarly optimistic about the beneficent character of death. The following poem is perhaps the most unambiguously hopeful she ever wrote: it begins by noting the bereavement of an actual death, but goes on to insist that the "society" of the living and the dead is only slightly abridged, since the "superior eyes" of the dead establish a meaningful reciprocity between themselves and the living. The poem is remarkable for its lack of bitterness, since the secret of immortality, after all, is still "foreclosed." The speaker gently characterizes the benighted condition of human perception as a "sleeping" from which we will wake to join in the higher society above:

> We miss Her, not because We see—
> The Absence of an Eye—
> Except it's Mind accompany
> Abridge Society
>
> As slightly as the Routes of Stars—
> Ourselves—asleep below—
> We know that their superior Eyes
> Include Us—as they go—
> (P 993)

Another poem also expresses a remarkably gentle vision of death and in the final stanza balances the lack of perceptual "evidence" of immortality with a statement of faith:

> They dropped like Flakes—
> They dropped like Stars—
> Like Petals from a Rose—
> When suddenly across the June
> A Wind with fingers—goes
>
> They perished in the Seamless Grass—
> No eye could find the place—
> But God can summon every face
> On his Repealless—List.[3]
> (P 409)

Such serene moments, it should again be stressed, are infrequent; more often Dickinson's characteristic anger at being "shut out" from heaven colors her faith that the "Members of the Invisible" do indeed exist:

> How noteless Men, and Pleiads, stand,
> Until a sudden sky
> Reveals the fact that One is rapt
> Forever from the Eye—
>
> Members of the Invisible,
> Existing, while we stare,
> In Leagueless Opportunity,
> O'ertakeless, as the Air—
>
> Why did'nt we detain Them?
> The Heavens with a smile,
> Sweep by our disappointed Heads
> Without a syllable—
> (P 282)

Dickinson's anger, however, is not an emotional cul-de-sac but rather a spur to her curiosity, her drive toward certain knowledge; and her sense of isolation, in turn, intensifies her confidence in the validity of her independent quest. Though her fascination with various concepts of immortality never left her, the death poetry—like her work as a whole—tends to focus upon physical evidence rather than whimsical supposition. Because the dead are "Members of the Invisible," therefore, their present existence is beyond the poet's concept of what is real: the dead are "Those fair—fictitious People" (P 499), and though Dickinson hopes that they exist "in places perfecter— / Inheriting Delight," she stresses that this immortal state is beyond even her "faint Conjecture" or "Estimate." The dead are "Past what Ourself can estimate—," and "That—makes the Quick of Wo!" (P 509). Another poem similarly stresses the unreal, fictitious quality of those who are "Repealed from observation":

> As Sleigh Bells seem in summer
> Or Bees, at Christmas show—
> So fairy—so fictitious
> The individuals do
> Repealed from observation—
> A Party that we knew—
> More distant in an instant
> Than Dawn in Timbuctoo.
> (P 981)

When Dickinson contemplates the dead as human individuals, therefore, rather than as possible inheritors of a new mode of life, she is plagued by a sense of their immeasurable distance from herself and by growing doubt. As she writes in a similar poem, she begins to view conventional notions of death and immortality with "narrow Eyes": "This timid life of Evidence / Keeps pleading—'I don't know.' " (P 696).

Because of her emphasis upon perceptual evidence, it should not be surprising that she so frequently writes about the physical manifestations of death, creating scenes that focus upon deathbeds, corpses, and funerals. Her imagination naturally converged upon the moment of perceptual transformation and upon those who are either dying or recently dead. But the more she retreats into the sphere of verifiable phenomena, the more despairing her view of death becomes: repeatedly she emphasizes the remoteness of the dead, their "arrogance"; and once again the imagery of eyesight and of light illustrates the progress of her thought. Two related poems, probably written in the same year, pretend to claim for the dead an independent, enviable status characterized by this sudden "arrogance" toward the living, a new and luxurious life of "idleness"—but these characterizations are clearly ironic, since the dead are shunning everything which Dickinson associates with bliss:

> What care the Dead, for Chanticleer—
> What care the Dead for Day?
> 'Tis late your Sunrise vex their face—
> And Purple Ribaldry—of Morning
>
> Pour as blank on them
> As on the Tier of Wall
> The Mason builded, yesterday,
> And equally as cool—
>
> What care the Dead for Summer?
> The Solstice had no Sun
> Could waste the Snow before their Gate—
> And knew One Bird a Tune—
>
> Could thrill their Mortised Ear
> Of all the Birds that be—
> This One—beloved of Mankind
> Henceforward cherished be. . . .
> (P 592)

In this poem the irony comes close to being heavy-handed: the absolute in-souciance of the dead, their inability to be "vexed" by sunrise or summer or birdsong, is related explicitly to their cool, stonelike repose, their "mortised" perception. The second poem also uses the rhetorical question (a familiar device in the death poetry) for ironic purposes, but here the execution is re-markably subtle and concise, focusing sharply upon the inert "idleness" and "independence" of the dead and contrasting this attitude with the symbolic noon of fulfillment:

> A long—long Sleep—A famous—Sleep—
> That makes no show for Morn—
> By Stretch of Limb—or stir of Lid—
> An independant One—
>
> Was ever idleness like This?
> Upon a Bank of Stone
> To bask the Centuries away—
> Nor once look up—for Noon?
> (P 654)

And in another poem Dickinson abandons irony, employing her familiar an-alogical technique to suggest the distance between the dead and "revela-tion"—here clearly related to earthly perception:

> As far from pity, as complaint—
> As cool to speech—as stone—
> As numb to Revelation
> As if my Trade were Bone—
>
> As far from Time—as History—
> As near yourself—Today—
> As Children, to the Rainbow's scarf—
> Or Sunset's Yellow play
>
> To eyelids in the Sepulchre—
> How dumb the Dancer lies—
> While Color's Revelations break—
> And blaze—the Butterflies!
> (P 496)

Dickinson's fascination with the stubborn repose of "eyelids in the Sep-ulchre" becomes even more pointed in poems dealing with an actual confron-tation between the speaker and a corpse; these are the poems which have earned Dickinson her reputation as a "morbid" writer, and in them her dramatic technique, her special ability to convey tense and highly momentous confrontations, becomes most chillingly effective. Robert Weisbuch has noted that Dickinson's well-known "Safe in their alabaster chambers" represents a "critique of faith" and that its vision of death is "simple, ironic, and horrifying."[4] This description applies to much of her death poetry, which so frequently employs an ironic method not to distance the horror but to emphasize it. One of Dickinson's most complex poems about an actual corpse employs the rhetorical question as well as another technique which serves to heighten the poem's irony: she casts her poem in the form of a riddle, never actually nominating death but approaching it by a circuitous and effective route:

It knew no Medicine—
It was not Sickness—then—
Nor any need of Surgery—
And therefore—'twas not Pain—

It moved away the Cheeks—
A Dimple at a time—
And left the Profile—plainer—
And in the place of Bloom

It left the little Tint
That never had a Name—
You've seen it on a Cast's face—
Was Paradise—to blame—

If momently ajar—
Temerity—drew near—
And sickened—ever afterward
For Somewhat that it saw?
(P 559)

Dickinson approaches her subject through a series of descriptions, noting the corpse's absence of feeling, then its absence of normal color—a color replaced by "the little Tint / That never had a Name." In the rhetorical question of the last five lines, however, the poem ironically contradicts itself. In the first stanza the speaker noted that death seems permanent—"It was not Sickness—then— / Nor any need of surgery"—but she finally wonders if the dead one is indeed "sickened." But this final horrifying sickness, of course, is of the spirit, caused by "Somewhat that it saw," the person's last perception of death's stiff stare.

The poem is a critique of faith because it blames the idea of "Paradise" for being simple-minded and for ignoring the tragic possibilities of death.

After the death of her mother, Dickinson described in a letter her hopeful response to the memory of her mother's corpse: "the illumination that comes but once passed upon her features, and it seemed like hiding a picture to lay her in the grave." The "illumination," however, was clearly a private one, for Dickinson herself remained in the dark: "We don't know where she is, though so many tell us" (L 785). The "picture" represented by the corpses in Dickinson's poems, moreover, is seldom an attractive one. Most frequently she contrasts the dead person with the anxious observation of the living, almost always taking note of the corpse's eyes:

> 'Twas warm—at first—like Us—
> Until there crept upon
> A Chill—like frost upon a Glass—
> Till all the scene—be gone.
>
> The Forehead copied Stone—
> The Fingers grew too cold
> To ache—and like a Skater's Brook—
> The busy eyes—congealed—
>
> It straightened—that was all—
> It crowded Cold to Cold—
> It multiplied indifference—
> As Pride were all it could—
>
> And even when with Cords—
> 'Twas lowered, like a Weight—
> It made no Signal, nor demurred,
> But dropped like Adamant.
> (P 519)

Clearly this insentient body creates a reaction of terror in the speaker, and the controlled poetry serves to heighten its effects: once the eyes have "congealed," the dead person's attitude seems one of "multiplied indifference," both toward the speaker ("It made no Signal") and toward its own fate ("nor demurred"). The body is "like Adamant" both in its inert weightiness and in what the speaker imagines to be an adamant refusal to communicate with the living. In the extremely effective final line, the word "dropped" signals the disappearance of both the corpse and the speaker's hopes.

Within the context of Dickinson's quest for knowledge, these rather macabre descriptions of physical death serve a crucial function: they deal directly with the most painful aspect of reality, preventing any swerve into fantasy or unballasted supposition; they assure, therefore, that any positive conclusions resulting from the poet's quest will be justified and earned. As Clark Griffith notes, "the perception of the dead is for Emily Dickinson a source of unremitting horror. She must ponder death through completely mature eyes for the simple reason that there is no pretense which can minimize the terrors of the corpse—and no averting of the eyes which will blind one to the dilemmas and uncertainties that the existence of the corpse elicits."[5] The central relationship in Dickinson's poetry between the eyes of her speaker and the eyes of the dead (or dying) person is nevertheless the focus of her attempt to solve these dilemmas and uncertainties. She hopes for some communicating flash between the dying person and herself that might provide her with insights unavailable to ordinary consciousness and perception. Griffith is correct, however, to suggest that such attempts frequently add to the poet's uncertainty:[6]

> I've seen a Dying Eye
> Run round and round a Room—
> In search of Something—as it seemed—
> Then Cloudier become—
> And then—obscure with Fog—
> And then—be soldered down
> Without disclosing what it be
> 'Twere blessed to have seen—
> (P 547)

Elsewhere she notes that the eyes seem to have been "wrenched / By Decalogues—away" (P 485), and in a poem written near the end of her life she recreates an identical dramatic situation, the poem's tone of desperation seeming even more intense as she addresses the dying person directly:

> Which question shall I clutch—
> What answer wrest from thee
> Before thou dost exude away
> In the recallless sea?
> (P 1633)

When Dickinson is dramatizing her own death, the results are similarly depressing. Two of her finest poems, "I heard a Fly buzz—when I died" (P 465) and "Because I could not stop for Death" (P 712), have been frequently and exhaustively analyzed, but the first may here be considered a kind of coda to Dickinson's imaginative drama of perception at the moment of death:

> I heard a Fly buzz—when I died—
> The Stillness in the Room
> Was like the Stillness in the Air—
> Between the Heaves of Storm—
>
> The Eyes around—had wrung them dry—
> And Breaths were gathering firm
> For that last Onset—when the King
> Be witnessed—in the Room—
>
> I willed my Keepsakes—Signed away
> What portion of me be
> Assignable—and then it was
> There interposed a Fly—
>
> With Blue—uncertain stumbling Buzz—
> Between the light—and me—
> And then the Windows failed—and then
> I could not see to see—
> (P 465)

This poem is grimly ironic in its brilliant contrasting of the conventional and pious sentiments attending the deathbed scene with a stark rendering of the gradual extinction of perception: a perception helplessly fastened to the blue uncertain stumbling of a common housefly, a symbol of the everyday unpleasantness of life and of the carrion the speaker will soon become.[7] In the final line of the poem, "I could not see to see," the first "see" refers to simple physical seeing, while the last is the more comprehensive seeing of perception and spiritual vision.[8] This relationship between the two types of seeing has seldom been acknowledged by the poem's commentators, and its implications make the poem one of total hopelessness: the speaker's experience implies that all "vision" inheres in the physical ability to see, and that death therefore brings an end to vision of any kind, and thus to being.

It should be stressed that all of Dickinson's imaginative approaches to death, as she herself noted, were "speculations": for all their variety, inventiveness, and dramatic force, her deathbed studies provide no concrete evidence of the precise effect of death upon perception; and it is in the absence of such evidence that her formulations tend to be generally grim, even nihilistic. This impasse, however, does not represent the end of the poet's great romance with death; she continued, as always, to generate confidence from her despair and to proceed stubbornly up the epistemological spiral in the hope of further insights. The actual experience of death, after all, is primarily important not as an event in Dickinson's future but as a daily pressure upon her spirit, and therefore the poems represent her attempt to cope with this pressure, both by acknowledging its force and by attempting to place it within the larger perspective of her attempt to live meaningfully. In his provocative study of death in modern literature, Lawrence J. Langer comments upon death as a component of consciousness in a way precisely applicable to Dickinson: "The moment of death is less important than the prospect of dying, and . . . the process, with the fear and pain and insights it induces, represents the period of significant experience for men. Measured against it, the moment of death is only a tiny, final station in an inward journey that can endure for many years."[9] In her poetry Dickinson repeatedly makes this "tiny, final station" dramatically large and present, and though this procedure risks despair, it also enables her to return to her actual, living moment with an enhanced and "reorganized" perception of life's value. If she speculates that death is a nihilistic void and an absolute end to perception, she can also conclude that her human perception—however limited and vulnerable to painful insight— is all the more precious by contrast. As one might expect, this contrast is frequently stated in terms of a ratio: as in the poem "I see thee clearer for the Grave" (P 1666), Dickinson claims that the "impassive stone" of the tomb only heightens her appreciation of her dynamic, creative perception.

This heightened awareness of the value of perceptual experience is Dickinson's major achievement in her romance with death. In his well-known study, *The Mortal No: Death and the Modern Imagination*, Frederic J. Hoffman describes this process of achieving experiential fruit from a philosophical stance that tends toward nihilism: "If death is a wall and not a doorway, the pace of experiences diminishes . . . and every detail of change is noted and treasured. Instead of a metaphysics dependent upon an infinite extension of the given, we get an ontology of objects and experiences. Death turns us toward life and forces us to admire or cherish it (even though we may despair of it as well), to begrudge the passing of time (which is signified by changes occurring in objects) and eventually to despair of conclusions."[10] Although Hoffman does not include Dickinson in his wide-ranging discussion, he lists attitudes toward experience which are among the most noticeable in her poetry—the cherishing of life, the anxiety over transience, the despair of final answers. In a crucial way, however, her stance differs from the one he describes. Although Dickinson does not posit "a metaphysics *dependent* upon an infinite extension of the given," her continuing emotional longing for such an extension makes the tension between her cherishing of life and her despairing of final conclusions all the more anguished and resonant. Death does turn her toward life, therefore, but it also leads her back to itself, so that death becomes the focal point of her "Convex—and Concave Witness," the generative locus of her unique double vision. Yet this vision, as has been suggested, embodies a pair of its own paradoxical impulses, since it was the horror of possible extinction that caused her to cherish life and the hope of immortality which spurred her wish to leave it altogether.

In her mature formulation of death as a pressure upon her daily existence, however, she combines these contradictory attitudes: while maintaining her hope of consciousness and vision beyond death, she resolves to make the most of her present existence—a resolve which frequently requires a bold rhetorical stance designed to diminish the power of death within her consciousness (this approach, of course, is the obverse of that in which she asserts her own exalted, monarchial status). She cannot employ the rhetoric which Donne uses, for instance, in his Holy Sonnets—especially "Death be not proud"—for simply to assert that "we wake eternally" a moment after death would be false to the complexity of her mature outlook, which maintained no such assurance. Rather than saying "Death, thou shalt die,"[11] she insists that the very absoluteness of death, its unchanging character, means that it has no ability to increase in stature—while Dickinson herself does have this ability and makes ample use of it. In this formulation, death is no longer an "Imperator" but rather becomes "democratic death" while Dickinson remains a queen.[12] The following poem contrasts the actuality and commonness of death with the possibilities of life, which is "a different Thing":

> A Toad, can die of Light—
> Death is the Common Right
> Of Toads and Men—
> Of Earl and Midge
> The privilege—
> Why swagger, then?
> The Gnat's supremacy is large as Thine—
>
> Life—is a different Thing—
> So measure Wine—
> Naked of Flask—Naked of Cask—
> Bare Rhine—
> Which Ruby's mine?
> (P 583)

Death is inevitable, absolute, but life represents continuous potential, an un-measured wine; the poem's final question implies that the wine of life must be refined, contained, and individuated to form the personal "Ruby" of identity and status.[13]

When Dickinson adjusts her focus from death back to life, she sees a constant and unpredictable suspension, a *process*; and often this process, because it seems to tease the poet's consciousness with hints of immortality even as it offers a paradigm of "annihilation," is seen as actively hostile:

Suspense—is Hostiler than Death—
Death—thosoever Broad,
Is just Death, and cannot increase—
Suspense—does not conclude—

But perishes—to live anew—
But just anew to die—
Annihilation—plated fresh
With Immortality—
(P 705)

In another poem Dickinson says she can never contemplate a dead person "Without the chance of Life / Afresh annihilating me" (P 1323), and in a poem quoted above, "To disappear enhances" (P 1209), she notes that the person who dies is "tinctured for an instant / With Immortality," and that the "sternest function" of death is to give us this suggestion of another realm and yet to "defy" our perception. This poem ends on a positive note, however, by stressing the ecstatic possibilities of human consciousness when reminded of its own transience and intensity. The daily routine of existential life, as the following poem claims, can be transformed into a continual "stimulus" when viewed within the context of death; only within the tormented human consciousness does the perceiver have the power to grow, to "repair":

To make Routine a Stimulus
Remember it can cease—
Capacity to Terminate
Is a Specific Grace—
Of Retrospect the Arrow
That power to repair
Departed with the Torment
Become, alas, more fair—
(P 1196)

Many poems of Dickinson's maturity stress this paradoxical relationship between the poet's unflinching acknowledgment of death and her heightened awareness of the possibilities of life, of its wavering, often rather friable dimensions;[14] typically, this uncertainty over the problems of consciousness and time brought painful as well as ecstatic insights, and as always she gives each outlook its proper due. This manner of viewing death, however, allows more than any other the possibility of "transcendence"—a transcendence located within time and seldom linked with assurance to anything beyond it, but nonetheless a claim for triumphant perceptual moments. "Death sets a Thing significant / The Eye had hurried by" (P 360), she writes in her most succinct expression of this concept: the poet implies that the significance of any perception lies in its being limited, necessarily curtailed, and that without death a life of perception would be a ceaseless and undifferentiated drifting from one perception to the next, with nothing to focus the eye's attention or lend meaning to the entire process.

One of Dickinson's most familiar deathbed studies, "The last Night that She lived" (P 1100), seems to resemble other poems in which the sudden remoteness of the dying person is contrasted with the anxiety of the onlookers. Here, however, the focus is not upon the experience of death, but rather upon the effect of death upon the living. As one might expect, Dickinson's attitude is complex, and the resulting poem is surely one of her finest:

> The last Night that She lived
> It was a Common Night
> Except the Dying—this to Us
> Made Nature different
>
> We noticed smallest things—
> Things overlooked before
> By this great light upon our Minds
> Italicized—as 'twere.
>
> As We went out and in
> Between Her final Room
> And Rooms where Those to be alive
> Tomorrow were, a Blame
>
> That Others could exist
> While She must finish quite
> A Jealousy for Her arose
> So nearly infinite—

We waited while She passed—
It was a narrow time—
Too jostled were Our Souls to speak
At length the notice came.

She mentioned, and forgot—
Then lightly as a Reed
Bent to the Water, struggled scarce—
Consented, and was dead—

And We—We placed the Hair—
And drew the Head erect—
And then an awful leisure was
Belief to regulate—
(P 1100)

In this poem, it is death which redeems the "Common Night" of ordinary existence: it not only sheds a "great light" upon the minds of the beholders but seems to make Nature itself somehow "different." All experience at this point becomes heightened, "Italicized." Thus the first two stanzas form a poem in themselves, arguing in remarkably colorless, prosaic language[15] the undeniable advantages of a perception whose relationship to death is overt, fully acknowledged. But the speaker's joyless, rather benumbed tone of voice is explained in the stanzas which follow: she and her companions meander in and out of the dying person's room, aimless and disconsolate; they are not experiencing ordinary grief, but rather a confusion made only the more hopeless by the great light of heightened perception. Although the common night has become suddenly momentous, they feel that to be alive is a "Blame"; they do not feel grief over the woman's death, but "Jealousy." At the moment of her death their souls are "jostled" in their painful inability to adopt a meaningful attitude toward the impending death or toward their own continuing life.

Implicit in the onlookers' confusion are several questions: Must we content ourselves with the intensity of our experience, its perceptual advantages, while consigning the corpse (and by extension, ourselves at some future time) to an unknown fate? Should we attempt imaginatively to follow after her, motivated by a jealous curiosity, abandoning the fruitless anxiety and barren ugliness of our present consciousness? Or is this state of uncertainty, our minds enlightened and our souls jostled, somehow profitable? This last possibility is the one suggested most strongly by the poem as a whole. The magnificent final stanza, following the rather perfunctory lines which describe the actual death,[16] shows that the onlookers have drawn only one conclusion from their experience: their sense of portentous, unregulated awareness will continue to influence their consciousness in the future, adjusting their perception of life's value and meaning:

> And We—We placed the Hair—
> And drew the Head erect—
> And then an awful leisure was
> Belief to regulate—

The art of this deceptively simple stanza should not go unremarked. The repetitions of the word "and" suggest a logical sequence of events—the final disposition of the corpse followed by a philosophical conclusion—and yet the lines ironically undercut this suggestion; the sequence of events in time occurs mechanically, ending in an immeasurable "leisure" of future time. For the onlookers, the woman's death has not made sense: in the first line their depressed weariness is suggested by the repetition of "We"—"And We—We placed the Hair"—and their new leisure is "awful" in both senses of the word; it is both awe-inspiring and horrible to contemplate. The final line is of special interest, since on the manuscript Dickinson lists two instructive variants for "Belief." The onlookers, at this point, face the onerous task of "regulating" their belief, since a return to their previous, less enlightened awareness is impossible. They are aware that their attitude toward both death and life must now become more complex, and they understand the cruel paradox of their situation: they sense the weight of meaningless time on their hands, yet they know they must employ this leisure by a conscious effort toward some new and higher belief. One of Dickinson's variants for "Belief" is "Our faith," a more specifically religious and orthodox phrase, and ultimately a more despairing one, since "faith" is by definition unchanging and cannot submit to regulation. Orthodox religion, therefore, is clearly not the answer. With her second variant Dickinson abandons irony and states her dilemma more starkly: this version reads, "And then an awful leisure was / With *nought* to regulate" (my italics). That Dickinson should list "nought" as a variant for "faith" and "belief" illustrates the total isolation of her vantage point.

We know, however, that the essential Dickinson is not a figure of mute despair but a wily mathematician. Throughout her elaborate rhetoric of attitudes toward death, she insists upon her ability to establish meaningful inferences from the enhanced perception of life which death provides her; in

addition, death allows these inferences to become more precise. The following poem deserves more attention than it has received, for it states concisely
the crucial function of death within the poet's consciousness:

> There is a finished feeling
> Experienced at Graves—
> A leisure of the Future—
> A Wilderness of Size.
>
> By Death's bold Exhibition
> Preciser what we are
> And the Eternal function
> Enabled to infer.
> (P 856)

The first stanza is a brief recapitulation of "The last Night that She lived,"
and Dickinson insists again upon the awful "leisure" that life becomes when
viewed in the context of death; moreover, she characterizes that future as a
wilderness which must be conquered by a continued and intensified quest
effort. The second stanza, however, goes on to form the characteristic Dickinson balance: despair at the complexity of quest is eased through the poet's
confidence in an "Eternal function," one in which death plays a necessary
role. The presence of death also serves to validate the poet's identity, since
death enables us to see "Preciser what we are." An inchoate sense of life's
meaning is therefore accompanied by a greater exactness of perception.

   The confidence of that second stanza is expanded and made rhetorically
complete in one of Dickinson's most important death poems; this is, in fact,
the poem of Dickinson's "bardic" stance, presenting her transcendence over
death in its character as an existential terror, an insuperable threat. The poem
employs Dickinson's familar imagery of light and focuses upon death as the
doorway, *within* consciousness, to a perception so glorified that it seems synonymous with transcendent poetic vision:

> The Admirations—and Contempts—of time—
> Show justest—through an Open Tomb—
> The Dying—as it were a Hight
> Reorganizes Estimate
> And what We saw not
> We distinguish clear—
> And mostly—see not
> What We saw before—

'Tis Compound Vision—
Light—enabling Light—
The Finite—furnished
With the Infinite—
Convex—and Concave Witness—
Back—toward Time—
And forward—
Toward the God of Him—
(P 906)

If death itself is "without estimate," it nevertheless enables the poet's human estimations to become more precise and more selective; her vision is adjusted, "reorganized," so that her perceptual values may be understood in their proper perspective. Death teaches her to perceive meaningfully: once its function is mastered, the perceiver can "distinguish clear" what is worth distinguishing and can easily discard what is not. Emerson had written that "The eye is the best of artists,"[17] and here Dickinson expresses her own sense of this selective, shaping function of perception. Her "Compound Vision," implying a simultaneous awareness of finite value and infinite possibility, represents a state of enlightened, reorganized consciousness, one which allows the eye to perform its transcendent function as the organ of visionary art.

"Death is potential to that Man / Who dies," Dickinson wrote, then added: "and to his friend" (P 548). The dying man's visionary potential is forward, toward the God of time, but his friend has a renewed perspective "Back— toward Time." Both kinds of potential, however, are available within consciousness, and Dickinson realizes that this visionary synthesis, this spiritual orientation within time, is the ultimate earthly reward of her quest effort. Her reward was made all the sweeter because her sense of mastery over the obstacles to quest, especially death, was balanced by a sense of continued vulnerability and the knowledge that unexpected pitfalls and intensified rewards always lay just ahead. Her attitude, then, is an appreciation of life's mystery controlled by her hard-won double vision, an understanding of her perception both in and out of time.

One of Dickinson's most memorable poems stresses this double vision as maintained in daily life. The poem speculates upon eternity and ultimate doom, but finally asserts the triumph of the isolated identity, synonymous for Dickinson with the isolated consciousness:

Two Lengths has every Day—
It's absolute extent
And Area superior
By Hope or Horror lent—

Eternity will be
Velocity or Pause
At Fundamental Signals
From Fundamental Laws.

To die is not to go—
On Doom's consummate Chart
No Territory new is staked—
Remain thou as thou art.
(P 1295)

The "absolute extent" of any day is the individual's fleeting experience of time, while its "Area superior" is a dimension added by the poet's developed consciousness, her compound vision: her awareness of herself within time can produce, as we have seen, either a hopeful or horrifying vision of her ultimate fate, but this poem itself shows the extent to which the two outlooks are compounded into a single vision. The poem's remarkable second stanza expresses a faith based upon the drama of her own individual consciousness; whether eternity represents an extension of the kind of fluid, mobile consciousness she has experienced in life, or a final "pause," a stasis of transcendent awareness, the conditions of eternity are governed by the same laws which govern the conditions of time. Her identity, therefore, cannot change in its essence, but will only ascend into a set of new conditions.[18] "To die is not to go," and there is no new "Territory": the process of individual growth and of epistemological quest, the poem implies, takes place within life, and eternity is only an enhancement or a continuation of these personally earned rewards.

One is returned again to the internalized nature of Dickinson's quest: death is ultimately viewed as a crucial way station of a continuing and mysterious journey. If to die was "not to go," death nonetheless represented a metamorphosis which the poet imaged repeatedly as a journey whose progress could never be said to end. Her concept of the crucial function of death within her ultimate quest, and her sense of its terror and adventure, is suggested by one of her most arresting prose remarks (L 332): "Dying is a wild Night and a new Road." This imaging of consciousness as a journey, and of death as an internalized transformation of the quest represented by the journey, shows Dickinson conceptualizing her poetic effort, once again, in terms of progress. In poems narrating the journey itself, Dickinson speculates upon—and in an important sense, experiences—the final and most complex stage of the poet's quest.

10   *Our Journey Had Advanced*

Many of Dickinson's poems make clear that she was wholly conscious of the nature of her poetic endeavor, that its conditions and goals represented a journey through stages of consciousness toward knowledge. Having asserted the complexity of her verbal "mathematics" and assessed the crucial role of death within her perceptual quest, one should finally emphasize that the quest romance itself, the arduous internalized journey, was the concept Dickinson herself employed when meditating upon her life's work and its possible fruition. "Paradise is no Journey," she wrote, "because it is within—but for that very cause though—it is the most Arduous of Journeys" (PF 99). Ultimately this self-consciousness served to sharpen her formulations of the relationship between perception and death, and to emphasize the precise nature of her quest as a whole.

As one might expect, Dickinson is capable of formulating two entirely opposing views of her quest and its ultimate result; these seemingly contradictory attitudes represent the polar extremes between faith and doubt, ecstasy and despair. That Dickinson's attitudes continually oscillated between the two extremes does not diminish their rhetorical validity or their genuineness as expressions of fleeting states of mind, but this fact does emphasize, once again, the fluctuation and indeterminacy of her progress. Such a poem as the following, therefore, expressing symbolically a triumphant vision of quest, also reminds us that "ecstatic instants" do not last, even though this particular poem shows no concern with transience:

Through the Dark Sod—as Education—
The Lily passes sure—
Feels her white foot—no trepidation—
Her faith—no fear—

> Afterward—in the Meadow—
> Swinging her Beryl Bell—
> The Mold-life—all forgotten—now—
> In Extasy—and Dell—
> (P 392)

The poem contains many familiar symbolic elements. The "Dark Sod" is the benighted human condition through which the white-robed quester "passes sure," realizing maximum profit from her "Education" in the realm of experience. The poet's "white foot" journeys upward toward her quest goal with complete faith in her own abilities and with no fear of a disappointing outcome; and the second stanza justifies her optimism. She has forgotten the "Mold-life," a phrase which has at least three relevant connotations: human life has the potential for evil and decay; its experiences shape, or mold, the individual who strives toward an ultimate reward; and it serves the typological function of *imaging* a life of consciousness that will differ from itself in degree but not in kind.[1] All that remains is "Extasy—and Dell," a heaven which is a state of consciousness—reminding us once again that "Heaven is . . . of the Mind" (P 370). And one additional element in the second stanza should be noted: unlike the first stanza, which comprises a complete sentence, the lines describing spiritual attainment are constructed around a participle, suggesting an infinite continuation of the ecstasy, its self-renewing life throughout eternity.

This wholly joyous vision of quest emphasizes the quester's identity, the purity and exalted spiritual status represented by her "whiteness." Dickinson's wholly negative vision of the journey also contains this emphasis, ending with the insistence that the poet is a "sham":

> Finding is the first Act
> The second, loss,
> Third, Expedition for
> the "Golden Fleece"—
>
> Fourth, no Discovery—
> Fifth, no Crew—
> Finally, no Golden Fleece—
> Jason—sham—too.
> (P 870)

The first line refers to the undervalued "daily Bliss" of the quester's immature state, which she loses in the course of experience and must seek to regain. But not only is the goal of her quest unattainable; she implies that the quest itself is a delusion and the quester deceived by her own charlatanism. The poem's disturbingly contemptuous tone, emphasized by the mechanical listing of the speaker's self-delusions, represents a disgust that is turned inward to cast doubt upon the speaker's own validity. Just as "Through the Dark Sod—as Education" shows the poet in possession of complete self-confidence and control, this poem represents a spiritual nadir, the moment when she is prepared to abandon all her efforts in despair.

The rhetorical identity of the above poems should again be stressed: Dickinson gives full expression to every stage of her quest, every emotional mood, every setback and advance. She insists, always, upon the complexity and seemingly patternless quality of the entire process. The aesthetic codifying of her experience, in fact, was always bothersome to her; even within individual lyrics, her art somehow distorted and ossified the truth. She wrote to Higginson: "While my thought is undressed—I can make the distinction, but when I put them in the Gown—they look alike, and numb" (L 261). In the following poem, written about the same time, she describes this frustration in terms of her own quest romance:

> No Romance sold unto
> Could so enthrall a Man
> As the perusal of
> His Individual One—
> 'Tis Fiction's—to dilute to Plausibility
> *Our* Novel—When 'tis small enough
> To Credit—'Tis'nt true!
> (P 669)

It disturbed her to "dilute to Plausibility" the splendidly various dynamics of her progress; on the manuscript she listed "contract" as a variant for "dilute," and the relative smallness of her art compared to the immensity of her undertaking seemed inappropriate, even though her lyric method best described the pattern of her thought. Ultimately, her solution lay in an underlying faith that the hundreds of rhetorical structures represented by individual lyrics, each presenting a facet of the truth, would give an accurate and honest picture of her experience when viewed as a whole. Her entire canon, therefore, represents the undiluted (and uncompleted) truth, the individual romance so "enthralling" to the poet herself.

Thus we are returned to the fact that the poet's identity stands out in isolated splendor as she conducts her private quest romance—her actual romance with death and her speculative romance with the "compound vision" of immortality, a vision curtailed and heightened by the limitations of perception within time. Dickinson characteristically refers to the romance as an "experiment" in the following poem, and again ends by stressing her soul's isolated identity:

> This Consciousness that is aware
> Of Neighbors and the Sun
> Will be the one aware of Death
> And that itself alone
>
> Is traversing the interval
> Experience between
> And most profound experiment
> Appointed unto Men—
>
> How adequate unto itself
> It's properties shall be
> Itself unto itself and none
> Shall make discovery.
>
> Adventure most unto itself
> The Soul condemned to be—
> Attended by a single Hound
> It's own identity.
> (P 822)

The poem begins with a statement about "Consciousness" and ends with one about "identity"; the poem's major claim is that they are synonymous. The "Consciousness that is aware" of both the sun and of death is the one best equipped to endure the quest journey, and to achieve that "Etherial Gain," as another poem describes it, which "One earns by measuring the Grave— / Then—measuring the Sun" (P 574). Harold Bloom remarks: "What matters in her is a vision that says only consciousness matters. Death interests her as a challenge to consciousness, but not as a challenge to any other capacity for heroism."[2] Despite the poet's loneliness, her sense that she is "condemned" to isolation, there is a sober joy in this "profound experiment," this "Adventure." In poems which describe the climax of the experiment, the focus is once again upon the isolated perceiver's confrontation with death and upon speculations about what may lie beyond.

One of Dickinson's major poems describing this climactic moment of the quest journey begins by noting the speaker's extreme weariness and ends with a question rather than an answer. Here too death is an "experiment":

I cross till I am weary
A Mountain—in my mind—
More Mountains—then a Sea—
More Seas—And then
A Desert—find—

And my Horizon blocks
With steady—drifting—Grains
Of unconjectured quantity—
As Asiatic Rains—

Nor this—defeat my Pace—
It hinder from the West
But as an Enemy's Salute
One hurrying to Rest—

What merit had the Goal—
Except there intervene
Faint Doubt—and far Competitor—
To jeopardize the Gain?

At last—the Grace in sight—
I shout unto my feet—
I offer them the Whole of Heaven
The instant that we meet—

They strive—and yet delay—
They perish—Do we die—
Or is this Death's Experiment—
Reversed—in Victory?
(P 550)

The internalized nature of the quest is again emphasized: "I cross till I am weary / A mountain—in my mind. . . ." The journey is one through limitless deserts, seas, and mountains, and it seems to the quester that the obstacles to her progress are of an "unconjectured quantity"; her mathematics, she implies once again, is "broken." The middle two stanzas narrate the stage at which confidence begins to balance despair, since nothing can defeat the quester's "pace," and she offers her familiar idea that her goal would have no value without a proportionate amount of danger and frustration:

What merit had the Goal—
Except there intervene
[*no stanza break*]

> Faint Doubt—and far Competitor—
> To jeopardize the Gain?

In the final two stanzas, however, an interesting problem arises. The speaker at last has her goal "in sight"—it is described, simply, as "the Whole of Heaven" (although a variant phrase stresses the transitional nature of this stage and can offer only "the Half of Heaven"). But the poet's feet have arrived at a curious impasse: "They strive—and yet delay— / They perish. . . ." And here the narrative seems to end, spurring the abrupt question with which Dickinson concludes the poem.

The last stanza of the poem is one of the most difficult Dickinson ever wrote, and contains ambiguities which are surely deliberate; it should be understood, however, that the narrative has passed beyond death between the penultimate and the final stanzas. The problematic nature of this transition in a dramatic poem is apparent in several of these quest lyrics, but it is important not to distort the poet's intentions. Yvor Winters sharply rebuked Dickinson for attempting to dramatize the departure from life in such poems as "Because I could not stop for death": "In so far as it concentrates on the life that is being left behind, it is wholly successful; in so far as it attempts to experience the death to come, it is fraudulent."[3] Other critics have defended Dickinson on this issue, but there is no doubt that the problem is a major one; the problem itself, however, must be accurately defined. Whether Dickinson's concept is "fraudulent" or not is beside the point; the problem is simply one of how to read the poem. Winters assumes that in such poems Dickinson is offering a speculation as a narrative fact, but actually the opposite is true. Since the drama is internalized, she is rather describing the final stage of her progress within consciousness, and then offering—in the appropriate form of a question—a speculation upon the nature of death itself.

In this light, the poem's final stanza may be read as an ambiguous description of a wholly internalized process:

> They strive—and yet delay—
> They perish—Do we die—
> Or is this Death's Experiment—
> Reversed—in Victory?

The burden of the poet's meaning falls upon the word "perish," and the ambiguity of the word is itself meaningful. Since this is the final word of the poem's narrative proper, does it indicate simple extinction, the end of the journey through absolute death? Such a possibility, though seldom denied in

Dickinson's work, is balanced in this poem by a more complex vision of death. The "perishing" of the poet's feet may simply mean that the journey itself, the walking, has come to an end—the poet's feet being synecdochic for the wearisome human effort of the quest. "Joy to have perished every step—," she wrote elsewhere, "To Compass Paradise—" (P 788). In this formulation, the quester's feet may be seen as part of the physical "Mold-life" which may now be forgotten as her awareness rises into the world of spirit. It is this possibility, in fact, which is suggested by the poet's final question: "is this Death's Experiment— / Reversed—in Victory?" Is this perception of death—within consciousness, in the act of writing this quest narrative—a mirror image of what lies beyond the "experiment" of death itself? And does this conscious reversing of the death experience—creating an "Open Tomb"— spell victory for the quester? The poem remains in the form of a question, but this complex vision of quest fulfillment, though presented as narrative, actually describes a pattern of fulfillment in consciousness, charting the attainment of "compound vision" in a viable (yet "experimental") assessment of death.

Another quest narrative, "I did not reach Thee," again recounts in full the pattern of the journey and maintains a surprisingly confident tone. The poem directly addresses God—"Sahara is too little price / To pay for thy Right hand"—but ends with the realization that death remains a barrier to full consciousness. The loss is explicitly stated in terms of perception:

> I did not reach Thee
> Bu my feet slip nearer every day
> Three Rivers and a Hill to cross
> One Desert and a Sea
> I shall not count the journey one
> When I am telling thee . . .
>
> . . . .
> We step like Plush
> We stand like snow
> The waters murmur new
> Three rivers and the Hill are passed
> Two deserts and the sea!
> Now Death usurps my Premium
> And gets the look at Thee—
> (P 1664)

In "Our journey had advanced," the poet offers an especially complex vision of the relationship between death and perception, and here the nature and quality of fulfillment are again ambiguous:

> Our journey had advanced—
> Our feet were almost come
> To that odd Fork in Being's Road—
> Eternity—by Term—
>
> Our pace took sudden awe—
> Our feet—reluctant—led—
> Before—were Cities—but Between—
> The Forest of the Dead—
>
> Retreat—was out of Hope—
> Behind—a Sealed Route—
> Eternity's White Flag—Before—
> And God—at every Gate—
> (P 615)

Even as she employs the imagery of a journey, she casts doubt upon its traditional valuations: she has reached a "Fork in Being's Road— / Eternity—by Term," thus suggesting that by her confrontation the nature of eternity itself must be redefined, renamed. Because she faces a "Fork" in the road, moreover, she implies that she has the power to make a deliberate choice. It is therefore clear that this poem describes another internalized journey; she is not dramatizing her actual death (after which, as she makes clear in other poems, she will be helpless within an unknown process) but is rather imaging her confrontation with death in consciousness. What are the two choices, then, represented by the "Fork"? Since the poem notes the fearfulness of what is conventionally termed "Eternity," the choices involve the quester's own courage and integrity: she may choose a conventional route, arranging a detour around the terror of the unknown and possible despair, or she may continue forward boldly and with full sight, redefining and renaming as she goes. By the beginning of the second stanza, she has already made her choice: though she feels a "sudden awe" and reluctance, her feet are nevertheless "leading" the way. At this point, she is able to view more clearly the conditions and the consequences of the choice she has made: "Before—were Cities—but Between— / The Forest of the Dead." This final obstacle, "The Forest of the Dead," represents a wilderness through which she must blaze a new and individual trail.

As for the road not taken, it is impossible to return to the easier, well-worn path. This is, after all, an "advanced" journey; there is no turning back from the forest of the dead.⁴ But when she confronts death in this reluctant, awe-struck moment, how does Dickinson conceptualize her future? In "I cross till I am weary," she declared ambiguously that her feet seemed to "perish." In this poem, however, the ambiguity lies in a peculiar blending of the concrete and the abstract: "Eternity's White Flag—Before— / And God—at every Gate." The lines are disturbing because they seem to offer a visual fulfillment with one hand and take it away with the other. The poem has already told us that eternity is only a human "term." Does "Eternity's White Flag" indicate that the mystery of time is surrendering to the advancing quester, the human mystery being replaced by definite spiritual knowledge? Or does the whiteness, as so often in Dickinson, simply represent the purity and inviolability of the mystery? The phrase describing "God—at every Gate" is similarly problematic, for if the image recalls the role of St. Peter, it also recalls that of Cerberus. Dickinson has no patience with intermediaries, of course, but God's own function cannot be defined: like the white flag, he can represent admittance into the world of spirit or the ultimate obstacle, stationed at the gate to prevent the quester's entering. This painful ambiguity, like the imagistic blending of the concrete and the abstract, represents the delicate suspense of her "compound vision": she remains poised at "that Odd Fork in Being's Road," continually attempting to define each world in terms of the other.⁵ The results, as always, involve deepening rewards and deepening pain.

Occasionally Dickinson tried to mitigate the pain simply by stressing the more hopeful vision of her destiny. She could look forward to the actual moment when "the Cheated Eye / Shuts arrogantly—in the Grave— / Another way—to see" (P 627). In one poem she places her hope in the principle of love:

> As plan for Noon and plan for Night
> So differ Life and Death
> In positive Prospective—
> The Foot upon the Earth
>
> At Distance, and Achievement, strains,
> The Foot upon the Grave
> Makes effort at conclusion
> Assisted faint of Love.
> (P 960)

As she phrased it in another poem, "Till Death—is narrow Loving . . ."

(P 907). But if love was the element which makes the human journey bearable, she nevertheless views the "scant heart" in the context of ultimate vision, which is "seeing God" and which therefore represents ultimate love.

In a poem discussed earlier, "I gained it so," Dickinson pictured such "Bliss" as the ultimate reward of an arduous journey: "I gained it so— / By Climbing slow— / By Catching at the Twigs that grow. . . ." That poem described the achievement of bliss within time, an "instant's Grace." A later poem, "What Twigs we held by," may be viewed as its sequel, since it describes the journey from the vantage point of "everlasting Light":

> What Twigs We held by—
> Oh the View
> When Life's swift River striven through
> We pause before a further plunge
> To take Momentum—
> As the Fringe
>
> Upon a former Garment shows
> The Garment cast,
> Our Props disclose
> So scant, so eminently small
> Of Might to help, so pitiful
> To sink, if We had labored, fond
> The diligence were not more blind
>
> How scant, by everlasting Light
> The Discs that satisfied Our Sight—
> How dimmer than a Saturn's Bar
> The Things esteemed, for Things that are!
> (P 1086)

This poem is not an easy wish-fulfillment, like many of Dickinson's early poems, for it takes into account the struggle of the quester's uphill journey and simply posits a happy ending, the reality of the "grace," or the love, which must assist "the Foot upon the Grave." This ecstatic conclusion to her journey not only involves everlasting light, but also a perceptual confrontation—seeing God—which inspires in Dickinson a characteristic awe. As she wrote in a letter near the end of her life, "I dare not think of the voraciousness of that only gaze and its only return" (L 969).

The prospect of this kind of perceptual fulfillment clearly aroused fear in her, whether she conceived of its occurrence within consciousness or after death: she distrusted mysticism, and she explicitly rejected the notion that after death her identity might be absorbed into God's. She feared the possible "voraciousness" of God's "only gaze"; this kind of fulfillment might "consume" her, as she noted in one poem, "For None see God and live" (p 1247). Even when speculating upon last things, she finds it difficult to abandon her concept of personal evolution and achievement, even in favor of the static, certainly higher form of being suggested by mystical tradition and by some of her own half-grudging apprehensions. She clung to the world of human seeing and human judgments, articulating a private faith in her own "estimations," her sense of a fundamental alignment between the world of her sensory perception and the larger, contextual world where consciousness could transcend the strictures of time and the flesh, and where death, forming its crucial link with the supernatural, seemed ripe with an ultimate, undiscovered meaning.

One of her poems dealing with perception and death offers a vision of their relationship in terms of a process, a final ripening:

There are two Ripenings—one—of sight—
Whose forces Spheric wind
Until the Velvet product
Drop spicy to the ground—
A homelier maturing—
A process in the Bur—
That teeth of Frosts alone disclose
In far October Air.
(p 332)

Though its imagery apparently refers to natural processes, the mode of this poem is symbolism in its pure form;[6] death is not even mentioned, and the reader is left to complete the work of the poem's suspended analogies. Even the relationship between the analogical components—the ripening of sight and the "homelier maturing"—is left implicit, but the first line of the poem suggests that these two ripenings are somehow the essential ones, the only ones that matter. What relationship, then, does the poem suggest between visionary fulfillment and the process of death? The relationship might seem, at first glance, to be an antagonistic one, since the "Velvet product" of vision seems threatened by the "teeth of Frosts." But the poem's rhetorical structure implies that a larger process subsumes the two apparently conflicting ones, and that the *meaning* of springtime fulfillment (visionary splendor) can only be "disclosed" by the autumnal realm of death. The poem is therefore a tiny, symbolic expression of Dickinson's theory of perception, envisioning death not as a hostile threat but as the crucial stage in a natural, inevitable process. Like both Emerson and Whitman, Dickinson views process as the condition of being, a condition which provides opportunities for fulfillment but which requires an utmost human effort toward further cycles of growth and renewal.

The poet's quest, in its broadest context, represents this highly conscious and carefully constructed "ripening" of her sight. Throughout Dickinson's canon, the relationship of perception to the homelier maturing of death is always implicit and deeply felt; her hard-won "compound vision" allowed her to conceive of the quest journey both within consciousness and as a figure of her ultimate destiny, each concept shedding light upon the other. The last words Dickinson wrote from her deathbed—"Called back" (L 1046)—suggest a return from one realm to the other, a passage from consciousness through the "open Tomb," but above all they suggest a continuing journey. In a letter written almost thirty years earlier, at the time when her poetry substantially began, she had exclaimed: "I wonder how long we shall wonder; how early we shall *know*" (L 190). It was on her journey of long and unceasing wonder, and in the act of exhaustively questioning her world and her destiny, that she arrived at the poems themselves—the artistic description of her quest, the richest of humanly possible answers.

Notes

Introduction

1   Thomas H. Johnson, ed., *The Poems of Emily Dickinson* (Cambridge: Harvard University Press, 1955), Poem 750. All subsequent references to Dickinson's poems are to this edition, and will be indicated in parenthesis by poem number (P). Dickinson's erratic spelling and punctuation are preserved; because the poet's lapses are well known, I have chosen not to distract the reader with the notation *sic*. References to Dickinson's letters (L) and prose fragments (PF) are to Thomas H. Johnson and Theodora V. W. Ward, eds., *The Letters of Emily Dickinson* (Cambridge: Harvard University Press, 1958), and will likewise be indicated by the letter number or prose fragment number assigned by the editors.

2   Bernard Rosenthal, *City of Nature: Journeys to Nature in the Age of American Romanticism* (Newark: University of Delaware Press, 1980), p. 19.

3   *The Variorum Walden*, ed. Walter Harding (New York: Twayne Publishers, 1962), p. 127.

4   *The Complete Works of Ralph Waldo Emerson*, Centenary ed., 12 vols. (Boston and New York: Houghton Mifflin, 1903–04), Vol. 1, p. 341. All subsequent references are to this edition and will be indicated by volume and page number.

5   Todd M. Lieber, *Endless Experiments: Essays on the Heroic Experience in American Romanticism* (Columbus, Ohio: Ohio State University Press, 1973), p.22.

6   Adrienne Rich, "Vesuvius at Home: The Power of Emily Dickinson," *Parnassus: Poetry in Review* 5 (1976): 54.

7   Sharon Cameron, *Lyric Time: Dickinson and the Limits of Genre* (Baltimore: Johns Hopkins University Press, 1979), p. 6.

8   David Porter, *Dickinson: The Modern Idiom* (Cambridge: Harvard University Press, 1981), p. 184.

9   Charles R. Anderson, *Emily Dickinson's Poetry: Stairway of Surprise* (New York: Holt, Rinehart & Winston, 1960), p. xiv.

10 Porter, *Dickinson: The Modern Idiom*, pp. 152, 6.

11 *The English Notebooks of Nathaniel Hawthorne*, ed. Randall Stewart (New York: Oxford University Press, 1941), p. 433.

12 Porter, *Dickinson: The Modern Idiom*, pp. 2–3. Roland Hagenbüchle, in "New Developments in Dickinson Criticism," *Anglia* 97 (1979): 470, remarks that Dickinson is "a

poet for whom all language is essentially heuristic, poetic knowledge definable only in terms of heuristic process, the poem itself a heuristic act. This heuristic act still needs demonstration and elucidation."

13   R. W. Franklin, ed., *The Manuscript Books of Emily Dickinson: 1883–1895* (Cambridge: Harvard University Press, 1981).

Chapter 1

1   *The Journals of Ralph Waldo Emerson*, ed. Edward W. Emerson and Waldo E. Forbes, 10 vols. (Boston and New York: Houghton Mifflin, 1909–14), Vol. II, p. 409. All future references to Emerson's journals are to this edition and will be cited by volume and page number.

2   In a key letter of April 1850 to her friend Jane Humphrey, Dickinson (aged 19) relates—in characteristically oblique language—her lack of orthodox commitment to a new, exciting preoccupation: "Christ is calling everyone here, all of my companions have answered, . . . and I am standing alone in rebellion. . . . I have dared to do strange things—bold things, and have asked no advice from any—I have heeded beautiful tempters . . ." (L 35). For a discussion of this letter as a guarded announcement of Dickinson's poetic vocation, see Richard B. Sewall, *The Life of Emily Dickinson* (New York: Farrar, Straus & Giroux, 1974), pp. 391–99.

3   In a journal entry of April 23, 1841, Emerson notes: "We forget daily our high call to be discoverers—we forget that we are embarked on a holy, unknown sea whose blue recesses we have a secret warrant that we shall yet arrive at the Fortunate Isles hid from men . . ." (*Journals*, V, 533–34). Dickinson, of course, has no confidence in this "secret warrant"; her own "Fortunate Isles" represent only one possibility among many.

4   Ruth Miller writes that the poem represents "precisely the questions that may be resolved by the poet. Whether it (death) is nothingness, whether it is troubled passage, or judgment or damnation, whether death is peaceful entry into Paradise, exactly what is the mooring that will hold the soul, it is the errand of the Bard to reveal." *The Poetry of Emily Dickinson* (Middletown: Wesleyan University Press, 1968), p. 155. William Robert Sherwood believes the poem suggests that "the poet's eye and the flight of his imagination are the only means by which [the] mystery may be penetrated." *Circumference and Circumstance: Stages in the Mind and Art of Emily Dickinson* (New York and London: Columbia University Press, 1968), p. 42.

5   See Harold Bloom, "The Internalization of Quest-Romance," in *Romanticism and Consciousness: Essays in Criticism*, ed. Harold Bloom (New York: Norton, 1970), pp. 3–24. Michael G. Yetman considers Bloom's seminal essay crucial to an understanding of Dickinson's quest: "The special importance of Professor Bloom's insight is that it is applicable not just to individual works but to an understanding of a poet's evolution. . . ." "Emily Dickinson and the English Romantic Tradition," *Texas Studies in Literature and Language* 15 (1973): 129–47. More recently, Joanne Feit Diehl has discussed in detail the relation between Bloom's theory of influence and Dickinson's place in Romantic tradition: "Dickinson and Bloom: An Antithetical Reading of Romanticism," *Texas Studies in Literature and Language* 23 (1981): 418–41. For a full discussion of Dickinson's relationship to Romantic tradition, see Diehl's *Dickinson and the Romantic Imagination* (Princeton: Princeton University Press, 1981).

6   As David Porter suggests in *The Art of Emily Dickinson's Early Poetry* (Cambridge: Harvard University Press, 1966), p. 17, we should avoid considering the body of Dickinson's poetry as "a random scattering of fragments out of which one is free to make his own mosaic"; to recognize at the outset the comprehensiveness of Dickinson's quest, and especially the often contradictory voices which describe it, is crucial in avoiding oversimplification.

7   *Walt Whitman: Complete Poetry and Selected Prose*, ed. James E. Miller, Jr. (Boston: Houghton Mifflin, 1959), p. 186. Todd M. Lieber remarks of this poem that "any sense of procession is lost entirely, and Whitman envisions himself as a particle adrift in a world of flux" (*Endless Experiments*, p. 106).

8   Joanne Feit Diehl comments on Dickinson's deliberate creation of innocent personae who are, surely, distinct from the poet herself: "Dickinson writes only songs of experience. Those poems which adopt a vision of the young innocent are often her most searing comments." Searing, that is, in light of the turmoil and confusion lying in wait for the "innocent." Most of these poems are ironic, however, only in contrast to later admissions of despair. As isolated lyrics they simply recreate, rather than mock, the innocence of the young quester. See Diehl, *Dickinson and the Romantic Imagination*, p. 16.

9   Thomas W. Ford remarks that the poem "shows the contradiction between observed fact and a religious hope for immortality," and also adds: "The poem is a good, or perhaps bad, example of just how sentimental and conventional some of her early verse could be." *Heaven Beguiles the Tired: Death in the Poetry of Emily Dickinson* (University: University of Alabama Press, 1966), p. 75. David Porter also feels that the poem reflects "stylistic weakness" (*Art of Emily Dickinson's Early Poetry*, p. 128). I would suggest that the poem's childish manner is appropriate to its underlying theme: the delusive nature of unquestioning faith.

10 The poet is also "barefoot," a condition that symbolizes the deracinated quester in many of Dickinson's poems and letters. For a discussion of this figure see Mary Ann C. McGuire, "A Metaphorical Pattern in Emily Dickinson," *American Transcendental Quarterly* 29 (1976): 83–85. In Poem 1113 (about 1867), Dickinson employs this figure in a startling line which recalls her earlier "bark" poems: "To walk on seas requires cedar Feet."

11 This awareness persisted throughout her life. In 1873, for instance, she writes apprehensively to her cousin, Perez Cowan: "I hope that you have Power and as much of Peace as in our deep existence may be possible. To multiply the Harbors does not reduce the Sea" (L 386).

12 Thomas W. Ford remarks: "Though obviously not based on observed fact, the poem describes the imagined sensation *in terms of sensation*" (*Heaven Beguiles the Tired*, p. 84; italics mine). This emphasis upon sense perception *as if* spiritual experiences were "based on observed fact" constitutes a chief hallmark of Dickinson's poetry, one that becomes even more evident in the later work.

13 Roy Harvey Pearce, *The Continuity of American Poetry* (Princeton: Princeton University Press, 1961), pp. 180–81.

14 Ibid., p. 181. This skepticism is reflected in another intriguing early poem, related through imagery to the poems under discussion. Here Dickinson describes the quest in relation to death, the dying person having "a faith in one he met not." The final stanza implies Dickinson's own lack of trust that the spiritual "Bay" represents any actual fulfillment:

Such trust had one among us,
Among us *not* today—
We who saw the launching
Never sailed the Bay!
(P 43)

15 Here again the work of Dickinson's contemporaries provides interesting parallels. In Whitman the relationship between perception and the unknown is described almost literally in terms of sweetness and light (*Complete Poetry and Selected Prose*, p. 26):

Clear and sweet is my soul, and clear and sweet is
    all that is not my soul.
Lack one lacks both, and the unseen is proved by the seen,
Till that becomes unseen and receives its proof in turn.

Closer to Dickinson's mood is the hero of Melville's *Mardi*, Taji, who is embarked upon a "chartless" voyage. Warned that "from the deep beyond, no voyager e'er puts back," he nevertheless continues onward with "eternity . . . in his eye." *The Writings of Herman Melville*, ed. Harrison Hayford, Hershel Parker, and G. Thomas Tanselle, 10 vols. (Evanston, Ill.: Northwestern University Press and the Newberry Library, 1968), Vol. III, p. 654.

16 Though the critic must always remain aware that Thomas H. Johnson's dating of the poems is approximate, it seems clear that the cluster of "bark" poems belongs among the earliest surviving manuscripts. Later poems do occasionally revive the metaphor. See, for instance, P 723 (about 1863): "It tossed—and tossed— / A little Brig I knew"; and P 1123 (about 1868):

The mind was built for mighty Freight
For dread occasion planned
How often foundering at Sea
Ostensibly, on Land. . . .

17 Joanne Feit Diehl remarks of this poem: "As the danger of her position increases, as her world is reduced to heaven and the abyss, to the stars and the sea, her own figure enlarges to fill the gap. Self assumes the gigantic proportions of one who touches the extremities of the universe. The radical severity of her world demands a self that will fill 'the Term between.' This giantism corresponds to the aims of the expanded self that desires to measure the abyss." *Dickinson and the Romantic Imagination*, pp. 180–81. Consciousness of this expanded self no doubt prompted two interesting "reminiscence" poems, both written about 1862. Poem 486 recalls a time when "I was the slightest in the House—" and P 476 begins by confessing, rather slyly, "I meant to have but modest needs. . . ."

18 Emerson, "Intellect," *Complete Works*: II, 342.

19 Robert Weisbuch, *Emily Dickinson's Poetry* (Chicago: University of Chicago Press, 1975), p. 3.

20 Yet another early poem also employs the sea / land metaphor and characterizes the speaker as one who is determined and hopeful in her search for answers:

Once more, my now bewildered Dove
Bestirs her puzzled wings
Once more her mistress, on the deep
Her troubled question flings—

Thrice to the floating casement
The Patriarch's bird returned,
Courage! My brave Columba!
There may yet be *Land!*
(P 48)

21 Emerson, "Experience," *Complete Works*: III, 75–76.

Chapter 2

1 It is surely significant that the image of the poet's bark surrounded by an unexplored ocean, so frequent in the early poems, turns up in the poet's letters as well: "I am so far from Land" (L 247); "I live in the Sea always and know the Road" (L 306); "I am pleasantly located in the deep sea, but . . . don't wait till I land, for I'm going ashore on the other side" (L 209). She began a letter to Susan Dickinson, with no further explanation: "At Centre of the Sea—" This letter was written from Cambridge, where she had gone to seek treatment for an eye ailment. The "Sea" reference perhaps indicates (in an image Sue would understand) the poet's sense of perceptual disorientation.

2 Emerson, *Nature, Complete Works*: I, 49.

3 This thesis is developed in John Cody, *After Great Pain: The Inner Life of Emily Dickinson* (Cambridge: Harvard University Press, 1971), pp. 291–356.

4 In this same letter she notes: "I had a letter—and Ralph Emerson's Poems—a beautiful copy—from Newton the other day. I should love to read you them both—they are very pleasant to me."

5 Cody, *After Great Pain*, p. 245. In a poem of about 1865 which uses language strikingly analogous to that in the letter to Sue, Dickinson stresses that it was her own "Heart" which made the choice of solitude:

Up Life's Hill with my little Bundle
If I prove it steep—
If a Discouragement with[h]old me—
If my newest step

Older feel than the Hope that prompted—
Spotless be from blame
Heart that proposed as Heart that accepted
Homelessness, for Home—
(P 1010)

6 Sewall, *Life of Emily Dickinson*, p. 165.

7 See especially the letter of June 1852 to Susan Dickinson (L 93). Albert Gelpi discusses the crucial importance of this letter in *Emily Dickinson: The Mind of the Poet* (Cambridge: Harvard University Press, 1965), pp. 1–3.

8 See Rebecca Patterson, *The Riddle of Emily Dickinson* (Boston: Houghton Mifflin, 1951).

9 Two excellent discussions of Dickinson's relationship to her own creative power are Rich, "Vesuvius at Home"; and Albert Gelpi, "Emily Dickinson and the Deerslayer: The Dilemma of the Woman Poet in America," reprinted in Sandra M. Gilbert and Susan Gubar, eds., *Shakespeare's Sisters: Feminist Essays on Women Poets* (Bloomington and London: Indiana University Press, 1979), pp. 122–34.

10 Sandra M. Gilbert and Susan Gubar, *The Madwoman in the Attic: The Woman Writer and the Nineteenth-Century Literary Imagination* (New Haven and London: Yale University Press, 1979), p. 583.

11 Sewall, *Life of Emily Dickinson*, p. 608, suggests that even members of Dickinson's immediate family were unaware of the extent of her engagement with poetry until after her death.

12 David Porter, *Dickinson: The Modern Idiom*, pp. 137, 294, 152. Porter's overemphasis of Dickinson as a modernist who focuses upon language as an end in itself, language having been robbed of any signifying power, is qualified by Albert Gelpi's recent comment in *The Tenth Muse: The Psyche of the American Poet* (Cambridge: Harvard University Press, 1975), p. 222: "The corpus of Dickinson's poems represents a complex psyche struggling to press her inner conflicts and contrarieties to clarity from moment to moment through the creative and reflective act of language."

13 Emerson, "Intellect," *Complete Works*: II, 342.

14 Cameron, *Lyric Time*, p. 1.

15 Emerson, *Nature, Complete Works*: I, 34–35. As David Porter remarks, "Dickinson is a world away from Emerson's confident Platonism. For she sought not examples of his reassuring metamorphosis of fact into Truth but rather the design of experience itself of which she was ignorant." *Dickinson: The Modern Idiom*, p. 159.

16 Emerson, "Montaigne; or, The Skeptic," *Complete Works*: IV, 156. Roland Hagenbüchle remarks: "in total contrast to Emerson's optimistic 'presentiments' of a progressively increasing knowledge, Dickinson knows that she cannot know. The knowledge which her poems express is a *docta ignorantia*; knowledge terminates in the act of knowing, more precisely, in the impossibility of knowing. If the infinite could be known, it would not be the infinite; this is a fundamental Romantic tenet." "Sign and Process: The Concept of Language in Emerson and Dickinson," *ESQ: A Journal of the American Renaissance* 25 (1979): 152–53.

The complex relationship between Dickinson and Emerson deserves a book-length study to itself, and here we can only remark upon the relationship as it touches upon Dickinson's quest for knowledge. The major critical commentators on the extent of Emerson's influence have been G. F. Whicher, *This Was a Poet* (New York: Charles Scribners and Sons, 1938); Albert Gelpi, *Emily Dickinson: The Mind of the Poet*; Hyatt Waggoner, "Emily Dickinson: The Transcendent Self," *Criticism* 7 (1965): 297–334; Karl Keller, *The Only Kangaroo Among the Beauty: Emily Dickinson and America* (Baltimore: Johns Hopkins University Press, 1979), pp. 148–83; and the work of Roland Hagenbüchle and Joanne Feit Diehl already cited. For a good summary of Dickinson's probable reading in the Emerson canon, see Jack L. Capps, *Emily Dickinson's Reading: 1836–1886* (Cambridge: Harvard University Press, 1966), pp. 111–18.

17 Emerson, "Montaigne; or, The Skeptic," *Complete Works*: IV, 185.

18 Ibid., p. 186.

19 Quoting Northrop Frye's contention that "the great Romantic theme is the attaining of

an apocalyptic vision by a fallen but potentially regenerate mind," Bernard Rosenthal insists upon a distinction that has special relevance to Dickinson: "Literary historians reasonably enough associate this regeneration with an 'Adamic myth,' but there must be no misunderstanding about the state of Adam in this myth as it took shape in America. Adam was fallen and not innocent." *City of Nature*, p. 19.

20 Discussing the effects of her Puritan heritage upon Dickinson, Thomas M. Davis remarks of the Puritan frame of mind: "Uncertainty, where it exists, is not attributable to the Creator; it is the consequence of the imperfect perception of the finite. Although the Puritans' soul-searching is genuine, the expressions of their fallen state and insufficiencies sincere, these are imbedded within a construct where even the sparrow does not fall without God's knowledge." "Emily Dickinson and the Right of Way to Tripoli," collected in Robert J. DeMott and Sanford E. Marovitz, eds., *Artful Thunder: Versions of the Romantic Tradition in American Literature* (Kent, Ohio: Kent State University Press, 1975), p. 212. In Dickinson, of course, "uncertainty" is very often actively blamed on the Creator; and yet she shares Puritan anxiety over "imperfect perception of the finite" which gives rise to her large number of poems focused upon minute natural particulars.

21 Clark W. Griffith, *The Long Shadow: Emily Dickinson's Tragic Poetry* (Princeton: Princeton University Press, 1964), p. 23. His discussion of Dickinson's "post-Romantic" identity, though perhaps overemphasizing Dickinson's fear and estrangement within nature, is often illuminating; see pp. 17–40, passim.

22 Roland Hagenbüchle remarks: "What Emerson and Dickinson share is the Romantic conviction that art is ultimately a religious expression in that it renders the experience of the numinous and the sublime, and at the same time recreates it in the mind of the reader." "Sign and Process," p. 152. Jeffrey L. Duncan rightly comments that "[Dickinson's] concern is epistemological and religious: what does the visible world tell us about the nature of the invisible world, the reserve of God?" He goes on, however, to remark that "Dickinson offers us the curious spectacle of poems deeply concerned with perception that are not at all perceptive, empirically speaking, and that do not pretend to be. . . . Dickinson feels little obligation to the empirical, if any. . . . She pays little attention to empirical matters of fact." "Joining Together / Putting Asunder: An Essay on Emily Dickinson's Poetry," *Missouri Review* 4 (1980): 111, 116, 117. Rather, I would argue that Dickinson's respect for the mystery and opacity of nature spurs her innate empiricism; as this and later chapters will try to demonstrate, her emphasis on empirical perception is the foundation of her epistemological / religious quest. Poems that seem to be concerned with perception but not "perceptive" are typically the speaker's confession of her own temporarily inadequate resources; but they do not imply indifference or defeatism.

23 Thomas M. Davis remarks that "There is about many of the poems of the late 1850's an exuberance and aura of flight and soaring distinctly Emersonian in cast." "Emily Dickinson and the Right of Way to Tripoli," p. 213. The Emersonian impulse, however, does recur (though infrequently) in the mature work as well. See Poem 790, "Nature— the Gentlest Mother is" and another curious lyric, apparently written in 1865, in which Dickinson momentarily escapes her pervasive feelings of enslavement to natural cycles:

Did We abolish Frost
The Summer would not cease—

> If Seasons perish or prevail
> Is optional with Us—
> (P 1014)

24   Emerson's "confidence" is often overemphasized, however. Todd M. Lieber writes: "[Emerson] reached his diagonal line, balancing, incorporating, and transcending the polarities of sensual and spiritual, social and private, self and not self. But Emerson knew that the diagonal line was not a path that could be followed or maintained without deviation. It was, in fact, no line at all, but rather a point, a position, a peak of experience that could be achieved only momentarily and only momentarily retained. The moments when nature seems transparent are evanescent. The immediacy of these visionary experiences endows them with a high degree of intensity, but also renders them fleeting and transient. At other times nature seems opaque, blank, a world totally unrelated to the thoughts of man." *Endless Experiments*, p. 14. Emerson himself complained: "When shall I die and be relieved of the responsibility of seeing a Universe I do not use? I wish to exchange this flash-of-lightning faith for continuous daylight, this fever-glow for a benign climate." "The Transcendentalist," *Complete Works*: I, 352–53. Dickinson too felt burdened by the "responsibility of seeing" and longed for "continuous daylight" (which becomes a pervasive image of fulfillment), and in this common frustration they are vitally linked. Stephen E. Whicher, Emerson's biographer, comments on the frustration in a sense applicable to Dickinson as well as to Emerson: "Any statement of truth is necessarily partial . . . and implies the potential truth of its opposite also. The essential thing is not any given insight but the vital capacity to move from one to the next according to the natural rhythm of thought. The life of the mind is a perpetual voyage of discovery. . . ." "Introduction" to *Selections from Ralph Waldo Emerson: An Organic Anthology* (Boston: Houghton Mifflin, 1957), pp. xviii–xix.

25   Diehl, *Dickinson and the Romantic Imagination*, pp. 162–64.

26   Inder Nath Kher, *The Landscape of Absence: Emily Dickinson's Poetry* (New Haven: Yale University Press, 1974). See especially his chapters "The Landscape of Absence: Mansions of Mirage" (pp. 47–84) and "Perception: The Billows of Circumference" (pp. 85–134).

27   Emerson, *Nature, Complete Works*: I, 48.

28   Ibid., I, 63.

29   Harold Bloom, ed., *Romantic Poetry and Prose* (New York: Oxford University Press, 1973), p. 148n.

30   Harold Bloom, *The Visionary Company: A Reading of English Romantic Poetry* (Ithaca: Cornell University Press, 1961), p. 125.

31   R. P. Blackmur, "Emily Dickinson's Notation," in Richard B. Sewall, ed., *Emily Dickinson: A Collection of Critical Essays* (Englewood Cliffs: Prentice-Hall, 1963), p. 82.

32   Kher, *Landscape of Absence*, p. 92, overemphasizes Dickinson's acceptance of her subjectivity: "Dickinson's theory of perception endorses the romantic view of the creative mind as projecting its own inner truth upon the forms of life. . . ." He quotes the well-known "To hear an Oriole sing" (P 526) but ignores a poem which states the opposite view, "Split the Lark—and you'll find the Music—" (P 861). Clearly, Dickinson vacillated on this problem (as did her American contemporaries). On p. 94 Kher quotes

approvingly from Albert Gelpi's *The Mind of the Poet*, p. 135: "[Dickinson] is concerned not with the 'Perfectness' of the ultimate reality 'that 'tis so Heavenly far' . . . but with the poet's perception, which more than compensates for the sacrifice of negligible phenomenal existence." It is a major contention of the present study that Dickinson was concerned with little else *but* "the ultimate reality" which is the object of her quest. Though she knows the quest object is "so Heavenly far," this indicates honest awareness—not indifference.

33   Vivian Hopkins, *Spires of Form: A Study of Emerson's Aesthetic Theory* (Cambridge: Harvard University Press, 1951), p. 27.

34   Weisbuch, *Emily Dickinson's Poetry*, p. 19.

35   Michael G. Yetman calls this "one of those apparently innocuous little poems . . . which is saved at the very end by a shift to a higher mood through metaphor. After describing playfully a childlike fear toward one of 'Nature's People,' in its last line the poem suddenly catapults us into the adult world of existential terror. . . ." He also remarks that the poem is a characteristic Romantic lyric because it depicts "the suddenness and psychological upheaval of the cognitive act." "Emily Dickinson and the English Romantic Tradition," p. 136. Also, it should be noted that the word "cordiality" almost always indicates an ambiguous, delicate relationship in Dickinson's poems: cf. "the Cordiality of Death" (P 286); "Back from the cordial Grave I drag thee" (P 1625); and the "cordial light" emitted by the gun in "My Life had stood—a Loaded Gun" (P 754).

36   For an explanation of the Shakespearean reference in this poem see Anderson, *Emily Dickinson's Poetry*, pp. 116–17.

37   The occasional ugliness of nature is another theme which separates Dickinson and Emerson. Emerson often expressed the idea that "Nature never wears a mean appearance" (*Nature, Complete Works*: I, 7–8). Dickinson, on the other hand, notes that "Nature, like Us is sometimes caught / Without her Diadem" (P 1075).

38   David Porter, "Emily Dickinson: The Poetics of Doubt," *Emerson Society Quarterly* 60 (1979): 86–93.

39   Weisbuch, *Emily Dickinson's Poetry*, p. 16.

40   Charles R. Anderson misreads this poem by assuming that "their Competeless show" refers to the poet's own splendors; but the reference is surely to the Northern lights, since the argument of the poem as a whole contrasts the individual's pathetic "strutting" against the magnificent self-sufficiency of the universe. William R. Sherwood, *Circumference and Circumstance* (pp. 206–07), corrects Anderson, notes the "invidious" contrast the poem asserts, and also adds with insight: "the poem *qua* poem slyly contradicts the poet's self-deprecation." Yet Sherwood himself considers this "The one poem in which Emily Dickinson seriously and coherently discusses the poet and the value of what he creates. . . ." I see the poem not as dealing with "the poet" but rather describing a representative individual and her adroit defenses against her own insignificance within nature.

41   In *Emily Dickinson: The Mind of the Poet*, p. 151, Gelpi notes: "The spider image occurs throughout American writing with revealing differences in image and association." He traces the image briefly from Edward Taylor through Whitman to Frost and Robert Lowell, and also notes that Dickinson's use of the image is unique. For an extended discussion of the image in Dickinson's poetry, see JoAnne De Lavan Williams,

"Spiders in the Attic: A Suggestion of Synthesis in the Poetry of Emily Dickinson," *Emily Dickinson Bulletin* 29 (1976): 21–29.

42   Sewall, *Life of Emily Dickinson*, pp. 398–99n.

Chapter 3

1   It should be noted that except for forms of "to be," the most recurrent verbs in Dickinson's canon relate directly to her perceptual and poetic quest: "know" (used 230 times), "go" (152), "see" (146), and "tell" (135). See S. P. Rosenbaum, ed., *A Concordance to the Poems of Emily Dickinson* (Ithaca: Cornell University Press, 1964), p. 865.

2   Sandra M. Gilbert and Susan Gubar have sensitively delineated the relationship between Dickinson and her highly various poetic personae. In Dickinson's poems, they write, we see "an almost complete absorption of the characters of the fiction into the persona of their author, so that this writer and her protagonist(s) become for all practical purposes one—one 'supposed person' achieving the authority of self-creation by enacting many highly literary selves and lives." They also assert that "[Dickinson's] terse, explosive poems are . . . the speech of a fictional character. . . . Indeed, understood as an elaborate set of dramatic monologues, her poems constitute the 'dialogue' in an extended fiction whose subject is the life of that supposed person who was originally called Emily Dickinson but who also christened herself, variously, Emilie, Daisy, Brother Emily, Uncle Emily, and simply Dickinson." *Madwoman in the Attic*, pp. 585, 583.

3   See, for example, John Emerson Todd's monograph *Emily Dickinson's Use of the Persona* (The Hague: Mouton, 1973). Also see Thomas R. Arp, "Dramatic Poses in the Poetry of Emily Dickinson" (Ph.D. dissertation, Stanford University, 1962), especially pp. 23–53.

4   Her characteristic intensity is illustrated in a letter to Mrs. Holland of March 2, 1859: "Complacency! My Father! in such a world as this, when we must all stand barefoot before thy jasper doors!" (L 204).

5   E. Miller Budick, "When the Soul Selects: Emily Dickinson's Attack on New England Symbolism," *American Literature* 51 (1979): 361, 360. Budick also notes (p. 360) that in this poem the persona, "who has opted for spiritual as opposed to physical seeing, discovers not only that her blindness is more encompassing than she had originally thought, but that the vision which remains to her is fragmented and chaotic." Budick concludes (p. 362) that the poem is one "of despair, an admission that the simultaneous stereoscopicity of eyesight and insight is unattainable. The persona may see, in one moment, with her physical vision, in another through the optics of her spiritualizing, transcendentalizing imagination. Yet, even if she oscillates between the two modes of seeing, it will be impossible to draw them into one harmonious simultaneity." This too, however, seems to ignore the poem's rhetorical structure: it does not deal with an "oscillation" but with a progression, showing that eyesight *leads* to insight; it has been precisely the speaker's delusion that she must renounce one in order to gain the other.

6   Miller, *Poetry of Emily Dickinson*, p. 278.

7   Sewall, *Life of Emily Dickinson*, p. 559.

8   Nor should one confuse this speaker's argument with the warnings Dickinson issues in her poems about poetry itself, also using the metaphor of eyesight: "The Truth must dazzle gradually / Or every man be blind" (P 1129), "None see God and live" (P 1247).

In these poems she is imaging the power of absolute truth, which requires the poet's mediation, rather than suggesting a renunciation of eyesight as a means toward knowledge.

9   Cody argues persuasively (*After Great Pain*, pp. 416–20) that her eye disease was largely psychosomatic, a result of emotional illness; in this light, "Before I got my eye put out" might indeed be read biographically as an expression of anxiety (resulting from what Dr. Cody calls "self-directed hostility") over her own excessive renunciatory impulses. This adds a special poignance to the poet's contempt for her speaker.

10   Cody rejects this possibility, asking "why was it a fear she 'could tell to none'?" But he provides his own answer: she surely hesitated before complaining of an illness which she perhaps sensed was psychological rather than organic. Her father's ultimate refusal to allow the continuation of her treatments is perhaps explained by this theory.

Richard B. Sewall remarks that "The nature of Emily's difficulty with her eyes is still a mystery." He notes Cody's theory that the problem was psychosomatic and adds: "Other suggestions point to physiological disorders: the early manifestations of Bright's disease (as her final illness was diagnosed) or strabismus (the inability to direct both eyes to the same object) or glaucoma." *Life of Emily Dickinson*, p. 606*n*. In a controversial essay, Jerry Ferris Reynolds suggests that Dickinson's general ill health was the major reason for her seclusion. Although his thesis often leads him far afield—into a suggestion, for instance, that the poem "I felt a Cleaving in my Mind" (P 937) describes a "violent headache"—he is more convincing in regard to her eye problems, which he believes the result of systemic lupus erythematosus. See Reynolds, " 'Banishment from Native Eyes': The Reason for Emily Dickinson's Seclusion Reconsidered," *The Markham Review* 8 (1979): 41–48. See pp. 44–45 for his discussion of Dickinson's eye disease, where he notes the relationship between lupus and the particular eye afflictions suffered by Dickinson.

11   Emerson, *Nature, Complete Works*: I, 10; my italics.

12   Ibid., I, 8.

13   Weisbuch (*Emily Dickinson's Poetry*, p. 174) misreads the poem by attempting to make it an expression of a biographical episode (Dickinson's courtship by Judge Lord). Of the final stanza he writes: "To paraphrase these badly crabbed lines, renunciation must renounce itself at the appropriate time. Dickinson . . . wishes to assure herself that, when the time is ripe, she can accept an ending to her quest." Here again the misreading is due to a misunderstood referent. When Dickinson writes, "Renunciation—is the Choosing / Against itself—" the word "itself" does not refer to "Renunciation" but to the chooser (this usage of "itself" is not unusual with Dickinson—see, for example, L 575: "Till it has loved—no man or woman can become itself"). To paraphrase the stanza: when one deliberately chooses self-deprivation, the self is justified (perceptually validated) through that choice and may then perceive in true perspective the relationship between a limited "Presence" and a larger, ultimate "Expectation." It should thus be clear that the poem has nothing to do with "an ending to her quest"—rather it defines a stance through which the quest may proceed meaningfully.

14   Jean McClure Mudge, *Emily Dickinson and the Image of Home* (Amherst: University of Massachusetts Press, 1975), p. 113. Inder Nath Kher writes that "By putting out the earthly eyes one experiences the sunrise on the inner landscape, with which even the sun, the 'Day's Great Progenitor,' cannot contend. By renunciation, one chooses against one's mortal longings. . . ." *Landscape of Absence*, p. 241. Again it should be stressed,

however, that the sun is here used to symbolize the visionary glory for which one must renounce the day itself. Although we are dealing with an "inner landscape," that landscape is exteriorized through the poem's imagery.

15   Kher, *Landscape of Absence*, p. 88.

16   Porter, *Art of Emily Dickinson's Early Poetry*, p. 24.

17   Gelpi, *Emily Dickinson: The Mind of the Poet*, p. 265.

18   Harold Bloom notes that "Dickinson's religion . . . was no more Christian than the faiths of Emerson, Thoreau, Whitman. Christian imagery she employed always to her own curious ends as she saw fit, free-style, picking it up or dropping it at will." *Figures of Capable Imagination* (New York: Seabury Press, 1976), p. 80.

19   Considerable critical confusion has resulted from the attempt to reconcile this poem with Dickinson's characteristic skepticism. Edwin Moseley, in "The Gambit of Emily Dickinson," *The University of Kansas City Review* 16 (1949): 17, finds in the poem a "severe calmness" which evokes "the Puritan's concern with the practical. . . ." On the other hand, Griffith (*The Long Shadow*, p. 4), complaining of the poem's popularity, calls it a "tinkling little credo." Later in his book (pp. 109–10) he returns to the poem and suggests that it is either ironic, or a kind of "whistling in the dark."

Though not citing this poem, Carole Anne Taylor notes that Dickinson is "fond of creating speakers whose spiritual role-playing exposes the psychology of self-deception." Relating Dickinson's subtle ironies to Kierkegaard's belief that "ironic tonal qualities could elucidate the structures of religious consciousness," she comments upon the relationship between Dickinson the quester and her "rich repertoire" of poetic voices: "For those supremely 'difficult' individuals who possess the requisite passion and imagination to give voices to their spiritual attitudes (primarily poets and philosophers), the passage in and out of ironic states of consciousness is a condition of life. Dickinson never puts on a mask to pose as someone else, yet she creates voices that assume distinct spiritual identity and project traits of mind and character through what they say. Her ironic voices are, of course, only part of a rich repertoire, but they illustrate her capacity for combining the fresh spontaneity of the lyric with self-conscious tonal qualities." Taylor, "Kierkegaard and the Ironic Voices of Emily Dickinson," *Journal of English and Germanic Philology* 77 (1978): 580.

Chapter 4

1   Diehl, *Dickinson and the Romantic Imagination*, p. 163.

2   Gelpi, *The Tenth Muse*, p. 264.

3   Porter, *Dickinson: The Modern Idiom*, p. 35.

4   Walt Whitman, *The Uncollected Poetry and Prose*, ed. Emory Holloway, 2 vols. (New York: Peter Smith, 1932), Vol. 2, p. 36.

5   William Mulder remarks: "To see New Englandly is, finally, to see inwardly, to search the landscape of the soul for signs of grace, an exercise congenial to the New England temperament since the Puritans fled old England." "Seeing 'New Englandly': Planes of Perception in Emily Dickinson and Robert Frost," *The New England Quarterly* 52 (1979): 556.

6   Emerson, *Nature, Complete Works*: I, 16–22.

7   Emerson, "Circles," *Complete Works*: II, 318.

8 Emerson, "The American Scholar," *Complete Works*: I, 86.

9 Martin Bickman, *The Unsounded Centre: Jungian Studies in American Romanticism* (Chapel Hill: University of North Carolina Press, 1980), p. 145.

10 M. H. Abrams, *Natural Supernaturalism* (New York: Norton, 1971), p. 184.

11 William James, *The Varieties of Religious Experience* (New York: The Modern Library, 1929), p. 372.

12 Richard Chase, *Emily Dickinson* (New York: William Sloane, 1951), p. 121.

13 Louise Bogan, "Emily Dickinson: A Mystical Poet," in Sewall, ed., *Emily Dickinson: A Collection of Critical Essays*, p. 138.

14 Andrew M. Greeley, *Ecstasy as Knowledge* (Englewood Cliffs: Prentice-Hall, 1974), pp. 57–58.

15 William Johnston, *The Still Point: Reflections on Zen and Christian Mysticism* (New York: Fordham University Press, 1970), pp. 124–25.

16 Emerson, "The Transcendentalist," *Complete Works*: I, 334.

17 *John Keats: Selected Poems and Letters*, ed. Douglas Bush (Boston: Houghton Mifflin, 1959), p. 288. For a full discussion of Dickinson's relationship to Keats, see Diehl, *Dickinson and the Romantic Imagination*, pp. 68–121.

18 Todd M. Lieber notes that for Emerson, too, such apprehensions are visionary triumphs, however fleeting, rather than the passive ecstasies of the mystic: "Although the images of ascension in Emerson's writing at times suggest a movement toward an increasingly intense and pure perception of the Absolute, Emerson is not a mystic, striving laboriously toward God, but rather a visionary who becomes aware of God's presence about him and within him in the successive repetition of epiphanic moments." *Endless Experiments*, p. 28.

19 Henry W. Wells has suggested that the poem is a "deliberate and almost line for line translation of [Shakespeare's] forty-third sonnet beginning 'When most I wink, then do mine eyes best see.' Emily merely drains off Shakespeare's baroque eloquence, leaving the terser New England statement, twelve short lines taking the place of fourteen long." *Introduction to Emily Dickinson* (Chicago: Hendricks House, 1947), pp. 126–27.

20 E. Miller Budick interprets Dickinson's poems about her soul as part of a large-scale ironic attack on "the symbolistic literalness of Puritanism and Transcendentalism," the soul's isolation indicating a division between self and world which Dickinson wishes to deplore: "The fulfillment of symbolism's potential reductiveness and destructiveness was achieved for Dickinson, in the American tradition, by the special, literalistic symbolofideism of the Puritans and Transcendentalists. In failing to recognize and accept the mortal limitations of humankind's fallen, physical vision and its worldly, material soul, these American idealists mistook forms for essences. . . . When, in Dickinson's poems, the soul selects its own society of self and arrogantly transforms its own world into a wholly complete and self-contained Puritan universe; or when it positions itself at the window pane of the poet's access to the physical creation and blinds her to the actual dimensions of the real world, then communication between the individual and the universe is destroyed. The soul and the cosmos become mutually exclusive elements in an irreparable dualism." Budick, "When the Soul Selects," p. 363. I view the "irreparable dualism" suggested in these poems to be the necessary condition of a more meaningful unity: that between the soul and spiritual vision. In this context, "the universe" becomes a negligible consideration.

21   Dickinson's mature technique in this poem heightens its effectiveness: after the exact rhyme at the end of stanza three, the final stanza suspends rhyme altogether. Aurally this describes the appropriation by the soul of the colossal substance, an undifferentiated expansiveness which at this point goes beyond linguistic restriction or denotation.

22   Gelpi writes: "For all her experience of the blaze of noon and the lightning-flash, for all her knowledge of the flower's ecstasy and the bee's power, she had to reject the kind of 'mysticism' which in Emerson became mistiness and in Whitman amorphousness." *Emily Dickinson: The Mind of the Poet*, p. 152.

Chapter 5

1   Emerson, *Nature, Complete Works*: I, 33.

2   Emerson, "Circles," *Complete Works*: II, 318.

3   Roland Hagenbüchle remarks, however, that Emerson's and Dickinson's techniques of experimentation differ sharply, Emerson's method being largely discursive, Dickinson's starkly dialectical: "In contrast to his generally discursive method, where opposites often stand in unresolved juxtaposition, she has developed a dialectical poetics capable of integrating in processual terms the paradoxical elements of experience into the movement of language and thought." "Sign and Process," p. 152.

4   Since the poem is crucial to this discussion, it is well at the outset to summarize this criticism and to place the various readings in perspective. Nat Henry misreads the poem by taking Dickinson's "ratio" too literally: after a great deal of mathematical computation he concludes that the "prize" must refer to living friends, not the recently dead. Thus he summarizes Dickinson's theme: "The sharpened remembrance of what is gone triggers fretful joy in what we still have left to lose." Laurence Perrine corrects Henry on the crucial point that the "prize" cannot refer to the living, but in a later discussion he similarly insists upon mathematic literalness with regard to the "ratio"—which is, he writes, "the *emotional value* of the *one recently lost friend* to the *collective emotional value* of the *friends who remain*." It is crucial, however, not to ignore Dickinson's warning that she is describing a "broken" mathematics; we must approach the poem's ratio on its own terms—through its imaginative contrast of emotional valuations—rather than through a literal mathematics.

The first stanza of the poem establishes *analogies*. Critical argument over the situation of the "persona"—in a churchyard (Henry), by a deathbed (Perrine)—is a wrong-headed one, for there is no persona, no lyric "I"; as to the generalized situation presented in lines 1 and 2, Perrine is accurate, but his description applies only to those two lines. The "we" of lines one and three is a universal we; Edgar F. Daniels rightly notes that the poem "makes universal the tendency to value what we haven't over what we have." But the poem does not, as Daniels claims, "satirize the reversal of priorities." It simply states the truth of this reversal.

See Nat Henry, "Dickinson's 'As by the dead we love to sit,' " *The Explicator*, January 1973, Item 35; Laurence Perrine, "Dickinson's 'As by the dead we love to sit,' " *The Explicator*, February 1975, Item 49; Laurence Perrine, "Dickinson's 'As by the dead we love to sit,' " *The Explicator* 37 (1978): 38; Edgar F. Daniels, "Dickinson's 'As by the dead we love to sit,' " *The Explicator* 35 (1976): 10.

5   Weisbuch, *Emily Dickinson's Poetry*, p. 14.

6   Griffith cites this poem as one which indicates a "scrupulously ironical outlook. She argues that since the actions of the world are themselves uncontrollable, the best the inhabitant of the world can do is to cultivate from within the ironist's rigidly controlled responses." *The Long Shadow,* p. 44. Although Dickinson is a master ironist, I do not see any irony in this poem; rather than a "rigidly controlled response," it seems to convey an open acknowledgment of abundant pain as a fact of experience.

7   David Porter writes that the "skein" is a "description" of the rainbow. *The Art of Emily Dickinson's Early Poetry,* p. 84. But Dickinson says that the skein "would suit" as well as a rainbow were it not for the rainbow's transience: thus she is contrasting a negligible permanent possession (a mere skein) with the actual rainbow.

8   Richard Wilbur, in his essay "Sumptuous Destitution," comments usefully on this poem: "To the eye of desire, all things are seen in a profound perspective, either moving or gesturing toward the vanishing-point. Or to use a figure which may be closer to Miss Dickinson's thought, to the eye of desire the world is a centrifuge, in which all things are straining or flying toward the occult circumference." Sewall, *Emily Dickinson: A Collection of Critical Essays,* p. 133.

9   Dickinson rejected these lines as unsuitable for her friend, surely realizing that they comprised a left-handed compliment at best. The idea that Anthon in herself cannot compare with the poet's idealized object of adoration is noticeably absent from the rather maudlin poem she composed as a replacement:

I shall not murmur if at last
The ones I loved below
Permission have to understand
For what I shunned them so—
Divulging it would rest my Heart
But it would ravage their's —
Why, Katie, Treason has a Voice—
But mine—dispels—in Tears.
(P 1410)

10 Another significant metaphor for fulfillment is that of food; "starvation" is analogous to poverty in such poems, and the operative principle of ratio is the same. In Poem 439, for example, Dickinson notes: "Undue Significance a starving man attaches / To Food," concluding that "It was the Distance— / Was Savory—". See also "I had been hungry, all the Years" (P 579) and "None can experience stint" (P 771).

11 Cynthia Chaliff, "The Psychology of Economics in Emily Dickinson," *Literature and Psychology* 18 (1968): 93.

12 Porter, *Dickinson: The Modern Idiom,* p. 114.

13 In reproducing this poem I have departed from the Variorum, which places a period at the end of line 8, and followed R. W. Franklin's suggestion that the punctuation should actually be a dash; study of the facsimile manuscript confirms Franklin's opinion. See *The Editing of Emily Dickinson* (Madison: University of Wisconsin Press, 1967), p. 16; and p. 149, n. 34.

14 These well-known lines provide a good example of such complaints:

Of Course—I prayed—
And did God care?
He cared as much as on the Air
A Bird—had stamped her foot—
And cried "Give Me". . . .
(P 376)

15 Emerson, "Swedenborg; or, The Mystic," *Complete Works*: IV, 121.

16 This poem's central image recurs in another poem which envisions Christ as the schoolmaster:

I shall know why—when Time is over—
And I have ceased to wonder why—
Christ will explain each separate anguish
In the fair schoolroom of the sky—
(P 193)

Some telling differences between the two poems should be noted, however: Christ is portrayed as a gentle explainer who justifies the poet's experience after she has ceased to need such justification—a fairly conventional vision of divine benevolence. In the later poem, however, the more dramatic (and frequently clashing) relationship between the quest poet and an omniscient Father focuses on a vision of justice which may be attained within human experience, thus enhancing that experience. Thus the infrequent, usually sentimental use of Christ in Dickinson's poems as compared with the pervasive, ambiguous, and powerful presence of God as "Father."

17 Note to Variorum Edition: II, 790.

18 Myron Ochshorn clarifies the focus of the poem: "Despite its New Testament symbolism, the poem has little to do with the Christian concept of redemption. Its stress is entirely on the possibility of happiness in the present world, not in any hereafter." "In Search of Emily Dickinson," *New Mexico Quarterly* 23 (1953): 98. This is perhaps an overstatement, since the faith with which Dickinson bleats to understand *is* concerned with a secure concept of the hereafter. But Ochshorn is right in adding: "The insight central in the poem is that great joy can come only where accompanied by great suffering. It is Dostoievsky's theme, not Christ's."

19 In "Dickinson's 'As Watchers hang upon the East,' " *The Explicator* 35 (1976): 5, Laurence Perrine notes that "if true" represents Dickinson's "characteristic doubt," and adds: "But the point here is that it makes little difference whether it is true or not. The real value of heaven is not in its actuality, but in the hope of its actuality, sweetening an existence which might otherwise be intolerable." Although this statement is accurate when applied to the effects of such hope upon life itself, it is surely going too far to imagine that it "makes little difference" to Dickinson what lies beyond death; she spent her entire life speculating on this problem.

20 It is surely significant that the most recurrent word in Dickinson's entire canon, with the single exception of the pronoun "I," is the word "as"—it appears 980 times. See S. P. Rosenbaum, *Concordance to the Poems*, p. 865.

21 Weisbuch, *Emily Dickinson's Poetry*, pp. 11, 12. Weisbuch's chapter on Dickinson's use of analogy is consistently brilliant and should be considered indispensable reading for anyone seriously grappling with Dickinson's poetry.

22 Emerson, *Journals*: V, 342 (italics mine). It should already be apparent that Emerson is a possible source for Dickinson's use of the mathematics metaphor. Early in his career he acknowledged the issue of "wanting mathematical certainty for moral truths," and stated an incremental theory that is strikingly similar to Dickinson's idea that her poems are both the means and record of a measurable progress: "This Book is my Savings Bank. I grow richer because I have somewhere to deposit my earnings; and fractions are worth more to me because corresponding fractions are waiting here that shall be made integers by their addition." *Journals*: III, 197, 246. See especially Poem 773, where Dickinson notes that her own wealth has "grown by slender addings / To so esteemed a size . . . ," and the first stanza of poem 843:

> I made slow Riches but my Gain
> Was steady as the Sun
> And every Night, it numbered more
> Than the preceding One. . . .

23 Griffith, in discussing Dickinson as an existential writer, notes her resistance to any "fixed views"—whether based upon her own "exact knowledge" or a surrender to the conviction that life is meaningless. He continues: "If the flowing of detail might suggest to Emily Dickinson that incoherency had triumphed, still by the *manner of the flowing*—by the fact of its *constancy*—she was forever drawn back to the idea that a Plan existed and could ultimately be spelled out" (italics mine). *The Long Shadow*, p. 263. It is this constancy of "manner," within the flux of time and experience, that Dickinson asserts through her ratios.

24 Weisbuch, *Emily Dickinson's Poetry*, p. 1.

25 In another poem, Dickinson pictures herself as a mathematician suddenly interrupted in her problem-solving, baffled by the "statelier sums" of a new problem which defies her human abilities:

> Low at my problem bending,
> Another problem comes—
> Larger than mine—Serener—
> Involving statelier sums.
>
> I check my busy pencil,
> My figures file away.
> Wherefore, my baffled fingers
> Thy perplexity?
> (P 69)

Chapter 6

1 *The Letters of Ralph Waldo Emerson*, ed. Ralph L. Rusk, 6 vols. (New York: Columbia University Press, 1939), Vol. III: 9–10. All subsequent reference to Emerson's letters are to this edition and will be cited by volume and page number.

Emerson had also noted, in "Experience": "I take this evanescence and lubricity of all objects, which lets them slip through our fingers then when we clutch hardest, to be the most unhandsome part of our condition. Nature does not like to be observed, and likes that we should be her fools and playmates." *Complete Works:* III, 49.

2   Yvor Winters, "Emily Dickinson and the Limits of Judgment," in Richard B. Sewall, ed., *Emily Dickinson: A Collection of Critical Essays*, p. 35.

3   Ibid., p. 36.

4   Paul J. Ferlazzo, *Emily Dickinson* (Boston: Twayne Publishers, 1976), p. 124. David Porter comments on the poem: "She is not celebrating the change but calibrating it, dissecting it, placing it in no system. In the starkest modernist way, the poem is an analysis without an explanation." *Dickinson: The Modern Idiom*, p. 260.

5   Thomas H. Johnson discusses the four existing versions of the poem—three in holograph, one a transcript made by Dickinson's cousin, Frances Norcross—and dismisses strong internal evidence that the three inferior stanzas were indeed added to the poem in later versions: "Emily Dickinson always shortened her poems if she made stanza changes in later fair copies—never lengthened them" (Variorum, II, 755). This statement is not accurate, however: see, for example, the two versions of Poem 433. The earlier version of 14 lines was evidently written about 1862; the later version of 24 lines, about 1865. The problematic three stanzas of the poem under discussion, though poetically inferior, have a clarity which the received text lacks, and it seems possible that Dickinson, recognizing the poem's obscurity, added them in the effort to clarify her theme. The fact that the longer version was sent to her Norcross cousins—certainly the most intellectually limited of her correspondents—would seem to support this view.

6   One suspects that Frances Norcross erred in transcribing line 11: "When sunrise is, that is it not" is meaningless; "that" should probably read "then."

7   Anderson finds in the opening comparison, "As imperceptibly as Grief," an indication of this larger awareness and outlook: "The manifest comparison is apt. Nothing lapses so imperceptibly as grief, for one never feels, or at least admits, any diminishing of it until the sudden realization that it has already gone. But the latent meanings should fit too, because the similarity of their vanishings implies some likeness in their essences. How then is summer a grief? Only for those whose eyes are set on autumn. There is indeed a recurrent note in her poetry that life is mostly pain, and death a release into some kind of eternal peace." *Emily Dickinson's Poetry*, p. 150.

8   In discussing Dickinson as "the poet of dread," Clark Griffith claims that "out of her aversion to time and change there emerge the darkest moments in Emily Dickinson's poetry." In his discussion (*The Long Shadow*, pp. 84–93) he uses "Further in Summer than the Birds" and "A light exists in Spring" as poems conveying this aversion. The result is a wholly one-sided reading which ignores entirely the tone and rhythm of these poems, their moments of quiet, even tender emotion and awe. He writes that in these poems time and change are seen "as deliberately malevolent, as treacherous forces which express . . . a profound contempt for the human observer's needs" (p. 88). They are "monstrous personifications, a pair of forces that have set out intentionally to persecute the human observer" (p. 89). As for the religious language in "Further in Summer than the Birds": "The consequence of this sort of language is one of investing temporality with a distinctively ceremonial guise. Emily Dickinson shows time and change beating down upon the human observer in the form of a grim, remorseless and overbearing ritual" (p. 91). Through such intemperate, distorted readings Griffith, eager to force Dickinson into the role of a relentlessly tragic poet he has conceived for her, invests these

poems with a paranoid fear and bitterness which they entirely lack. Time and change are painful forces to Dickinson, but in poems such as these she grows through her profound, complex perception of their tragic beauty, not through a mere ugly reaction to the pain itself.

9 Variorum Edition: III, 1061–62.

10 Elizabeth F. Perlmutter, "Hide and Seek: Emily Dickinson's Use of the Existential Sentence," *Language and Style: An International Journal* 10 (1977): 117–18. Perlmutter's discussion relates directly to Dickinson's concern with transience and more largely to her emphases upon perceptual confrontation and upon violations of spatial and temporal order: "Dickinson used the existential sentence to arrive at a poetic form that offered respite from the poetry of concentrated selfhood and the fixed conventions of self, place, and time. The form itself could thus stand as a guarantee that, should the self fail to maintain the stability of its perception, the world, as an array of mysterious particulars, would still be 'there,' drawing the mind toward its elusive, tantalizing disclosures" (p. 118).

11 In her valuable psychological and critical study, *Emily Dickinson and the Image of Home*, p. 89, Jean McClure Mudge made use of her unique vantage point (she has been Resident Curator at the Dickinson Homestead) to comment on this poem: "A double mahogany sleigh-style bed dominated [Dickinson's bedroom], placed as it was on the east wall with advantageous, though veiled, views of Main Street and Austin's grounds. . . . Waking one morning, she doubtless conceived the poem 'The Angle of a Landscape— / That every time I wake— / Between my Curtain and the Wall / Upon an ample Crack.' Into this crack, she fitted a bough of apples, a chimney, a hill, a weathervane, and finally a steeple. She may have piled the scene on purpose but the delight of doing so seems motivated by a more serious purpose than cataloguing the landscape. Except for the bough of apples, replaced by a snow-burdened branch in another season, all the other subjects of her view 'never stir at all,' as she claims in the last line of the poem. Controlled, structured, dependable, above all trustworthy objects, so much in contrast to Dickinson's own inner life. . . . Once again, Emily seems to be seeking supports which she does not find within herself, her room, her house, but rather ones which could only be bestowed by Nature or by God, not immune to change but perhaps more stable than the poet."

12 Sharon Cameron remarks: "In the 'Bough of Apples—' forming its own angle, the subject comes to light readily enough, however deceptively it appears on the wrong side of the horizon, but most poems are not so quick to distinguish the landscape from the linear displacements of the speaker's angle of vision. At a more subtle level of obliquity, entire landscapes can seem like indirect renderings of something larger of which they are a mere part. Landscapes are thus generally symbolic in the poems, bearers of more meaning than a given speaker can interpret (as in 'There's a certain Slant of light'), or they are deficient of meaning, unable to rise to its occasion (as in 'A Light exists in Spring'), and this excess or deficit indicates a profound discrepancy between the multitudinous lines of the world and the optics of a central vision that, more often than not, they may be accused of baffling." *Lyric Time*, p. 5.

13 Robert Weisbuch calls this the "sage-sufferer compound," a seemingly self-contradictory stance through which Dickinson, as a "wounded dialectician," is able "to charge

hypothesis with feeling, to add a note of experiential authority to logic." *Emily Dickinson's Poetry*, p. 65.

Chapter 7

1　Porter, *Dickinson: The Modern Idiom*, pp. 152, 294.
2　Sherwood, *Circumference and Circumstance*, p. 230.
3　Hagenbüchle, "New Developments in Dickinson Criticism," p. 453.
4　Porter, *Dickinson: The Modern Idiom*, p. 184.
5　Bickman, *The Unsounded Centre*, p. 145.
6　David C. Estes, " 'Out upon Circumference': Emily Dickinson's Search for Location," *Essays in Literature* 6 (1979): 207.
7　One poem of 1862 describes the specific disillusionment which led to this power. It begins, "I meant to have but modest needs— / Such as Content—and Heaven"; it notes that she had been naive enough to "take the Tale for true— / That 'Whatsoever Ye shall ask— / Itself be given You'—". The poem ends bitterly:

But I, grown shrewder—scan the Skies
With a suspicious Air—
As Children—swindled for the first
All Swindlers—be—infer—
(P 476)

8　Albert Gelpi remarks: "All she can say with certainty is that a fundamental flaw condemns her to contingency and in the end to obliteration. Her contingency stems from her inability to find a fixed center in herself and nature; the something lost is her connection with the All." *The Tenth Muse*, p. 238.
9　Rich, "Vesuvius at Home," p. 52.
10　Rebecca Patterson, in her intriguing chart of "Emily Dickinson's Gems," illustrates the frequency with which Dickinson employed the pearl image. According to the chart, the pearl appears on 31 occasions in her poems, 16 of them—more than half—in poems of 1862. See Patterson, *Emily Dickinson's Imagery* (Amherst: University of Massachusetts Press, 1979), p. 76.
11　Rebecca Patterson notes the inventiveness Dickinson displays in her use of the pearl image and discusses its varying symbolic values. Ultimately she focuses upon Sue Dickinson as the central figure in the poet's life and interprets the pearl as a symbol for Sue— the poet's great love, lost forever when Sue married Austin Dickinson. This argument, however, unnecessarily limits the scope of Dickinson's pearl image. While the pearl may refer, on occasion, to her feeling for Sue—or for another romantic lover—the autobiographical meaning is always secondary to Dickinson's larger themes. And even in an autobiographical context, I believe that Dickinson most often uses the pearl to symbolize an aspect of her own selfhood rather than to confer value upon another. See Patterson, *Emily Dickinson's Imagery*, pp. 85–93.
12　Jean Mudge notes: "The poem 'Essential oils are wrung' . . . hints of the bureau's use as a vault for the poet's unknown writings, protecting her treasure of insights, her 'essential oils.' " *Emily Dickinson and the Image of Home*, p. 92.
13　For example, Theodora Ward says of this poem: "The pearl is used as only one of several

ways of estimating the value of the person whom she names in the final lines a 'Monarch.' " *The Capsule of the Mind: Chapters in the Life of Emily Dickinson* (Cambridge: Harvard University Press, 1961), p. 62.

14 Realizing that this poem was written in 1861, just before the commencement of Dickinson's *annus mirabilis* when she would write 366 poems, the reader can easily share in her sense of excitement. Inder Nath Kher remarks of this poem: "Dickinson shows readiness to invest the spiritual earnings of her lifetime in order to gain one pearl, which symbolizes the precious gift of her art and identity." *Landscape of Absence*, p. 244.

15 Vivian R. Pollak notes: "This poem embodies both the pathetic sense of her loss and the reasons for it," and adds: "the pearl is the price of consciousness." " 'That Fine Prosperity': Emily Dickinson's Use of Economic Metaphors," *Modern Language Quarterly* 34 (1973): 173.

16 The poem's imagery recalls another poem dealing with renunciation versus easy fulfillment:

Did the Harebell loose her girdle
To the lover Bee
Would the Bee the Harebell *hallow*
Much as formerly?

Did the "Paradise"—persuaded—
Yield her moat of pearl—
Would the Eden *be* an Eden,
Or the Earl—an *Earl*?
(P 213)

Robert Weisbuch, in his brilliant explication of this deceptively "simple" poem (*Emily Dickinson's Poetry*, pp. 16–18), concludes that it illustrates Dickinson's "negative law": "That law includes God, includes essence itself. By the time we derive the law, its imaging has hit upon so many areas of consciousness—social, libidinal, natural, mythic, cosmological—that whatever areas have not been hit feel the shot nonetheless" (p. 17). This poem, moreover, clarifies Dickinson's identification of her consecrated poetic identity with her sexual identity.

17 For a discussion of Dickinson's possible debt to Robert Browning's *Paracelsus* for the Malay / pearl figure, see Capps, *Emily Dickinson's Reading*, pp. 89–91.

18 Porter, *Art of Emily Dickinson's Early Poetry*, pp. 10–11. Thomas H. Johnson notes, moreover, the extent of Dickinson's metrical skill in this poem itself: "Here she uses three varieties of rhyme: identical, exact, suspended. The idea of the poem juxtaposes the tyro and the artist, and the form does likewise for the two stanzas. The alternate iambic dimeter-trimeter regularity of the first stanza is abandoned in the second, where the meter follows its own convention, striking out in a new direction. Most interesting are the two final lines. The thought of line seven concerns the artist whose craft is learned; that of line eight, the learner. It can hardly be a matter of chance that the metric patterns of the two lines enforce the thought by reversing the beat thus: ∪--∪ / -∪∪-." *Emily Dickinson: An Interpretive Biography* (Cambridge: Harvard University Press, 1955), p. 110.

19 Richard Chase comments rather oddly that "in this poem her subject is death. For the poem says in effect: 'What need I care for earthly wealth and earthly position, who am dying and who in death will be crowned a queen?' For the 'ample sea' is immortality;

the rubies are missiles from whose wounds we slowly die." *Emily Dickinson*, pp. 172–73. It is difficult to see in what sense the rubies of the poems are "missiles" which wound the speaker. Rather they are symbols, like her queenly status, of her own self-esteem as poet. She is writing not about death but about ecstatic life in poetry.

20   Michael R. Dressman, "Empress of Calvary: Mystical Marriage in the Poems of Emily Dickinson," *South Atlantic Bulletin* 42 (1977): 40.

21   Griffith, *The Long Shadow*, p. 176.

22   It is interesting to note that Dickinson switches to a masculine pronoun when speaking of the woman's inner, aggressive, creative self: "But only to *Himself* be known / The Fathoms they abide." For discussions of this characteristic identification of masculine identity with Dickinson's poetic identity, see Cody, *After Great Pain*, pp. 121–23; Mudge, *Emily Dickinson and the Image of Home*, pp. 34–35; and Gelpi, *The Tenth Muse*, pp. 247–58. Mudge sees the masculine and feminine traits in Dickinson's character as deriving directly from the poet's parents: "[Edward Dickinson's] special contribution to his older daughter was to her private self, the inner woman whose desire for independence reached the same heights as her father's, if it did not exceed his" (p. 35). Gelpi discusses her masculine identification as a form of "animus connection."

23   Chase, *Emily Dickinson*, p. 94.

24   John Cody writes: "The abnormal prolongation of latency experienced by Emily Dickinson really represents an inability to resolve the problems of the oedipal period. This dilemma, in turn, was founded on an earlier severe conflict in the oral sphere, involving the maternal-deprivation syndrome. . . . Underlying all the frustrated yearning for maturity and the clinging to childhood that characterize Emily Dickinson's adolescent and young adult years is always this deeper problem, which made the failure of her hopes for a normal life unavoidable." *After Great Pain*, p. 121. Although this comment helps to explain the "loss" of Dickinson's early years, it does not take into account the success of her effort to mature artistically.

25   Rich, "Vesuvius at Home," p. 58.

26   Another poem also shows an acute feminist awareness:

When a Lover is a Beggar
Abject is his Knee—
When a Lover is an Owner
Different is he—

What he begged is then the Beggar—
Oh disparity—
Bread of Heaven resents bestowal
Like an obloquy—
(P 1314)

27   Daniel B. Shea, discussing Dickinson in the context of American spiritual autobiography, writes that "Emily Dickinson has been described as turning the experience of defeat into gains for consciousness; pain and perception are intimately associated in the tragic economy of loss. The theme is indeed a familiar one in her poetry and the very existence of the poetry is evidence of the theme's validity. Yet there is no definitive Emily Dickinson poem, no structural point in her gathered writing at which one can say that here,

climactically, vision outruns suffering." *Spiritual Autobiography in Early America* (Princeton: Princeton University Press, 1968), p. 262. I would suggest that because of its broad thematic scope and its tone of confident resolution, "One Blessing had I than the rest" is just such a poem, though the emphasis is not upon vision "outrunning" suffering but upon the poet's consciousness having attained a permanent understanding of their relationship. Carole Anne Taylor writes that the poem "utilizes an ironic logic common in Dickinson's poems, setting up expectations in the developmental stanzas which are suddenly and bitterly disappointed in the last stanza." "Kierkegaard and the Ironic Voices," p. 572. In response, I would again stress the *tone* of the poem. Unlike many of Dickinson's poems of "bitter disappointment," this one displays a tone of resignation and an acceptance of the limitations of mortal consciousness. The final stanza signals an end to bitter speculations, as well as the poet's decision to make the most of unavoidable conditions.

28   Pollak, " 'That Fine Prosperity,' " pp. 161–79. Though overemphasizing Dickinson's concern with making *social* commentary through her use of economic metaphors, this article nevertheless contains valuable insights into Dickinson's method, asserting that "Dickinson uses [the] concepts of want and wealth and price and labor to work out a notion of subjective valuation and to delineate an intangible estate" (p. 163).

29   Richard Wilbur remarks of this stanza: "We often assent to the shock of a paradox before we understand it, but those lines are so just and so concentrated as to explode their meaning instantly in the mind. They did not come so easily, I think, to Emily Dickinson. Unless I guess wrongly as to chronology, such lines were the fruit of long poetic research; the poet had worked toward them through much study of the way certain emotions can usurp consciousness entirely, annulling our sense of past and future, cancelling near and far, converting all time and space to a joyous or grievous here and now. It is in their ways of annihilating time and space that bliss and despair are comparable." Richard Wilbur, "Sumptuous Destitution," in Sewall, ed., *Emily Dickinson: A Collection of Critical Essays,* p. 128.

30   In a famous letter to T. W. Higginson, Dickinson notes, "You inquire my Books—For Poets—I have Keats—and Mr and Mrs Browning. For Prose—Mr Ruskin—Sir Thomas Browne—and the Revelations" (L 261).

Chapter 8

1   Louise Bogan, "Emily Dickinson," p. 141.

2   Porter, *Dickinson: The Modern Idiom,* pp. 188, 190.

3   Typical of those critics who attempt to make Dickinson's concern with death appear normal is Millicent Todd Bingham, in *Emily Dickinson's Home* (New York: Harper Brothers, 1955), pp. 179–80: noting the prevalence of disease and early death in nineteenth-century New England, she writes that "the Dickinson orchard adjoined the burying ground where the final rites took place. Every funeral procession must pass their house. The wonder is not that Emily as a young girl thought and often wrote about death, but that any buoyancy of spirit remained." Even Jean McClure Mudge, writing in 1975, leans toward this view: "One of the few aspects of Emily's mind which dates her for most modern readers is her constant curiosity and apprehension about the end of life. . . . Nineteenth-century New England was still plagued with the empirical rea-

sons which had caused Puritans two centuries before to be perpetually contemplating life under the omnipresence of death. Arduous winters and uncontrollable epidemics, no matter the season, might carry off many of Emily's closest friends and relatives in a single year." *Emily Dickinson and the Image of Home*, p. 192.

But, even granting a more pervasive presence of death in daily existence than prevails today, this attitude is naive, especially from a psychoanalytic point of view; and it ignores a multitude of biographical facts. John Cody notes, for instance, that "Throughout her life Emily Dickinson displayed an avid interest in death scenes. She thirsted for details"; he quotes numerous passages from her letters in which "the idea of death is introduced out of context by means of the flimsiest of transitional passages"; and he quotes other revealing passages, such as this sentence from a letter to Austin (L 53): "Vinnie tells me she has detailed the *news*—she reserved the *deaths* for me." He notes certain strange aspects of Dickinson's behavior: at age twenty-six, for example, she clipped out of the newspaper an advertisement for tombstones. Dr. Cody concludes: "The religious influences, the literary ones, and repeated actual confrontations with death undoubtedly made their contributions to Emily Dickinson's preoccupation with mortality. But it should be apparent that these forces, in their convergence on the poet, found fertile psychological ground." His discussion of the psychodynamics of Dickinson's death-obsession is both judicious and illuminating. *After Great Pain*, pp. 272–76.

Emily Stipes Watts, in *The Poetry of American Women from 1632 to 1945* (Austin: University of Texas Press, 1977), p. 126, comments on the intensity of the death poetry by relating it to that of women's elegiac verse of the early nineteenth century.

4   A poem written about ten years later presents a similar situation—the attitude of a person about to die—but reaches a precisely opposite conclusion: life becomes all the more precious in ratio to the imminence of death. The doomed person does not walk home with "gayer sandals," but rather is "famished" in his awareness of what he is losing:

Which was to famish, then or now—
The difference of Day
Ask him unto the Gallows led—
With morning in the sky
(P 1125)

5   Weisbuch, *Emily Dickinson's Poetry*, p. 91.
6   Emerson, "The Divinity School Address," *Complete Works*: I, 120.
7   Pearce, *Continuity of American Poetry*, pp. 180–81.
8   Weisbuch, *Emily Dickinson's Poetry*, p. 83.
9   Judith Banzer, " 'Compound Manner': Emily Dickinson and the Metaphysical Poets," *American Literature* 32 (1961): 417.
10   Bloom, "Internalization of Quest-Romance," p. 18.
11   Harold Bloom, "Death and the Native Strain in American Poetry," *Social Research* 39 (1972): 454.
12   Emerson, *Journals*: IV, 343–44.
13   Charles Anderson offers a different reading. He considers these "humorous verses," in which Dickinson wishes to "satirize her own attempt at an inside view of death." I find no humor in the poem, and if it is satirical, then Dickinson is surely satirizing the speak-

er's *evasion* of death, not the poet's own attempt to intuit death's meaning. See Anderson, *Emily Dickinson's Poetry*, pp. 232–33.

A later poem, "I never hear that one is dead," may serve as a gloss upon this one, since its subject is precisely the same: the terror of full consciousness. The last two stanzas are as follows:

Beliefs are Bandaged, like the Tongue
When Terror were it told
In any Tone commensurate
Would strike us instant Dead

I do not know the man so bold
He dare in lonely Place
That awful stranger Consciousness
Deliberately face—
(P 1323)

Dickinson did, however, know a woman who was "so bold."

14 "This is Night—now," she warns in a letter to Mrs. Holland, "but we are not dreaming" (L 525).

15 Charles Anderson notes the ambiguity of the "fond Ambush": "The modern meaning of this adjective is loving; etymologically it means foolishly naive and credulous." But then, inexplicably, he calls the poem's conclusion a "pretended nightmare of nihilism." I consider the poem's initial statement of truth to be "pretended" in order to state the reality of Dickinson's private nightmare. See Anderson, *Emily Dickinson's Poetry*, p. 264. As Clark Griffith notes, the poem conveys Dickinson's "deeply rooted sense of dread." As the poem progresses, "its facade of unconcern goes to pieces, exposing beneath its set features a residue of pure fear." *The Long Shadow*, p. 76.

16 Albert Gelpi comments upon the complexity of this figure in Dickinson's work: "In the pattern of her mind, since 'The Test of Love—is Death,' then death itself came as a lover; since death was crowned with power, he came as a lover-king; since death justified the 'Guilt' of Love, he came as a lover-redeemer. . . . In several poems it is impossible to identify the 'him' as lover, death, or Christ." Gelpi concludes: "The significant fact is that Emily Dickinson did not make the distinction in her own mind." *Emily Dickinson*, p. 113.

17 In one poem the two lovers do not even speak to one another, but communicate wholly through eye contact; the organs of perception become those of communication as well, so that the speaker's entire destiny has evolved into this single perceptual relationship:

It was a quiet way—
He asked if I was his—
I made no answer of the Tongue
But answer of the Eyes—
And then He bore me on
Before this mortal noise. . . .
(P 1053)

18 Joanne Feit Diehl comments: "Given a protean form, death becomes, of course, easier

to confront than if perceived as an undifferentiated, amorphous force recognized solely by its effects. Through the creation of this shadowy Stranger, Dickinson projects an 'other' whom she can approach and with whom she may speak. Such a strategy allows her to relinquish the role of passive victim for the more aggressive act of confronting the powers of silence itself." "Dickinson and the American Self," *ESQ: A Journal of the American Renaissance* 26 (1980): 3.

19ʹ I believe that Ruth Miller errs in saying that the poem "carries the soul farther past the experience of death, . . . leaving the factor of time behind. The soul has survived, it has not descended, and waits now to traverse the vast distance to the place of redemption." She concludes that "Mortal knowledge is finished but immortal faith has replaced it." *Poetry of Emily Dickinson*, pp. 283, 285. Rather the poem marks the moment when mortal knowledge can *begin*, since the speaker "knows the worst," has faced the cold truth, and can proceed on her imaginative "Holiday."

20 Emerson, *Journals*: II, 517.

Chapter 9

1 See for example, Ford, *Heaven Beguiles the Tired,* pp. 69–92; and Griffith, *The Long Shadow,* pp. 111–49.

2 Although I will organize my discussion of the death poetry to conform to this progress as if it were a single movement, it should be emphasized that the progress is cyclic rather than linear.

3 Ford, who believes this poem is about the Civil War, says that "observed fact and religious faith clash" in the final stanza. *Heaven Beguiles the Tired,* p. 132. His description would serve for many Dickinson poems, but here the poet's declared faith insists upon a mysterious harmony, not a true "clash," between what she sees and what is ultimately true.

4 Weisbuch, *Emily Dickinson's Poetry,* pp. 112, 110.

5 Griffith, *The Long Shadow,* pp. 125–26.

6 Another poem stressing perception expresses a fear that it is the living, not the dead, who are "out of sight," suggesting that the perceiving consciousness is totally isolated from knowledge:

Three Weeks passed since I had seen Her—
Some Disease had vext
'Twas with Text and Village Singing
I beheld Her next

And a Company—our pleasure
To discourse alone—
Gracious now to me as any—
Gracious unto none—

Borne without dissent of Either
To the Parish night—
Of the Separated Parties
Which be out of sight?
(P 1061)

7 Robert Weisbuch's discussion of this poem is typically astute. He concludes that the poem "stresses the hurt of pain, the finality of death, the blank of uncertainty. It is the climactic poem of Dickinson's world of veto." *Emily Dickinson's Poetry*, pp. 99–102.

8 Another poem about the moment of death, Dickinson's single poem dealing with suicide, notes that the suicide feels "as if / His Mind were going blind" (P 1062).

9 Lawrence J. Langer, *The Age of Atrocity: Death in Modern Literature* (Boston: The Beacon Press, 1978), p. 21.

10 Frederic J. Hoffman, *The Mortal No: Death and the Modern Imagination* (Princeton: Princeton University Press, 1964), p. 4.

11 John Donne, *Selected Poetry*, ed. Marius Bewley (New York: New American Library, 1966), pp. 269–70.

12 She also realized, however, that the democratic realm of death could make her queenliness count for nought:

Not any higher stands the Grave
For Heroes than for Men—
Not any nearer for the Child
Than numb Three Score and Ten—

This latest Leisure equal lulls
The Beggar and his Queen
Propitiate this Democrat
A Summer's Afternoon—
(P 1256)

13 Here Dickinson uses the ruby because its color makes it an appropriate concretization of the unmeasured wine, but the ruby may be considered synonymous with the pearl image discussed earlier. Again Dickinson uses her mathematics to "measure" the value of life and to emphasize the status of her own identity and achievement.

14 It should be noted that most of these poems come after the period of the poet's greatest creativity (1861–63), a time when Dickinson most often emphasized the horror and possible finality of death; by contrast, the later poems are noticeably serener and more amenable to a positive viewpoint.

15 Clark Griffith notes that the poem is deliberately "ugly, about as barbarously ugly, indeed, as lyric poetry can be while still retaining its essentially lyric features." Griffith's extensive discussion of this point is useful, concluding that Dickinson's "technique [is] in perfect consonance with the point of view that it expresses," and that the style of the poem creates "an atmosphere of rigidly curbed hysteria." *The Long Shadow*, pp. 115–19.

16 Griffith notes that these particular lines "must be *under*read, so to speak—read in such a way that they emerge as blunt, literal statements of fact." Ibid., p. 117.

17 Emerson, *Nature, Complete Works*: I, 15.

18 Thomas H. Johnson notes: "Here is no mystical, transcendental identification with the divine, but rather an echo of the trumpet voice of the seers and prophets, who speak not visions only, but a judgment: identity cannot be lost." *Emily Dickinson: An Interpretive Biography*, p. 254.

Chapter 10

1 This last meaning of "mold" as a reproduced image was common in Dickinson's time. In her third letter to T. W. Higginson, in July 1862, she denies his request for a photograph and then comments: "It often alarms Father—He says Death might occur, and he has Molds of all the rest—but has no Mold of me . . ." (L 268).

2 Bloom, "Death and the Native Strain," p. 455.

3 ̇ Yvor Winters, "Emily Dickinson and the Limits of Judgment," in Richard B. Sewall, ed., *Emily Dickinson: A Collection of Critical Essays* (Englewood Cliffs: Prentice-Hall, 1963), p. 33.

4 Dickinson's mixed feelings about her continuing journey are described by Clark Griffith (*The Long Shadow,* pp. 139–40): "Ranging imaginatively down the road to the afterlife, Emily Dickinson proceeds with something less than the saint's assurance. But neither are her movements to be characterized as completely unwilling. 'Reluctance' and 'awe' are underlain by implied eagerness. As image balances out image or concept is made to match concept, all three emotions—awe, reluctance, *and* eagerness—are yoked together into a mixed, yet inextricably mixed, feeling about the destination ahead."

5 Geoffrey Hartman comments on the "suspended" quality of the poem's action: "In this little quest-romance Eternity is always *before* you. . . . The conception [of Eternity], obviously, is a motivating one in terms of the poem. The poet sees to see. Her mode is infinitive. Each stanza infers that one step which is not taken—into epiphany, or invisibility." Hartman concludes: "Her destiny—or is it her choice—seems to be to stay . . . on the threshold of vision." *Beyond Formalism* (New Haven: Yale University Press, 1970), pp. 349–50.

6 For a discussion of the poem's literal referents, see Laurence Perrine, " 'There are two Ripenings—one—of sight—,' " *The Explicator* 31 (1973), Item 65.

Bibliography

Abrams, M. H. *Natural Supernaturalism*. New York: Norton, 1971.

Anderson, Charles R. *Emily Dickinson's Poetry: Stairway of Surprise*. New York: Holt, Rinehart & Winston, 1960.

Arp, Thomas R. "Dramatic Poses in the Poetry of Emily Dickinson." Ph.D. dissertation, Stanford University, 1962.

Banzer, Judith. " 'Compound Manner': Emily Dickinson and the Metaphysical Poets," *American Literature* 32 (1961): 415–33.

Bickman, Martin. *The Unsounded Centre: Jungian Studies in American Romanticism*. Chapel Hill: University of North Carolina Press, 1980.

Bingham, Millicent Todd. *Emily Dickinson's Home*. New York: Harper Brothers, 1955.

Blackmur, R.P. "Emily Dickinson's Notation," in Richard B. Sewall, ed., *Emily Dickinson: A Collection of Critical Essays*. Englewood Cliffs: Prentice-Hall, 1963.

Bloom, Harold. "Death and the Native Strain in American Poetry," *Social Research* 39 (1972): 447–62.

————. *Figures of Capable Imagination*. New York: Seabury Press, 1976.

————. *The Visionary Company: A Reading of English Romantic Poetry*. Ithaca: Cornell University Press, 1961.

————, ed. *Romantic Poetry and Prose*. New York: Oxford University Press, 1973.

————, ed. *Romanticism and Consciousness: Essays in Criticism*. New York: Norton, 1970.

Bogan, Louise. "Emily Dickinson: A Mystical Poet," in Richard B. Sewall, ed., *Emily Dickinson: A Collection of Critical Essays*. Englewood Cliffs: Prentice-Hall, 1963.

Buckingham, Willis J. *Emily Dickinson: An Annotated Bibliography*. Bloomington: Indiana University Press, 1970.

Budick, E. Miller. "When the Soul Selects: Emily Dickinson's Attack on New England Symbolism," *American Literature* 51 (1979): 349–63.

Cambon, Glauco. "Emily Dickinson and the Crisis of Self-Reliance," in Myron Simon and Thornton H. Parsons, eds., *Transcendentalism and Its Legacy*. Ann Arbor: University of Michigan Press, 1966.

Cameron, Sharon. *Lyric Time: Dickinson and the Limits of Genre*. Baltimore: Johns Hopkins University Press, 1979.

Capps, Jack L. *Emily Dickinson's Reading: 1836–1886*. Cambridge: Harvard University Press, 1966.

Chaliff, Cynthia. "The Psychology of Economics in Emily Dickinson," *Literature and Psychology* 18 (1968): 93–100.

Chase, Richard. *Emily Dickinson.* New York: William Sloane, 1951.

Cody, John. *After Great Pain: The Inner Life of Emily Dickinson.* Cambridge: Harvard University Press, 1971.

Daniels, Edgar F. "Dickinson's 'As by the dead we love to sit,' " *The Explicator* 35 (1976): 10–11.

Davis, Thomas M. "Emily Dickinson and the Right of Way to Tripoli," in Robert J. DeMott and Sanford E. Marovitz, eds., *Artful Thunder: Versions of the Romantic Tradition in American Literature.* Kent, Ohio: Kent State University Press, 1975.

Dickinson, Emily. *The Letters of Emily Dickinson.* Edited by Thomas H. Johnson and Theodora Ward. 3 vols. Cambridge, Mass.: The Belknap Press of Harvard University Press, 1958.

———. *The Poems of Emily Dickinson.* Edited by Thomas H. Johnson. 3 vols. Cambridge, Mass.: The Belknap Press of Harvard University Press, 1955.

Diehl, Joanne Feit. "Dickinson and Bloom: An Antithetical Reading of Romanticism," *Texas Studies in Literature and Language* 23 (1981): 418–41.

———. "Dickinson and the American Self," *ESQ: A Journal of the American Renaissance* 26 (1980): 1–9.

———. *Dickinson and the Romantic Imagination.* Princeton: Princeton University Press, 1981.

Donne, John. *Selected Poetry,* ed. Marius Bewley. New York: New American Library, 1966.

Dressman, Michael R. "Empress of Calvary: Mystical Marriage in the Poems of Emily Dickinson," *South Atlantic Bulletin* 42 (1977): 39–43.

Duncan, Jeffrey L. "Joining Together / Putting Asunder: An Essay on Emily Dickinson's Poetry," *Missouri Review* 4 (1980): 111–29.

Emerson, Ralph Waldo. *The Complete Works of Ralph Waldo Emerson,* Centenary Edition, 12 vols. Boston and New York: Houghton Mifflin, 1903–04.

———. *The Journals of Ralph Waldo Emerson.* Edited by Edward W. Emerson and Waldo E. Forbes. 10 vols. Boston and New York: Houghton Mifflin, 1909–14.

———. *The Letters of Ralph Waldo Emerson.* Edited by Ralph L. Rusk. 6 vols. New York: Columbia University Press, 1939.

———. *Selections from Ralph Waldo Emerson: An Organic Anthology.* Edited by Stephen E. Whicher. Boston: Houghton Mifflin, 1957.

Estes, David C. " 'Out upon Circumference': Emily Dickinson's Search for Location," *Essays in Literature* 6 (1979) : 207–18.

Ferlazzo, Paul J. *Emily Dickinson.* Boston: Twayne Publishers, 1976.

Ford, Thomas W. *Heaven Beguiles the Tired: Death in the Poetry of Emily Dickinson.* University: University of Alabama Press, 1966.

Franklin, Ralph W. *The Editing of Emily Dickinson.* Madison: University of Wisconsin Press, 1967.

———, ed. *The Manuscript Books of Emily Dickinson: 1883–1895.* Cambridge: Harvard University Press, 1981.

Gelpi, Albert. "Emily Dickinson and the Deerslayer: The Dilemma of the Woman Poet in America," in Sandra M. Gilbert and Susan Gubar, eds., *Shakespeare's Sisters: Feminist Essays on Women Poets.* Bloomington and London: Indiana University Press, 1979.

———. *Emily Dickinson: The Mind of the Poet*. Cambridge: Harvard University Press, 1965.

———. *The Tenth Muse: The Psyche of the American Poet*. Cambridge: Harvard University Press, 1975.

Gilbert, Sandra M. and Susan Gubar. *The Madwoman in the Attic: The Woman Writer and the Nineteenth-Century Literary Imagination*. New Haven and London: Yale University Press, 1979.

———, eds. *Shakespeare's Sisters: Feminist Essays on Women Poets*. Bloomington and London: Indiana University Press, 1979.

Greeley, Andrew M. *Ecstasy as Knowledge*. Englewood Cliffs: Prentice-Hall, 1974.

Griffith, Clark W. *The Long Shadow: Emily Dickinson's Tragic Poetry*. Princeton: Princeton University Press, 1964.

Hagenbüchle, Roland. "New Developments in Dickinson Criticism," *Anglia* 97 (1979): 452–74.

———. "Sign and Process: The Concept of Language in Emerson and Dickinson," *ESQ: A Journal of the American Renaissance* 25 (1979): 137–55.

Hartman, Geoffrey. *Beyond Formalism*. New Haven: Yale University Press, 1970.

Hawthorne, Nathaniel. *The English Notebooks of Nathaniel Hawthorne*. Edited by Randall Stewart. New York: Oxford University Press, 1941.

Henry, Nat. "Dickinson's 'As by the dead we love to sit,' " *The Explicator*, January 1973: Item 35.

Hoffman, Frederic J. *The Mortal No: Death and the Modern Imagination*. Princeton: Princeton University Press, 1964.

Hopkins, Vivian. *Spires of Form: A Study of Emerson's Aesthetic Theory*. Cambridge: Harvard University Press, 1951.

James, William. *The Varieties of Religious Experience*. New York: The Modern Library, 1929.

Johnson, Thomas H. *Emily Dickinson: An Interpretive Biography*. Cambridge: Harvard University Press, 1955.

Johnston, William. *The Still Point: Reflections on Zen and Christian Mysticism*. New York: Fordham University Press, 1970.

Keller, Karl. *The Only Kangaroo Among the Beauty: Emily Dickinson and America*. Baltimore: Johns Hopkins University Press, 1979.

Kher, Inder Nath. *The Landscape of Absence: Emily Dickinson's Poetry*. New Haven: Yale University Press, 1974.

Langer, Lawrence J. *The Age of Atrocity: Death in Modern Literature*. Boston: The Beacon Press, 1978.

Lieber, Todd M. *Endless Experiments: Essays on the Heroic Experience in American Romanticism*. Columbus, Ohio: Ohio State University Press, 1973.

McGuire, Mary Ann C. "A Metaphorical Pattern in Emily Dickinson," *American Transcendental Quarterly* 29 (1976): 83–85.

Matthiessen, F. O. *American Renaissance: Art and Expression in the Age of Emerson and Whitman*. New York: Oxford University Press, 1968.

———. "The Problem of the Private Poet," *Kenyon Review* 7 (1949): 584–97.

Melville, Herman. *The Writings of Herman Melville*. Edited by Harrison Hayford, Hershel Parker, and G. Thomas Tanselle. 10 vols. Evanston, Ill.: Northwestern University Press and the Newberry Library, 1968.

Miller, Ruth. *The Poetry of Emily Dickinson*. Middletown: Wesleyan University Press, 1968.

Moseley, Edwin. "The Gambit of Emily Dickinson," *The University of Kansas City Review* 16 (1949): 11–19.

Mudge, Jean McClure. *Emily Dickinson and the Image of Home*. Amherst: University of Massachusetts Press, 1975.

Mulder, William. "Seeing 'New Englandly': Planes of Perception in Emily Dickinson and Robert Frost," *The New England Quarterly* 52 (1979): 550–59.

Ochshorn, Myron. "In Search of Emily Dickinson," *New Mexico Quarterly* 23 (1953): 94–106.

Patterson, Rebecca. *Emily Dickinson's Imagery*. Amherst: University of Massachusetts Press, 1979.

———. *The Riddle of Emily Dickinson*. Boston: Houghton Mifflin, 1951.

Pearce, Roy Harvey. *The Continuity of American Poetry*. Princeton: Princeton University Press, 1961.

Perlmutter, Elizabeth F. "Hide and Seek: Emily Dickinson's Use of the Existential Sentence," *Language and Style: An International Journal* 10 (1977): 109–19.

Perrine, Laurence. "Dickinson's 'As by the dead we love to sit,' " *The Explicator*, February 1975: Item 49.

———. "Dickinson's 'As by the dead we love to sit,' " *The Explicator* 36 (1978): 32–33.

———. "Dickinson's 'As Watchers hang upon the East,' " *The Explicator* 35 (1976): 4–5.

———. " 'There are two Ripenings—one—of sight—,' " *The Explicator* 31 (1973): Item 65.

Pollak, Vivian R. " 'That Fine Prosperity' : Emily Dickinson's Use of Economic Metaphors," *Modern Language Quarterly* 34 (1973): 161–79.

Porter, David. *The Art of Emily Dickinson's Early Poetry*. Cambridge: Harvard University Press, 1966.

———. *Dickinson: The Modern Idiom*. Cambridge: Harvard University Press, 1981.

———. "Emily Dickinson: The Poetics of Doubt," *Emerson Society Quarterly* 60 (1979): 86–93.

Reynolds, Jerry Ferris. " 'Banishment from Native Eyes': The Reason for Emily Dickinson's Seclusion Reconsidered," *The Markham Review* 8 (1979): 41–48.

Rich, Adrienne. "Vesuvius at Home: The Power of Emily Dickinson," *Parnassus: Poetry in Review* 5 (1976): 49–74.

Rogers, B. J. "The Truth Told Slant: Emily Dickinson's Poetic Mode," *Texas Studies in Literature and Language* 14 (1972): 329–36.

Rosenbaum, S. P., ed. *A Concordance to the Poems of Emily Dickinson*. Ithaca: Cornell University Press, 1964.

Rosenthal, Bernard. *City of Nature: Journeys to Nature in the Age of American Romanticism*. Newark: University of Delaware Press, 1980.

Sewall, Richard B. *The Life of Emily Dickinson*. New York: Farrar, Straus & Giroux, 1974.

———, ed. *Emily Dickinson: A Collection of Critical Essays*. Englewood Cliffs: Prentice-Hall, 1963.

Shea, Daniel B. *Spiritual Autobiography in Early America*. Princeton: Princeton University Press, 1968.

Sherwood, William Robert. *Circumference and Circumstance: Stages in the Mind and Art of Emily Dickinson*. New York and London: Columbia University Press, 1968.

Taylor, Carole Anne. "Kierkegaard and the Ironic Voices of Emily Dickinson," *Journal of English and Germanic Philology* 77(1978): 569–81.

Thoreau, Henry David. *The Variorum Walden*. Edited by Walter Harding. New York: Twayne Publishers, 1962.

Todd, John Emerson. *Emily Dickinson's Use of the Persona*. The Hague: Mouton, 1963.

Waggoner, Hyatt. "Emily Dickinson: The Transcendent Self," *Criticism* 7 (1965): 297–334.

Ward, Theodora. *The Capsule of the Mind: Chapters in the Life of Emily Dickinson*. Cambridge: Harvard University Press, 1961.

Watts, Emily Stipes. *The Poetry of American Women from 1632 to 1945*. Austin: University of Texas Press, 1977.

Weisbuch, Robert. *Emily Dickinson's Poetry*. Chicago: The University of Chicago Press, 1975.

Wells, Henry W. *Introduction to Emily Dickinson*. Chicago: Hendricks House, 1947.

Whicher, G. F. *This Was a Poet*. New York: Charles Scribners and Sons, 1938.

Whitman, Walt. *The Uncollected Poetry and Prose*. Edited by Emory Holloway. 2 vols. New York: Peter Smith, 1932.

———. *Walt Whitman: Complete Poetry and Selected Prose*. Edited by James E. Miller, Jr. Boston: Houghton Mifflin, 1959.

Wilbur, Richard. "Sumptuous Destitution," in Richard B. Sewall, ed., *Emily Dickinson: A Collection of Critical Essays*. Englewood Cliffs: Prentice-Hall, 1963.

Williams, JoAnne De Lavan. "Spiders in the Attic: A Suggestion of Synthesis in the Poetry of Emily Dickinson," *Emily Dickinson Bulletin* 29 (1976): 21–29.

Wilner, Eleanor. "The Poetics of Emily Dickinson," *ELH* 38 (1971): 126–54.

Wilson, Suzanne M. "Structural Patterns in the Poetry of Emily Dickinson," *American Literature* 35 (1963): 53–59.

Winters, Yvor. "Emily Dickinson and the Limits of Judgment," in Richard B. Sewall, ed., *Emily Dickinson: A Collection of Critical Essays*. Englewood Cliffs: Prentice-Hall, 1963.

Yetman, Michael G. "Emily Dickinson and the English Romantic Tradition," *Texas Studies in Literature and Language* 15 (1973): 129–47.

Index to Poems Discussed

The poems are alphabetized according to first lines. Numbers in parentheses are those assigned by the Variorum Edition.

General Index

Abrams, M. H., 64

Analogy: as structural principle in Dickinson's poetry, 83–87, 97–98, 162, 202 (n. 4), 204 (n. 21)

Anderson, Charles R., 7, 197 (n. 40), 206 (n. 7), 212–13 (n. 13), 213 (n. 15)

Anthon, Kate Scott, 88, 203 (n. 9)

Banzer, Judith, 149

"Barefoot" image, 36, 119, 123, 191 (n. 10), 198 (n. 4)

Bark image in Dickinson's poetry, 14–19, 33, 48, 82, 119, 121, 191 (n. 10), 192 (n. 16), 193 (n. 1)

Bible: Book of Revelations, 139; Matthew, 140

Bickman, Martin, 64, 122

Bingham, Millicent Todd, 211 (n. 3)

Blackmur, R. P., 35

Bloom, Harold, 34, 149, 190 (n. 5), 200 (n. 18)

Bogan, Louise, 65

Bowles, Samuel, 122

Browning, Robert, 209 (n. 17)

Budick, E. Miller, 50, 198 (n. 5), 201 (n. 20)

Cameron, Sharon, 5, 7, 31, 207 (n. 12)

Chaliff, Cynthia, 89

Chase, Richard, 65, 134, 143, 209–10 (n. 19)

Christ, Jesus, 113, 204 (n. 16)

Christian imagery, 6, 14, 200 (n. 18)

Cody, John, 51, 193 (n. 3), 199 (n. 9), 210 (n. 24), 212 (n. 3)

Consciousness: as divisive element in quest, 66; as spiritually debilitating, 67; diffuses concentration upon essences, 73; imaged as a journey, 175–76; terror of full consciousness, 213 (n. 13)

Cowan, Perez, 191 (n. 11)

Daniels, Edgar F., 202 (n. 4)

Davis, Thomas M., 6, 195 (n. 20, n. 23)

Death, 5, 19; as chief focus of Dickinson's poetry, 92, 100–101, 211–12 (n. 3); Dickinson's obsession with, 143; directly related to Dickinson's creative impulse, 144; impervious to "mathematics," 144; physical aspects of, 149, 160–61; fear of, 151; internalized, 151–52; personification as romantic lover, 153, 213 (n. 16); perceptual confrontation with, 153, 162–64; the dead as "lures," 154; accepting reality of, 155; clinical observation of, 155; effects upon human perception, 156; as doorway to visionary fulfillment, 157; as purgatorial experience, 158; as beneficent phenomenon, 159; presence of corpses in Dickinson's death poetry, 161–66, 170–73; dramatization of Dickinson's own death, 165–67; as an end to vision, 166; as a daily pressure upon the spirit, 167–68; heightens appreciation of creative perception, 167; as continual stimulus, 169;

About the Author

Greg Johnson has taught most recently at Emory University, where he earned the Ph.D. in 1979. His essays, reviews, fiction, and poetry have appeared in numerous journals, including *The Georgia Review, Virginia Quarterly Review, The Hollins Critic, Southwest Review,* and *Ontario Review.* He lives in Atlanta.